Evidence and Religious Belief

Evidence and Religious Belief

EDITED BY
Kelly James Clark
and Raymond J. VanArragon

OXFORD
UNIVERSITY PRESS

OXFORD
UNIVERSITY PRESS

Great Clarendon Street, Oxford ox2 6DP

Oxford University Press is a department of the University of Oxford.
It furthers the University's objective of excellence in research, scholarship,
and education by publishing worldwide in

Oxford New York

Auckland Cape Town Dar es Salaam Hong Kong Karachi
Kuala Lumpur Madrid Melbourne Mexico City Nairobi
New Delhi Shanghai Taipei Toronto

With offices in

Argentina Austria Brazil Chile Czech Republic France Greece
Guatemala Hungary Italy Japan Poland Portugal Singapore
South Korea Switzerland Thailand Turkey Ukraine Vietnam

Oxford is a registered trade mark of Oxford University Press
in the UK and in certain others countries

Published in the United States
by Oxford University Press Inc., New York

© the several contributors 2011

The moral rights of the authors have been asserted
Database right Oxford University Press (maker)

First published 2011

British Library Cataloguing in Publication Data

Data available

Library of Congress Cataloging in Publication Data
Library of Congress Control Number: 2011929292

Typeset by SPI Publisher Services, Pondicherry, India
Printed in Great Britain
on acid-free paper by
MPG Books Group, Bodmin and King's Lynn

ISBN 9780–19–960371–8

1 3 5 7 9 10 8 6 4 2

To George Mavrodes
In gratitude

Contents

Notes on Contributors

JEFF CERVANTEZ is a Ph.D. candidate in Philosophy at the University of Tennessee.

KELLY JAMES CLARK (editor) is Professor of Philosophy at Calvin College.

E. J. COFFMAN is Assistant Professor of Philosophy at the University of Tennessee.

THOMAS M. CRISP is Associate Professor of Philosophy at Biola University.

C. STEPHEN EVANS is University Professor of Philosophy and Humanities at Baylor University.

WILLIAM HASKER is Professor of Philosophy Emeritus at Huntington University.

JOHN HICK is Professor of Philosophy Emeritus at Claremont Graduate University.

THOMAS KELLY is Associate Professor of Philosophy at Princeton University.

JAMES ROSS was Professor of Philosophy at Pennsylvania University.

WILLIAM ROWE is Professor of Philosophy Emeritus at Purdue University.

ANDREW SAMUEL is Assistant Professor of Economics at Loyola University, Maryland.

CHRIS TUCKER is Lecturer in Philosophy at the University of Auckland.

RAYMOND J. VANARRAGON (editor) is Associate Professor and Chair of the Philosophy Department at Bethel University.

WILLIAM J. WAINWRIGHT is Distinguished Professor Emeritus at the University of Wisconsin Milwaukee.

LINDA ZAGZEBSKI is George Lynn Cross Research Professor of Philosophy and Kingfisher College Chair of the Philosophy of Religion and Ethics at the University of Oklahoma.

Introduction

Questions about the relation between evidence and religious belief have been front and center in recent philosophy of religion. This book takes up three of them. One question asks whether religious belief needs to be based on evidence in order to justified, rational, or warranted. A second asks how what evidence we have for or against religious belief can depend on other factors, including our desires, attitudes, and background beliefs. A third question asks what evidence there actually is for and against particular religious beliefs. In this introduction we will sum up some of the contemporary discussion of these questions, in order to provide some background and context for the chapters to come.

1 Evidentialism and Reformed epistemology

The first question, we said, has to do with whether religious belief, in order to enjoy certain kinds of positive epistemic status, must be based on evidence. This topic has been among the most hotly debated in the last thirty years, and prominent philosophers have staked out positions that are diametrically opposed to each other. We'll briefly explore them here. On one side, evidentialists, whose contemporary adherents follow such luminaries as David Hume and W. K. Clifford, claim that religious belief must only be held on the basis of evidence, and that if it isn't, then such belief is deficient and irrational. On the other side, so-called Reformed epistemologists, echoing (from a distance) the pronouncements of John Calvin, claim that religious belief need not be based on evidence and should instead be thought of as properly basic, so that, for example, belief in God can serve as evidence without needing any itself. Religious beliefs can enjoy positive epistemic status, say Reformed epistemologists, but that status typically comes from something other than evidence. (And maybe it *has to* come from something else: many Reformed epistemologists hold that the evidence for religious claims is insufficient to justify belief in them.)

Evidentialists themselves fall into different camps: some believe that the evidence favors religious belief like belief in God, and some do not. For both camps the arguments for God's existence, in their many guises, are of great significance. If successful, they constitute the rock on which theistic religious beliefs can safely be built; but if not, then such beliefs should be abandoned even if they are true. Hence the project of Natural Theology, understood roughly as the attempt to produce an argument for God's existence that would compel any rational person to accept it, is for evidentialists an enterprise where a great deal is at stake.

For Reformed epistemologists, the value of arguments for God's existence (and for other religious beliefs) is obviously limited. Not only are they unnecessary for rational belief in God, but, some allege, there may even be something wrong or impious with the pursuit of them, something reflecting a lack of faith or trust in God. Indeed, searching for evidence for God, and having one's belief depend on acquiring it, may be like perversely having one's belief that other people have minds depend on acquiring a convincing philosophical argument that they do. More modestly, some Reformed epistemologists suggest that arguments can 'prepare the way' for belief in God or perhaps help to shore up the faith the believer already has; but for the most part whatever positive epistemic status religious belief has comes from elsewhere.

Alvin Plantinga has been as responsible as anyone for pursuing this line of reasoning, and in the last twenty years he has developed a full-blooded theory of knowledge that bolsters the Reformed epistemologist's contention about the proper place of evidence. On Plantinga's theory, often called *proper functionalism*, all beliefs that have warrant— that quality enough of which turns true belief into knowledge—get it by virtue of the degree to which they are the products of properly functioning, reliably truth-aimed cognitive faculties, operating in the sort of environment for which they were designed.[1] For example, a visual belief acquires warrant not from being based on evidence but instead by virtue of how it is produced. Although some beliefs produced by our cognitive apparatus are first acquired on the basis of evidence, their connection to evidence is not fundamentally what gives them warrant. We may even cite evidence in explaining why we believe as we do; but in fact the evidence is almost incidental to the warrant that the beliefs have.

This theory in hand, Plantinga has gone on to argue that if belief in God is produced by the *sensus divinitatus*, a faculty which, by hypothesis, is part of our natural cognitive endowment and which generates belief in God in response to certain kinds of experiences, then that belief has warrant. This faculty does not require arguments as inputs—it produces foundational beliefs, beliefs that aren't themselves based on other beliefs, even though they can quite properly be used as evidence for other beliefs. Further, Plantinga argues, if specifically Christian beliefs (belief in the incarnation, atonement, trinity) are produced by the supernatural work of the Holy Spirit in us, they too have warrant despite the fact that evidence plays no role in their acquisition. Such beliefs are produced by properly functioning faculties and on that account they enjoy the same epistemic status that ordinary perceptual beliefs enjoy. Or at least they can enjoy that status, provided they are in fact produced in that way. An important part

---

[1] Plantinga, *Warrant and Proper Function* (New York, Oxford University Press, 1993).

of his book *Warranted Christian Belief*[2] contains Plantinga's argument that if God exists and specifically Christian beliefs are true, then those beliefs probably are produced in those ways and hence probably are warranted. Critics, both Christian and not, have protested that it would be really nice if Plantinga would provide evidence that Christian beliefs are in fact true so that we might determine whether they are warranted; but Plantinga contends that the evidence available is not sufficient to settle the matter. Fortunately, on his view, such evidence is not needed, either.

Thus we have two positions, evidentialism and Reformed epistemology, offering opposing answers to the central question of whether religious belief must be based on evidence in order to be rational, justified, or the like. In recent years both positions have faced challenges. Here we shall consider a challenge to evidentialism and some responses which may serve to bridge the gap between it and Reformed epistemology. Doing so will help to set the context for the essays in Part I of this book.

2 Challenge and responses

An important challenge to evidentialism has been to its overall viability as an epistemological theory. The suggestion that all beliefs require evidence in order to be justified raises the specter of a vicious regress, particularly when the evidence in question must be *propositional*—that is, must take the form of other beliefs. (If so, then a belief must be justified by another, which must be justified by another, and so on ad infinitum, leaving it unclear how any belief could acquire justification in the first place.) That indeed is how Reformed epistemologists, led again by Plantinga, have often construed evidentialism.[3] And they have not done so without reason. As Laurence Bonjour argued, a justification for a belief is a reason to think the belief is true, and it seems an essential feature of such reasons that they have propositional content and take the form of beliefs themselves.[4] To avoid the regress, most evidentialists endorse some version of foundationalism and grant that certain beliefs need not be held on the basis of propositional evidence but instead can serve as the foundations of a doxastic system, passing justification (and other desirable epistemic properties) on to other beliefs without acquiring it from other beliefs themselves. Foundationalisms come in a variety of flavors, depending on their claims about how justification gets passed up the chain and, more importantly for our purposes, about what sorts of beliefs can serve in the foundation, and why.

Plantinga, in his original attack on evidentialism, chose what he labeled 'classical foundationalism' as his target. Classical foundationalism states that only beliefs which

² New York, Oxford University Press, 2000.
³ See especially Plantinga, 'Reason and Belief in God' in Alvin Plantinga and Nicholas Wolterstorff (eds.), *Faith and Rationality* (Notre Dame, IN, Notre Dame Press, 1984), pp. 16–93.
⁴ Laurence Bonjour, 'Can Empirical Knowledge Have a Foundation?' (1978), *American Philosophical Quarterly* 15, pp. 1–14.

are incorrigible, self-evident, or evident to the senses can be justified without appeal to other beliefs; beliefs not justified in this fashion must be properly inferred ultimately from those. As Plantinga and others have pointed out, this version is fraught with difficulty, in part because it so restricts the content of foundational beliefs. It seems that many of our ordinary, widely-accepted beliefs turn out to be unjustified—and even unjustifiable—on this account; and hence classical foundationalism leads to skepticism. (It also leads to self-referential difficulties, since belief in classical foundationalism cannot be justified by its own standard.) Moreover, the picture of belief acquisition and justification proposed by classical foundationalism does not seem to fit with the way that people's belief systems actually work. If our epistemological theories don't match with epistemic reality, what is their point?

The challenge to evidentialism, then, is directed at its general viability as an account that adequately applies to our epistemic lives and doesn't, when conjoined with some form of foundationalism, lead to skepticism. In different ways, the first two chapters in Part I of this volume carry on this challenge. In the first chapter, James Ross offers a damning indictment of the notion that all our beliefs must be based on evidence and contends, in defense of ordinary believers, that all human belief systems are fundamentally faith-based. In the second, Linda Zagzebski argues that in the face of the failure of strong foundationalism and for other reasons besides, a certain degree of self-trust is necessary to leading a productive epistemic life. But the reasons we have for epistemically trusting ourselves can also be turned into reasons for trusting others, and this, Zagzebski continues, leads us to a *consensus gentium* argument for God's existence. The fact that belief in God is so widespread, together with our reasons for trusting others, gives us reason to adopt such belief ourselves.

The challenge to evidentialism has not gone unanswered. An important recent response has been to spell out more carefully—and perhaps more permissively—what can count as evidence for a belief. The Reformed epistemologist paints evidentialism into a corner on this point, restricting evidence to propositional evidence and saddling the evidentialist with classical foundationalism on top of all that. While some evidentialists have followed the strict classical line,[5] it's probably fair to say that the restriction doesn't fit well with the way that we speak about evidence in ordinary life. Suppose I walk into a room and see a group of people in it. I don't explicitly *infer* from my visual experience that there are people there; instead, as the Reformed epistemologist insists, I have the experience and (at least if I am attentive to it) simply find myself with the belief that there are people in the room. The belief is produced in me automatically. On the Reformed epistemologist's construal of 'evidence' this belief is not based on it; on his account, the classical foundationalist would label this a basic belief in so far as it is one that is 'evident to the senses.' Yet this construal seems mistaken. Of course I believe on evidence: I *see* the people, I *experience* them, and then I believe that they are there.

---

[5] See, for example, Richard Fumerton, 'Classical Foundationalism' in Michael DePaul (ed.), *Resurrecting Old-Fashioned Foundationalism* (Lanham, MD, Rowman and Littlefield, 2001), pp. 3–20.

Indeed, it seems that experiences can themselves serve as evidence that can justify belief. Evidentialists need not restrict evidence to propositional evidence. Earl Conee and Richard Feldman, prominent contemporary defenders of evidentialism, embrace this sort of approach in the following passage:

Some philosophers have argued that only believed propositions can be part of the evidence one has. Their typical ground for this claim is that only believed propositions can serve as premises of arguments. Our view differs radically from this one. We hold that experiences can be evidence, and beliefs are only derivatively evidence . . . all ultimate evidence is experiential.[6]

Many contemporary epistemologists would agree that experiences can constitute evidence, and they include as candidates for experiential evidence perceptual experiences as well as intuitions concerning math, morality, and what is possible in the broadly logical sense.

In the third chapter of this volume, C. Stephen Evans explores ways in which experiences can serve as evidence, and then develops the notion of 'natural signs' to attempt a reconciliation between evidentialists and Reformed epistemologists. Natural signs, which include experienced features of the natural world and the experiences of those features, can function non-inferentially to produce warranted belief in God, as Reformed epistomologists affirm. (In the broader sense of 'evidence', of course, these signs can also count as evidence.) Evans tries to show, however, that these very same signs can also be the basis for acceptance of the arguments for God's existence, and thus can be the source of propositional evidence as well.

Another recent view of evidence that is particularly permissive concerning the justificatory power of experience is called *phenomenal conservatism*. It holds that, in the absence of defeaters, if it seems to S that P, then S has justification for P—no matter what P is and no matter how that seeming is caused. In favor of this permissive stance, Michael Huemer has argued that denying phenomenal conservatism is self-defeating and leads to skepticism. He contends that the view best captures the internalist intuition that for a belief to be justified, the believer must have access to what justifies it.[7] On this view, if it seems to S that the New York Yankees are the best team in Major League Baseball, then, in the absence of defeaters, S is justified in believing that the Yankees are the best team. The same goes for religious beliefs.

---

[6] 'Evidence' in Quentin Smith (ed.), *Epistemology: New Essays* (Oxford, Oxford University Press, 2008), pp. 87–8. Note that Conee and Feldman do not just acknowledge the possibility of experiential evidence; they contend that ultimately that is the *only* kind of evidence.

[7] Defense of this view can be found in recent papers by Michael Huemer, including 'Compassionate Phenomenal Conservativism' (2007), *Philosophy and Phenomenological Research* 74, pp. 30–55; and 'Phenomenal Conservatism and the Internalist Intuition' (2006), *American Philosophical Quarterly* 43, pp. 147–58; and his book *Skepticism and the Veil of Perception* (Lanham, Rowman & Littlefield Publishers, 2001). Earl Conee expresses sympathy with the view, which he calls 'seeming evidentialism' but it isn't clear whether he actually endorses it. See his 'First Things First' in Earl Conee and Richard Feldman (eds.), *Evidentialism* (New York, Oxford University Press, 2004).

In the fourth chapter of this book, Chris Tucker explores phenomenal conservatism and its implications for religious beliefs and argues that, if it is true, then the evidentialist demand for evidence does not in fact impose a significant constraint on justified religious beliefs. One might find such a claim boring because conservatism seems too permissive to take seriously. Tucker replies to this objection at length; he also contends that phenomenal conservatism has advantages over Plantinga's proper functionalism and suggests ways in which the functioning of the *sensus divinitatus* might be re-described in keeping with this more permissive evidentialism. Thus the fourth chapter, like the third, serves to bring Reformed epistemologists and evidentialists closer together.

3 Evidence evaluation

Essays in the first part of the book consider whether religious belief, if it is to be justified, rational, or warranted, must be based on evidence; and they do so by exploring both the general viability of evidentialism and the nature of evidence itself. Essays in the second part explore how what evidence we acquire, and how we assess it, can depend on a variety of factors including desires, attitudes, and other beliefs that we hold.

The notion that the acquisition and assessment of evidence can depend on prior beliefs and attitudes is commonplace. What appears as strong testimonial evidence to one person may be seen differently by another who believes the testifier to be a liar. A preconceived notion about the location of the doctor's office may cause one to misinterpret directions or misread a map. In contentious political matters, a candidate's success in graduate school may be taken by supporters as evidence of a strong intelligence and work ethic, but by opponents as evidence of lax standards at the particular school or favoritism extended on account of the candidate's deceptive charm. Similarly, one may consider a commentator to be a reliable source on a particular topic, but upon finding her to be aligned with an opposing political movement, one may have a defeater (or, better, think one has a defeater) for the original belief and cease to put any stock in the commentator's pronouncements. Thus evidence-assessment can differ from person to person, depending partly on their background beliefs and attitudes.

We can also see examples of this with religious belief. A person might give up belief in the resurrection upon becoming increasingly committed to the notion that miracles cannot happen. On the other side, a person who is open to the possibility of miraculous divine intervention in the world might find the evidence for the resurrection to be compelling and come to believe it on that account.[8] A person disillusioned with her pastor could display a negative attitude towards the pastor's beliefs, and gradually find Christian belief less plausible on account of that. On the other hand, a person might

---

[8] Thus Stephen Davis, in defense of his belief in the resurrection in Michael Peterson and Raymond VanArragon (eds.), *Contemporary Debates in Philosophy of Religion* (London, Blackwell, 2003), argues not that the resurrection happened, but instead that it is rational for some people—depending on their background beliefs—to believe that it did.

find certain atheists or unbelievers insufferable, and be drawn to the arguments for God's existence or to the witness of theists because of that.[9]

In the case of belief in God, what accounts for the differences in assessments of the evidence on the part of believers and unbelievers? (We'll understand evidence to be either propositional or experiential.) There are explanations of such disagreement available on both sides, some charitable and some not, but it might help us to sample briefly three suggestions, from a theistic perspective, of what might be going on in cases where people appear to lack evidence for God's existence, and cases where they have it.

Consider first Pascal's Wager. By hypothesis, the person considering whether to take the wager and choose belief in God is in a position of evidential gridlock: only pragmatic considerations can guide her choice. The considerations in question, of course, have to do with prospects for the afterlife should God happen to exist, the idea being that one is infinitely better off believing under those conditions than not. But if she decides on those grounds that it would be prudent to embrace belief, how can she do it? It's not like she can just flip a switch and begin to believe. Pascal's solution to this problem is quite remarkable:

> But at least learn your inability to believe, since reason brings you to this, and yet you cannot believe. Endeavour, then, to convince yourself, not by increase of proofs of God, but by the abatement of your passions. You would like to attain faith and do not know the way; you would like to cure yourself of unbelief and ask the remedy for it. Learn of those who have been bound like you, and who now stake all their possessions. These are people who know the way which you would follow, and who are cured of an ill of which you would be cured. Follow the way by which they began; by acting as if they believed, taking the holy water, having masses said, etc. Even this will naturally make you believe, and deaden your acuteness. "But this is what I am afraid of." And why? What have you to lose? But to show you that this leads you there, it is this which will lessen the passions, which are your stumbling-blocks. (*Penseés*, 233)

By acting as if you believe, your conviction will grow, and you'll come to believe just as the saints do. On Pascal's view, the passions prevent us from seeing the evidence properly; if they are abated, then we can see what is in fact right before our eyes. Thus committing to belief in God and adjusting one's passions accordingly will enable one to see the evidence that God exists (and more particularly evidence for the Christian faith), evidence that will convict one of its truth.

A second theistic suggestion traces back to Reformed epistemology, and particularly to Plantinga's view that belief in God can serve as a foundational belief in a person's doxastic system. According to Plantinga, the *sensus divinitatus*, a faculty that is part of our natural cognitive equipment, takes certain kinds of experiences as input and then produces beliefs about God as output. Typical output beliefs may include the belief

---

[9] We can see some of this in the 'spiritual autobiography' of Peter van Inwagen, who tells of how, prior to converting to Christianity, he was put off by the anti-religious attitude of academics who 'thought they were so smart.' See 'Quam Dilecta' in Thomas Morris (ed.), *God and the Philosophers* (New York, Oxford, 1994), pp. 31–60.

that *God is wondrous*, produced on the occasion of witnessing a beautiful sunset, or, upon sinning, the belief that *God is unhappy with me*. The important point here, the point which explains why some see evidence (understood broadly) for God where others don't, is that the *sensus divinitatus* doesn't work the same in everyone. Indeed, damage to it is one of the cognitive effects of sin—not necessarily the sin of the particular person whose faculty is damaged, but the sinful condition into which we are all born.[10] In addition, people can be raised in ways that make them ignore the deliverances of the *sensus divinitatus*, or they can make conscious decisions with the same result. Similarly, they can form beliefs that serve as defeaters for those deliverances, which might further impede the faculty's function. On Plantinga's view, then, the malfunctioning of the *sensus divinitatus* can make it difficult for some people to come to warranted beliefs about God, unless God intervenes and repairs the faculty or conveys the relevant information in another way.

A third example that helps to explain from a theistic perspective why some people have evidence for God that others lack comes from recent debates over divine hiddenness.[11] Proponents of the argument from hiddenness against the existence of God focus on people who seek after God with great determination, who cry out to God but hear nothing in response. God remains hidden to them. If God existed, the argument goes, this would not happen; and more generally, the failure of God to make God's existence clearer to the world constitutes strong evidence that God does not exist. One response to this argument, suggested by Paul Moser,[12] is that critics are demanding evidence in the wrong way and are not appropriately positioned to see the evidence even if it is there. On the Christian view anyway, God does not want from people the mere belief that God exists; instead God wants commitment—God wants a relationship—which is only possible with people who are oriented appropriately towards God. (This fits with Pascal's suggestion that commitment and attitude adjustment will eventually result in convicting evidence and firm belief.) Thus God may have good reason to withhold evidence from people who seek God with an attitude unsuited to God's own aims. Those so confident in following whatever evidence may be available from an objective or disinterested perspective may be guilty of 'cognitive idolatry', demanding such evidence when God in fact is in control of the evidence and has reasons for handing it out more judiciously.

These issues are taken up in the fifth and sixth chapters of this book. In the fifth chapter, William Wainwright explores the person-relativity of religious arguments, the way in which evidence can work differently for different people, and considers some implications of person-relativity for the rationality of religious belief. One implication

---

[10] See Plantinga, *Warranted Christian Belief*, esp. pp. 199–240.

[11] See Daniel Howard-Snyder and Paul Moser (eds.), *Divine Hiddenness: New Essays* (New York, Cambridge University Press, 2001). See also the Schellenberg/Moser debate in Michael Peterson and Raymond VanArragon (eds.), *Contemporary Debates in Philosophy of Religion* (London, Blackwell, 2003), pp. 30–58.

[12] See for example 'Cognitive Idolatry and Divine Hiding' in *Divine Hiddenness: New Essays*.

in particular, he argues, is that it deflates the objection to belief in God which claims that agnosticism is preferable to belief in the face of a lack of objectively conclusive evidence for God's existence.[13] In the sixth chapter, E. J. Coffman and Jeff Cervantez explore the hiddenness argument against God's existence and offer a detailed critique of Moser's response to it. They argue that his response, and particularly the notion that God purposefully withholds evidence, is vulnerable in so far as it depends on certain highly controversial epistemological claims.

We have been discussing the way that the evidence a person uses in belief formation—what evidence he has, how he sees and assesses it—can depend in part on his background beliefs and attitudes. But some theists have argued that religious belief affects evidence in another way as well: by strengthening the overall epistemic position of the believer. In doing so they have in effect turned on its head the evidentialist demand that justified religious belief must be based on evidence, by claiming that only with religious beliefs of some kind can a person have any evidence for anything. In the seventh chapter of this volume, Thomas Crisp explores this line of argument; we shall set it up by considering two versions of the argument that are less modest than his.

First, the argument that having evidence depends on religious belief is found implicitly in Descartes, who (on the usual understanding) thought that only by demonstrating the existence of God could he trust that his cognitive faculties supplied him with true beliefs when he used them properly. Without such grounding, Descartes couldn't trust himself at all since, for all he knew, an evil demon could be deceiving him into falsely believing as he did and making the world seem to him vastly different than what it really was. Thus God played an essential role for Descartes as he attempted to rebuild the belief structure which he had laid waste at the beginning of the *Meditations*.

An argument similar to this has been defended in recent years by Plantinga, the so-called Evolutionary Argument against Naturalism.[14] This argument claims that a naturalist who accepts that her cognitive apparatus has been fashioned blindly by the evolutionary process has reason to doubt the reliability of that apparatus and hence has a defeater for everything she believes. Everything? Yes, Plantinga argues, because there are all sorts of ways in which our ancestors' (and our) belief systems could have promoted survival-enhancing behavior while being on the whole wildly false. Thus the naturalist should realize, upon reflecting on her beliefs about human origins, that

---

[13] This objection has recently been pressed by John L. Schellenberg in '"Breaking Down the Walls that Divide:" Virtue and Warrant, Belief and Nonbelief' (2004), *Faith and Philosophy* 21, pp. 195–213.

[14] For discussion of the argument, see James Beilby (ed.), *Naturalism Defeated* (Ithaca, NY, Cornell University Press, 2002). The chapters by Ernest Sosa and James Van Cleve are especially helpful in highlighting similarities between Plantinga's argument and Descartes'. See also Plantinga's discussion of the argument in *Warranted Christian Belief*, pp. 199–240; and Blake Roeber, 'Does the Theist Have an Epistemic Advantage over the Atheist? Plantinga and Descartes on Theism, Atheism and Skepticism' (2009), *The Journal of Philosophical Research* 34, pp. 305–28.

she has no undefeated evidence for anything she believes (including that!). Her epistemic position is woeful through and through.

Both arguments about the poor epistemic standing of naturalists have of course been controversial, even among theists, but again they highlight a different way in which one's religious beliefs, or lack of them, might affect the kinds of evidence one has and the type of justification that one's beliefs may enjoy. Crisp's essay in Chapter Seven presents a new and more modest argument along the lines of Plantinga's evolutionary argument. Crisp does not argue that naturalists have, in their view of human origins, a defeater for every belief that they hold; he instead argues that they have a defeater for certain key premises that some of them use in arguments for God's non-existence. Crisp contends that such arguments—arguments that have, as Crisp puts it, 'recondite premises'—cannot rationally be accepted as forceful by those most inclined to propound them.

The second part of the book thus considers, from different angles, ways in which the evidence for and against religious belief can depend on the passions, attitudes, and other beliefs the person considering it has.

4 Evidence and Religious Belief

The final section of this book considers the central question of what evidence there is for and against religious belief. The chapters provide discussion of new and amended arguments. Little needs to be said by way of background for them. Two chapters consider arguments for belief in God. Thomas Kelly in Chapter Eight explores *consensus gentium* arguments for God's existence (a version of which is defended by Linda Zagzebski in the second chapter). Does the 'common consent' of humanity—the fact that belief in God is widespread—constitute evidence that God exists? Kelly James Clark and Andrew Samuel, in Chapter Nine, contribute a pragmatic argument to show that belief in God is better than the alternatives for grounding moral motivation. The tenth chapter of the book, by William Rowe, contends that reflection on the notions of divine goodness and freedom can sensibly lead one to the conclusion that God does *not* exist. The final chapter, by William Hasker, explores the views of philosopher John Hick, who seems to take the variety and nature of human religious experiences to constitute evidence for the existence of individual divine beings. That chapter concludes with a response from Hick, where he acknowledges and clarifies his view that there may be intermediaries between human beings and the ultimate divine reality.[15]

---

[15] Special thanks to Chris Tucker for helping with this introduction.

PART I

Exploring the Demand for Evidence

1

Willing Belief and Rational Faith

James Ross

The point of this paper is that the rationality of Christian faith is more properly a question of whether it is a kind of rational reliance yielding commitments that, if true, are knowledge, rather than whether it is item by item evidentially justified.

The reliances of faith are usually unexamined because philosophical attention is on the justification of individual propositional beliefs, like the existence, omnipotence and benevolence of God. But for most Christians those are just parts of their religious construal of the world, not items individually sustained by evidence or mere coherence, but rather themselves bedrock forms of interpretation of everything else. For Christian believers are willingly committed to the promise of everlasting life with God (cf. Gal. 1.16; 1 Cor. 15.5-3-4; Heb. 1.10-12; John 3.16, 17.3; and Matt. 25.31-33) and motivated to believe (as a committed form of life) by it. For instance, Aquinas in one of his analyses of faith, D.V.14.1, said 'we are moved to believe what God says because we are promised eternal life as a reward if we believe.' He put his finger on what is common between religious faith and ordinary cognition in general.

I devote only a section of this paper to the criticism of evidentialism as a basic account of knowledge and the remainder of the essay to characterizing generally, not just in religious contexts, some aspects of the habitual willing reliance that yields knowledge,[1] in particular, (i) briefly why I think rational reliance is a transformation of animal cognition, (ii) that cognitive reliance is for reward, as is animal cognition, and (iii) that one's life-forming faiths may (indeed probably) conflict and have gaps.

Those are only a selection of the features one might want to examine, some of which I explore elsewhere.[2] But the basic message is that Christian faith is a form of the

---

[1] Of course, truth is also required for knowledge, but is not under inquiry here.

[2] 'Believing for Profit' in Gerald D. McCarthy (ed.), *The Ethics of Belief Debate* (Atlanta, Georgia, AAR Studies in Religion, 41, Scholars Press,1985), pp. 221–35. See also 'Aquinas on Belief and Knowledge' in William A. Frank and Gerard J. St Bonaventure (eds), *Essays Honoring Alan B. Wolter* (New York, Franciscan Institute Press, 1985), pp. 243–69; 'Adjusted Prospects for Philosophical Theology: Reason and Reliance' in E. Long (ed.), *Prospects for Natural Theology* (Washington, D.C., CUA Press, 1990); and 'Rational Reliance' (1995), *Journal of the American Academy of Religion* LXII/3, pp. 769–98.

characteristically human reliance that potentially generates knowledge, and not some outlier among modes of believing.

1 Cognition by reliance

Ours is animal cognition transformed by understanding and freedom. Our knowledge, like that of other higher animals, originates in sensation that by complex biological programming turns sensation and desire into perceptive action that is instinctively aimed at the animal's benefit (survival and reproduction); in primates that structure develops by maturation, and improves (or may be damaged) by conditioning and learning. In humans the platform, pretty much common to hominids, is transformed by understanding and freedom to serve specifically human functions that require under-standing and the ability to act with a grasp of what one acts for. By freedom here I mean the ability to act from a grasp of what the actions are for.

Animals generally do what they want.[3] Anyone who has trained a dog or a horse, or even tried with a cat, knows habituation is best achieved by reward. And as Aristotle observed, animals, and humans, sense because they want to (if you are able to, you want to see, hear), and act because they want to (by desiring and even in flight/fight), to relieve (satisfy) desire, but, as Aquinas observed, without a grasp of what their actions are for.

Our own constant cognition is by habitual willing reliance on perception, memory, imagination, reasoning and action aimed at our uses and peculiarly human satisfactions, most markedly, when we are doing explicit thinking in action, like crafts, physics, philosophy, literature, mathematics and art. But even scratching what we take to be a mosquito bite involves willing (unreflective) intelligent reliance on proprioceptive hand movements, imagination and past experience. We know what we are doing, even unre-flectively. One does not have to be attentive to act intelligently and willingly, as we can see when someone adjusts his stance while talking to us or turns to see another speaker.

I don't here further examine the premise that human understanding and action is carried out on a platform of constant animal cognition that is largely but not wholly encompassed in our understanding and comprehending desire. I expect that to be obvious on reflection, and to have been finally in the last century acknowledged and initially explored scientifically, after having been ignored, even denied, by early modern mechanist philosophers and appreciated by many of the ancients (and medievals).[4]

---

[3] Aristotle and Aquinas both emphasized this. In fact, Aquinas called animal willing 'imperfect voluntari-ety' (because it lacks grasp of what the action is for). See Aquinas, *Summa Theologiae* I-II, q.6, a.2 on animal voluntarism: 'It is essential to the voluntary act that its principle be within the agent together with some knowledge of the end . . . Imperfect knowledge of the end consists in mere apprehension of the end, without knowing it under the aspect of "end," or the relationship of an act to the end. Such knowledge of the end is exercised by rational animals through their senses and their natural estimative power . . . whereas the imperfect voluntary is within the competency of even irrational animals.'

[4] Margaret Dauler Wilson, 'Animal Ideas' (Nov 1995), *Proceedings and Addresses of the American Philosophical Association* Vol. 69, No. 2, pp. 7–25. See also Richard Sorabji, *Animal Minds and Human Morals: The Origins of the Western Debate* (Ithaca, NY, Cornell University Press, 1993).

Our standing, reaching, bending, head motions, turning, and so on, are willing, but mostly without reflective awareness (though still intelligent and sub-aware), though many of their components (e.g. the movement of tendons and bones in hand positions) are not accessible for focal attention while the actions are being performed for their usual ends. So those component movements are only to be called 'intelligent' derivatively. Of course some of them can be brought to conscious attention and intelligent modification, e.g. by persons learning musical instruments or sports, but not all of them and not all at once.

We, like other animals, rely willingly and with satisfaction on our faculties, on sight, hearing, touch, etc, and we gain things expected or imagined by using them. For humans, every sense (mode of perception) may even be a mode of love, and a pleasure in itself. ('I love the feel of velvet, the sound of strings, the smell after rain, and sunlight.')

For humans, acquired reliance (in contrast to basic animal reliance which we also have) is typically rational; that is, it is (i) objectively effective for benefits we seek, and (ii) accessible to our understanding as effective for specifically human aims, though we are sometimes subject to irrational reliance, too: to habits that conflict with reasoned examination or are ineffective for any human good (or interfere with the necessary ones); those are our vices of commitment, like greedy credulity.[5] Such vices, though, require some understanding (imperfect understanding), and so do not afflict other animals. Other animals act only from uncomplicated desire. But humans act from desire that involves at least some understanding of what the desire is *for*. That is both the source of freedom and the origin of illusory ends and of evil.[6]

Uncorrupted reliance that yields convictions that are true, and does so not by mere coincidence but because of the utility of the reliance for reaching truth, yields knowledge (cognition). Not always, of course. But if I lean on a banister in the dark to guide my way down the stairs, the utility is a consequence of the knowledge conveyed. Generally, knowledge is rational certainty about what is actually so, held not by happenstance or mistake but in a suitable causal dependence on what is so. My hypothesis here is that core Christian belief, if true, meets that condition (cf. Galatians 1.16, 'even we have believed in Christ Jesus in order to be justified by faith in

---

[5] That's because humans tend to be in some ways careless, superficial, gullible, superstitious, stubborn, lazy, uncritical or venial, prejudiced and intolerant. We act from desires, say for great wealth and power, that Epicurus considered unnatural and unnecessary.

[6] There is a traditional distinction between 'actus hominis' and 'actus humanus,' that is, between the act of some human (say when he's bumped in a line and bumps the next person), and a human action, when the person is aware and doing it.

I leave unsettled for now whether we ever have merely animal cognition, or whether there is always conception involved, though my hypothesis is that within each packet of rational reliance involving action, there remains a platform of animal cognition that does not rise to intelligent consciousness: e.g. when I am typing, there are movements of my arm and hand and finger muscles of which I am unaware (unless they are injured), but which fall within animal cognition and desire, to make the movements.

Christ, not by works of the law' and Aquinas *De. Ver.* 14.1, cited above). So we need to know more about what that condition is.

Our knowledge is not typically *scientia*, a grasp of the systematic *why* of the thing, but is, rather, what we also call cognition (*cognito*), the intelligent apprehension *that* something is so (like knowing the date or one's age, or that one can lift the cup or climb the stairs), an apprehension that is not just accidentally related to its being so, but rather is systematically useful because it conveys what *is* so. That's why it is knowledge.

Moreover it almost never happens in wholly separate items of belief, as epistemologists seem to think, but happens against a background of cognition in clusters. Our awareness of where we are and what is around us is like that. Our own bodily existence is unreflectively known in a cluster of cognition. Our recognition of others by sight or voice is like that, too. Rational reliance is like well-fitted glasses; it continually does something of value to us.

2 Reliance and reward

We rely on what rewards us, or what we expect to, whether it be something remembered, imagined, naturally inclined to, or learned. We rely on our cars, tools, computers, telephones, books and sources, etc., and call poor ones unreliable. So too with eyesight, hearing, touch, smell, taste, and so too, with the perceptions thereby, and also with memory, imagination (unreliable if not trained and matured), and acquired skills and informants of all kinds. The very relying is typically satisfying because the activity involved is pleasing, as I said, and its outcome is (expected to be) something useful like recognizing things, or some other good, like finding our way, knowing what to wear, finding a telephone number, dialing a phone, or typing a sentence. Even reaching for a cup involves cognitive reliance on far more than we can recite (that it is solid, that it is of anticipated weight, has a back, won't crumble, won't suddenly leak, and so on), reliance that goes beyond presented evidence and employs imagination (to anticipate what is 'not yet') and memory, too.

Sane humans commit to things and to *sources* for what they can get out of doing so: whether it is to dates on newspapers, labels on food, displays in stores, signs on highways, advice from attorneys, or opinions of stock analysts, and, especially we rely on what we take to be natural regularities, that chairs hold us, stairs don't melt, and so on. Indeed, as I mentioned, natural trust is a basic animal instinct that can be reinforced or damaged.

Among our learned and satisfying reliances are the indispensable ones leading to mastery of the kinds that require entering a community of training and trust (faith), like the crafts, technologies, sciences, art, engineering, chemistry, and so on. Religion practiced is like that too. Even learning to speak, to count and to write is like that, as is the acquisition of social graces. The most distinctive human accomplishments of advanced society are products of *communities of mastery*: the sciences, arts, crafts, technologies, sports and even the economies, the banking and political systems.

Those are communities with their own standards of entry, accomplishment and certification by masters who *rely* on their own judgment in certifying others to judge. Religious faith, with its instruction of children and converts and Baptism and Confirmation, and professions of faith at worship, is more like circles of mastery than like a simple reliance on a newspaper or the color of the sky.

Generally, the satisfaction, utility and indispensability of a mode of reliance is not the *reason* why some belief it yields is true—though we *maintain* some reliances because the yielded beliefs are or tend to be true—but rather, it explains our *taking* what it yields to be true and may be a reason why we *think* it is true (if it does not clash too obviously or too much with what else we know—and sometimes even then: e.g. nothing can falsify the love of God or capitalists' faith in free markets). And, sharpening what I said above, when the reliance is rewarding *because* the outcome is truth, then it surely yields knowledge. Habitual rational belief is not a matter of evidence; it is a matter of reward.

2.1 Uncompelled belief

If that weren't so, we could not explain the rationality of uncompelled believing.[7] Most of our commitments are uncompelled by evidence or insight that we have. Reliance has to be for what we get out of it in the way of what turns out to be so, e.g. the car does take me to work. Articulating reasons or evidence, as becomes central to social practices like science, law, detective work and business, is a refinement and extension of the simpler systems of reliance (on senses, memory, the word of others), and one especially adapted to circumstances where mere reliance is imperfect and needs calibration, not the other way around.

Most of our believing is uncompelled. For the evidence we have, especially if we are thinking of formulated belief, is not sufficient strictly to preclude error, and the most basic of our judgmental and continuing awareness of self, world, and others is not even formulated propositionally, said to oneself, or reflectively attended to, the way one can attend to the motion of one's hand to pick up a tiny screw. It is only philosophers who would assert 'the world is real' or 'I exist' or 'there are other minds.' Everyone (except some adolescents for a while) has such commitments, but few have a need or use to formulate and express them. The rest just rely on them, rely in action. We know it is reliance because of our surprise when the unattended to fails (e.g. a floor is not solid, or a cup sticks to the saucer). Such habitual cognition is a default condition of healthy intelligent beings. Reliance on what we expect to give what we want is our defeasible, default condition.

It is a long-lasting Platonic hangover, revived by Descartes, to suppose that in order to know something we have to be in circumstances where our believing could not possibly be in error given the basis on which we hold it (or be so structured that no basis is even relevant). Instead, all we have to do for knowing is get it right and not by

---

[7] It won't do to suppose it is by chance because its regularity is obvious.

some mere coincidence or improbability or happenstance, but in some systematic relation between our being committed and our commitments' being so. We are rewarded both by the pleasure of getting things right and by what we get in the way of our aims in action and society thereby. For the most part, we believe as we do for what we get out of it.[8]

3 Evidentialism, both epistemic and moral

Evidentialism fails to describe prerequisites for rational belief, and a fortiori for knowledge, first, because the principle is itself not evidentially justifiable, as Plantinga pointed out. It cannot be established a priori by revealing a contradictory denial, or established inductively by observation because most of the evidence would come by report, by reliance. And most of all, induction which is the very guide of life always goes beyond the evidence at hand and thus intrinsically involves reliance (even if, as Goodman proposed, it is reliance on entrenched meaning).

So it is not true that a person is always unjustified (i.e. acting contrary to reason) in claiming to know something for which he has insufficient evidence to assure (logically entail? establish beyond reasonable doubt? establish by clear and convincing evidence?) its truth. In any induction one is relying on something, say, the expectation of regularity, the entrenchment of a predicate, one's prior experience, or one's skill at a craft.

Induction requires reliance. One can think of attempts to justify induction as attempts to explain why it is rational to rely on an observed sample for unobserved multitudes. And note how damning it is to say someone's extrapolation *relies* on a few non-representative cases.

Evidentialism either as a moral or prudential constraint that one is failing in a duty to minimize error makes avoiding mistakes an unqualified moral or prudential duty, when, of course, it is a positive duty only in cases where there is strict liability or a duty of due diligence (of high care) or one ordinary care (to avoid foreseeable harm, say). There are areas where one should prudently rely on experience and skill, not wait on item by item evidence, and there are emergencies that require relying on even slender likelihoods, even where one is required to disregard evidence, and rely on instruction instead.[9] The prudential/ethical form of evidentialism, that you 'ought' not to believe anything on less than sufficient evidence, has little ground for the 'ought' and no account of 'sufficient' that is short of truth. So evidentialism in both forms is both self-refuting and untrustworthy. Instead evidential structures, experience and

---

[8] That's what I call 'believing for profit' by transformation of Augustine's title '*De Utilitate* Credendi', 'On the Profit of Believing' (as a British translation put it). See 'Believing for Profit' cited note 2 above.

[9] There are even occasions when rationality *requires* ignoring the evidence of one's senses, e.g. small-plane pilots in a nosedive from good altitude are instructed to disregard the way it looks and push down on the stick (contrary to appearances that would say pull the nose up). Backing up a trailer by using a mirror is like that, too. That may apply on occasion to matters of love as well.

science most notably, are extensions of the structures of rational reliance to include things also understood.

4 Clustered reliances amount to faiths

One's life is organized by local reliances, by faith in clocks, in trains, in phone books, in Fords, in doctors, in the government to pay its debts, in the justice system, in democracy, in capitalism, in modern medicine. One's faiths aren't likely to be altogether consistent or fully harmonious with one another. They are aimed at satisfactory (or more) living. Such clustered strands of reliance form the fabric of one's life. When the strands weave together (i) to involve habitual willing reliance on (their) suppositions as to what is so, (ii) to interpret what is the success, the fulfillment, of one's own life, and that of humanity, (iii) to determine the range of one's preferred caring (family, church, party, movement) and the proportions of one's efforts and preoccupation, and (iv) to confer one's own value and worth, one's self-regard, and the order of one's regard for others, even if the weave is rough, they make one's global or life-faith.

Prominent in such fabrics are faiths like atheistic naturalism, agnostic humanism, and Orthodox Judaism, and the various forms of Christianity, Hinduism, Islam, and other large-scale interpretations of life. Few of us could with accuracy lay out in detail our life-scale global faith because it has too many strands (covering everything from health, personality, profession, science, religion, politics, loyalties, etc.), but it is there, the whole fabric of our operative commitments that are not arrived at and sustained by the evaluation of evidence.

A fulfilled human being has to rely on regularities, sources, and interpretations, and aim at rewards for whose accomplishment s/he has not compelling evidence. And a fulfilled life has to have certain dominant themes about which one cannot hold up commitment to await evidence. We hold such commitments unreflectively (usually) for the good they do us (or we think they do). About doing that, whether haphazardly or coherently, we have no choice, though we do what we do willingly. So everyone has to have faiths, either orderly and comprehensive, or ragbag, inconstant, and jumbled. There does not seem to be a neutral standpoint from which to evaluate such global commitments, but from any of the internally respectable ones, certain others quite opposed can be seen to be at least subjectively rational because, given the objectives they are aimed at, they can be seen to be effective.[10]

There is a difference in the quality of life for a widow who thinks she can still benefit her husband by prayer, from the widow who sadly thinks that like her dead cat, her husband was boxed and dropped, and entirely ceased to be. There is a difference of life quality in a person who thinks he belongs to the inevitable march to a perfect communist society or the perfect capitalist one, and the one who thinks he belongs to the faithful

---

[10] Of course, Augustine criticized pagan virtues as not being virtues at all because not aimed at the right objective. I think we might be more generous now.

practicing love and awaiting the Messiah, and between those two and one who thinks human history is as meaningless as an ant hill. But for the persons involved, each may be reasonable and effective.

The free man's defiance of dogma and pursuit of rational contentment, or the existentialist's bleak determination to help mankind by his example, or the Communist's belief that economic equality would bring human fulfillment, hope for the dictatorship of the proletariat, or philosophical naturalist's certainty that human cooperation is all we have, is no less a faith, held for what one gets out of it, than the Christian's, and no more or less rationally accessible from without than any other reflective and careful commitment by which one construes one's life. If any such global faith is rational, orthodox Christianity—the fall of humans into sin and alienation from God, the redemptive sacrifice by divine intervention, and the offer of and enablement of each for unending life with God—is.

The fact that Russell, Lucretius, Epicurus, and Carl Sagan were satisfied with naturalist coherence and led just and reasonable lives, does not make their living any more rational than J. S. Bach's writing his 'St. John Passion' in deep faith in redemption and resurrection. And the love and pursuit of science and philosophy, and literature and the arts, has no greater achievements among the irreligious and the agnostic than it has among the devout and convinced.

In so far as any of those are coherent and in accord with the rest of what their practitioners know, and are aimed at and are effective for genuine human flourishing, the competing faiths are alike subjectively rational, and so far as additionally they accord with and are effective toward what is genuinely human fulfillment they are objectively rational as well. The superiority goes to the one(s) that are true. For a global faith can be reasonable and rational for its adherents even when it is not true, provided it delivers the goods it is aimed at, confers value, as described above, and does not consciously, constantly and seriously conflict with one's manner of life.

So it may well be that the wise Epicurean, the reserved Stoic and the ardent Christian are all objectively rational in their faiths (for they are not ragbag materialists or incoherent hedonists with cruel and empty aims), and all may provide avenues to genuine human flourishing; it is the one whose commitments track reality that knows.

A global faith is self-confirming; it accepts, or devalues or puts aside evidence to fit itself. Try persuading a free-market believer that justice requires comprehensive public regulation, or telling a Biblical literalist that geology and biology establish facts contrary to a literal reading of the six days of Genesis. In that respect a global faith is like any comprehensive craft; it restricts the access from outside itself. But the feature that protects it from outside assault may also be the feature that preserves it in error.

Where global faiths rub against one another, say, items from religion with items from science, or materialism against human spirituality, the insiders often evaluate the situation differently from the outsiders, the way herbal medicine was long dismissed by licensed professionals.

Faiths may also be separated by unbridgeable cultural differences. So attitudes to the world that are animist or pantheist in culture (about half of mankind) are generally irreconcilable with either Western monotheism or Western materialism. It is not a matter of reasons or evidence, but a matter of construal, of interpretation and evaluation, like circles of mastery in arts, only here it is culture. Global faiths are generally insulated from decisive external critiques, the way high art, science and sophisticated crafts are protected by their circles of mastery from decisive outside assault. I leave the issue of conflicts for another occasion.

5 Conclusion

For now, we need only consider that Christian faith (I leave out disputes among its adherents about its content) as a form of life aimed at respectful love and care of mankind and at life unending with God is on a par in its cognitive structure with human knowing in general, and compared with other philosophies of life (to use an old phrase for it), is like them a system of rational reliances aimed at human fulfillment, which, if true, amounts to knowledge.

A good deal of the learned contempt for religion might be shamed if the critics realized that such interpretative living is structurally the same as the secular faiths they prize, and may be superior because it is true.

2

Epistemic Self-Trust and the *Consensus Gentium* Argument

Linda Zagzebski

1 Introduction

In this paper I want to explore the reasonableness of religious belief as a consequence of the reasonableness of self-trust. I will argue that the natural desire for truth makes epistemic self-trust a requirement, and consistent epistemic self-trust commits us to epistemic trust in others. One of the consequences of this argument is that trust in the self supports the traditional *consensus gentium* argument for the existence of God. The fact that so many people in so many cultures in so many ages of the world have believed in a deity gives each of us a defeasible reason to believe in God that arises from a rational demand of the self. But the commitment to trust in others also shows why religious disagreement poses a particular threat to our own beliefs in matters of religion.

2 The need for self-trust

My starting point is the assumption that human beings have natural desires, desires that are part of every pre-reflective self. The idea that there are natural desires occurs repeatedly in both Western and non-Western philosophy, and it is presumed in many fields of study, although some scholars attempt to reduce them to a few basic ones such as the desire for pleasure and the avoidance of pain. I will not make any claims about the scope of natural desires, but I want to focus on a particular desire, the desire for truth, because I think it enjoys a certain primacy in the map of our desires, and if the desire is reasonable, there are some interesting consequences. If the desire for truth is natural, then virtually everyone has the desire, but I do not deny that there may be some exceptions. It is possible that the Pyrrhonian skeptics succeeded in giving it up, but even they recognized that skepticism is not the natural way to be since they thought they had to go through therapy to get there. So with a few possible exceptions, I think it is fair to say that everyone desires truth.

We do not need to assume anything controversial about truth to make this assumption about the natural desire for truth. My point is compatible with a deflationary view of truth according to which the word 'true' adds nothing to what can be stated without it. So according to some philosophers, if I want to know whether 'Hostas prefer shade' is true, that is just to say that I want to know whether Hostas prefer shade. We can express my question without the word 'true.' But that affects only the wording of my point, not its substance. It means that the natural desire for truth is the desire to have my questions answered. I want to know who or what something is, or whether something is the case, or how something works. When I say there is a natural desire for truth, I just mean that it is natural to ask questions and to want answers to them. Sometimes I don't even know enough to know what question to ask. The desire to be shown the question to ask as well as its answer is also part of what I mean by the desire for truth. What I am calling the desire for truth is the satisfaction of the questioning urge. So my claim that there is such a natural desire for truth does not depend upon the position that the word 'true' cannot be eliminated from our discourse, nor does it depend upon the idea that there is a single object—truth, which is the aim of the questioning urge.

In addition to the natural desire for truth, I think there is a natural belief that the natural desire for truth is satisfiable. I live my life as if I can get answers to my questions, so I think that the desire for truth can be, and often is, satisfied. I trust my faculties and my environment sufficiently to think that I believe many truths, and I rely upon those faculties and those truths in the normal conduct of my life. The faculties I use in forming beliefs may operate on the environment directly, or they may operate on the testimony of others. It is not only natural to rely upon my own faculties, but it is also natural to believe what other people tell me. So the natural trust with which I start includes trust in the relation between my faculties and my environment, and trust in the faculties of many other people. Philosophers raise the question whether it is reasonable to have trust in this general, basic way, but it is clear that trust is the starting point. It is a component of the pre-reflective self.

I do not know how common it is to reflect upon one's desire for truth or one's belief that the desire is satisfiable, but philosophers reflect upon everything. That might be what is most characteristic of philosophy. It is interesting to investigate what happens to a disciplined self-reflective being who reflects upon the belief that truth is attainable. Does she gain or lose confidence in it? Does she decide that the belief is justified? What does that do to her trust in herself and others?

A number of philosophers have observed that there is no non-circular way to determine that the natural desire for truth is satisfiable, or to put the claim in the preferred idiom, there is no non-circular way to tell that our belief-forming faculties are reliable as a whole. For instance, Richard Foley argues that there is no answer to the radical skeptic and the project of strong foundationalism failed, so there is no non-circular guarantee that our epistemic faculties and procedures are suited to discover truths.[1] We can do everything epistemically that we are supposed to do, including following the evidence scrupulously, and we have no assurances that the results will give us the truth or even make it probable that we will get the truth. We therefore need self-trust in our epistemic faculties taken as a whole, together with our pre-reflective opinions. Self-trust is necessary, and since it is a state to which we are led by a process of rational self-criticism, it is also rational.

For Foley, self-trust is a state to which we must move when we reflect upon the skeptical hypotheses and the failure of responses to them, particularly the failure of foundationalism. He implies that trust is a state to which we retreat because we do not have adequate justification, or as he sometimes puts it, a 'guarantee' of the reliability of our faculties and opinions taken as a whole.

William Alston offers a more detailed and subtle argument for a related conclusion about circularity in his 1986 paper, 'Epistemic Circularity,' repeating part of the argument of that paper with modifications in his book, *Beyond Justification* (2005).[2] Alston argues that as long as the issue is the reliability of broad sources of belief, the attempt to establish the reliability of beliefs deriving from that source will inevitably take us back to the source from which we started (2005, pp. 209–10). Full reflective justification for any belief is impossible (2005, p. 344). An interesting difference between Alston and Foley is that Alston does not think that the problem of epistemic circularity is necessarily tied to the threat of skepticism. He says that the specter of skepticism is a 'dramatic' way to put the issue, 'but it is not necessary for a calm, fully mature consideration of the problem' (2005, p. 216).[3] I think this is an important point. A person who aims to be fully reflectively justified in her beliefs need not be a person who is afraid that the alternative to full reflective justification is skepticism. She may just be a person who takes reflective self-consciousness as far as she can. She is doing what every self-reflective being does, only she is doing it more thoroughly. In making the attempt to go as far as she can in disciplined self-consciousness, she notices that she runs up against the problem of epistemic circularity. But she need not be motivated by fear of skepticism.

Like Foley, Alston concludes that self-trust is inescapable, and like Foley, Alston thinks of self-trust as the outcome of a sophisticated line of argument. We are forced into it by careful reflection on the human epistemic condition. If we could be fully reflectively justified in our beliefs, presumably we would not need to 'take' our faculties to be reliable and our beliefs to be credible. We would not need self-trust because we would have something in principle better, but impossible to achieve.

---

[1] Richard Foley, *Intellectual Trust in Oneself And Others* (Cambridge, Cambridge University Press, 2001).

[2] William P. Alston, 'Epistemic Circularity' (1986), *Philosophy and Phenomenological Research* 47, pp. 1–30; idem., *Beyond Justification: Dimensions of Epistemic Evaluation* (Ithaca, NY, Cornell University Press, 2005).

[3] He says, however, that he will pursue the discussion in the next few pages in terms of the 'more dramatically attractive' skeptical challenge. His response to epistemic circularity two pages later is therefore framed as a reply to the Pyrrhonian skeptic.

My approach to the need for self-trust is somewhat different. I have suggested that there is a natural desire for truth and a natural belief that the desire is satisfied. This belief is pre-reflective. Before we reflect upon the justification of our beliefs or the reliability of our faculties, we already trust ourselves and our environment, including other people. Trust is the condition of the pre-reflective self; it is not just for intellectually sophisticated persons who have reflected on skepticism and epistemic circularity and who conclude that we cannot be fully reflectively justified in our beliefs. Trust is the state from which we begin and we may ask ourselves whether we can escape it. Alston's arguments indicate that the answer will always be no.

What would happen if, *per impossibile*, we could escape epistemic circularity? What if someone thinks upon reflection that strong foundationalism succeeds, or that there is some other answer to skepticism, or that there is some way to achieve full reflective justification? Will they trust their faculties less than the person who thinks there is no answer to the skeptic?

Clearly it depends upon what trust is. Foley implies that trust is a fall-back state to which we retreat when we lack the proof we really want, and Alston seems to have a similar view, although he says very little about the state of trust. This way of looking at trust makes a lot of sense in certain contexts. For instance, people often say they trust their mates when they lack proof of fidelity. But trust in your spouse need not be a state to which you retreat when you lack the proof you would prefer to have. If you had proof, would you have less trust? In such a case you would not have to 'fall back' on trust, but it seems to me that typically, you would still have the *disposition* of trust because the point of trust is that it does not depend upon proof, not that it requires the lack of proof. Similarly, I think that trust in one's epistemic faculties does not depend upon the outcome of philosophical arguments. If we could escape epistemic circularity by getting a guarantee that our faculties get us the truth, that would be like the case in which you have proof of your spouse's fidelity. I don't see that trust would disappear. The difference is that epistemic circularity makes self-trust essential, whereas it would be non-essential but still natural if we were able to escape the epistemic circle.

Is there any difference between the pre-reflective state of self-trust and the self-trust we have after reflection on epistemic circularity? Again, that depends upon the necessary conditions for trust. I think that trust has two components that can be separated. First, when I trust x I treat x as trustworthy—deserving of trust. Second, I believe that x is trustworthy. If the trust in question is epistemic trust in myself, that means that I both treat my epistemic faculties and beliefs as trustworthy, and I believe that they are trustworthy. If I rely upon my faculties, as I necessarily do, I am treating them as if they are trustworthy, but it is possible for a person to respond to the problem of epistemic circularity by treating her faculties as trustworthy without believing they are trustworthy. Such a person would have one of the components of self-trust but not the other.

For the purposes of this paper I will not claim that this response is unreasonable, but will merely mention my reason for thinking that it is reasonable to believe ourselves to be trustworthy. To treat something as deserving of trust without believing it deserves trust creates dissonance in the self that becomes noticeable once we start reflecting. When I become aware of self-trust, I am pressured within myself to either stop trusting myself or to believe that I am trustworthy. It is possible to accept the dissonance or to not notice it, so I do not insist that it is impossible to live a normal life without believing that our epistemic faculties are trustworthy. But the self-reflective person at some point will become aware of the dissonance if she does not believe her faculties are trustworthy, and will then have to decide whether to accept the natural belief that her natural desire for truth is satisfiable or else live with dissonance. I propose that it is reasonable to resolve the dissonance by not only trusting our faculties, but also believing that they are trustworthy. I will return to the issue of what it means to be reasonable.

The awareness of epistemic circularity is not the deepest reason why we need epistemic self-trust. Epistemic circularity is relevant to the natural desire for truth only if we make certain assumptions about the nature of mind and the universe, and if we make those assumptions, we need to trust them. We observe the problem of epistemic circularity when we want truth—our questions answered, and we notice that the process of attempting to answer those questions can never be completed. But this would not be a problem unless (1) there is a connection between truth and what we do when we attempt to answer our questions, and (2) what we attempt to do can never be completed. The discovery of epistemic circularity is the discovery of (2), but what about (1)? The assumption that there is a connection between getting truth and what we do when we attempt to answer our questions is the deeper reason for self-trust.

To see why, suppose we resisted or gave up the desire to complete the task of finding reasons, and thus found epistemic circularity non-threatening. Then we would be forced to face the fact that the problem is not just that we cannot *complete* the search for reasons, but that we have to trust that there is *any* connection between reasons and truth. If the process of getting reasons were completed, then we would have the reasons we seek, but we would still need to trust that reasons are the sorts of things that give us the answers to our questions, that connect us to truth. And why do we trust reasons? Because looking for reasons for our beliefs is what a self-reflective person does when she is trying hard to get the truth. We trust reasons in virtue of our trust in the connection between trying to get the truth and succeeding.

The situation would be unchanged if we accepted a strong form of foundationalism. What foundationalism gives us is the completion of the search for reasons, but we would still need trust in whatever power in us produced the foundational beliefs in an attempt to answer our questions, and whatever it is in us that gives us the foundational cognitive structure. We trust reasons at all only because we trust ourselves when we are making the effort to get truth.

Let us call the quality of trying hard to get the truth *epistemic conscientiousness*. I think of this quality as the self-reflective parallel to the natural desire for truth. It is not just a vague, unspecified, and possibly unconscious desire, but a conscious desire accompanied by the attempt to satisfy it with all of one's available powers. I have argued that we need trust that there is a connection between the natural desire for truth and the satisfaction of that desire using the faculties that any person has, reflective or pre-reflective, but once a person becomes reflective, she will think that her trustworthiness is greater if she makes a greater effort, summoning her powers in a fully conscious and careful way, and exercising them to the best of her ability. What I am calling conscientiousness is the state or disposition to do that.[4] We trust that there is a connection between trying and succeeding, and the reflective person thinks that there is a closer connection between trying hard and succeeding. But it would not be reasonable to trust conscientiousness unless it was already reasonable to place a basic trust in the faculties we are using when we are conscientious. I would not be trustworthy when I am trying hard in using my faculties unless my faculties were already generally trustworthy. So it would not be reasonable to trust myself when I am conscientious and for the reason that I am conscientious unless it was already reasonable for me to trust my faculties in a very basic way.

I assume that conscientiousness comes in degrees. Trying a little is natural and requires no special self-reflection. It is probably an automatic accompaniment to the natural desire for truth. But trying hard requires considerable self-awareness and self-monitoring.

There are certain things we do when we monitor our beliefs. One of the things we do (but not the only thing) is to expect ourselves to have reasons for our beliefs. A conscientious person might not expect reasons for every belief, but having reasons is something conscientious persons expect of themselves, and we trust the connection between reasons and truth because we have a more basic trust in ourselves when we are being conscientious, and we trust the connection between conscientiousness and the possession of reasons.

The same point applies to trust in evidence (which I assume is closely related to reasons for belief). We do not have evidence that evidence leads to truth. We might think that we have evidence that evidence leads to truth, but what we mean is that we have evidence that evidence leads to more evidence, enough that at some point we say that the matter is settled. In any case, why should we pay attention to the evidence that evidence leads to truth unless we trust evidence? And what do we trust it for? To get to truth. We trust the evidence that evidence leads to truth, and we trust it because looking for evidence that something is true is what self-reflective persons who want the truth do, and we trust that. Like our trust in reasons, our trust in evidence is dependent upon our trust in ourselves when we are being conscientious. We have evidence that conscientiousness leads to truth; that is, we have evidence that trying to get truth leads to truth, but we trust that evidence because of a more basic trust in the relation between conscientiousness and truth.

---

[4] Note that as I define conscientiousness, it does not have any relation to duty.

So is it reasonable to trust ourselves epistemically? I have argued for two levels of epistemic self-trust, one a basic trust in our faculties, and the other a particular trust in ourselves when we self-consciously exercise those faculties to the best of our ability—when we are epistemically conscientious. We have reasons for thinking that our faculties give us truth, but the reasons are circular. We also have circular reasons for thinking that conscientiousness leads to truth. In both cases we lack non-circular reasons, but we lack non-circular reasons for any of our beliefs, so we do not lack something we can get. The belief that our faculties are trustworthy as a way to get to truth is one of the components of epistemic self-trust, and so one of the components of epistemic self-trust is reasonable. The other component is an attitude, a way of treating our faculties. We treat them as trustworthy. That is reasonable also, assuming the following principle: If it is reasonable to believe x is trustworthy, it is reasonable to treat x as trustworthy. There is a parallel argument for the reasonableness of trusting ourselves when we are conscientious.

If we are reasonable in trusting ourselves when we conscientious, we have another ground for the reasonableness of basic trust in our faculties. We would not be trustworthy when we are conscientious unless our faculties were already basically trustworthy. So the following principle gives us the conclusion that it is reasonable to have a basic trust in our faculties: If it is reasonable to trust x and x would not be trustworthy unless y is trustworthy, it is reasonable to trust y.

To summarize this section, we have a natural belief that our natural desire for truth is satisfiable, and a natural trust in the faculties and processes in ourselves that produce beliefs. There is no rational way to escape this natural self-trust, given the fact that the search for reasons for our beliefs leads to epistemic circularity, and the more basic fact that we have no way to tell that there is any connection at all between reasons and truth without trust in ourselves when we are conscientious. This means that a self-reflective person trusts herself in advance of reasons to trust herself, but she trusts herself more when she is conscientious and for the reason that she is conscientious. She trusts reasons and evidence because of her trust in herself when she is conscientious.

3 The need for trust in others

Natural epistemic trust in ourselves is inescapable, but what about the natural trust in other persons? Many philosophers think that it is not only escapable, but that epistemic self-reliance represents an intellectual ideal. Trusting only our own faculties and not those of others is a quality Elizabeth Fricker calls intellectual autonomy.[5] Almost everyone, including Fricker, agrees that if we did not depend upon others, we would have far less knowledge because we would have far fewer beliefs, but it does seem possible not to rely upon others, whereas it is impossible not to rely upon

---

[5] Elizabeth Fricker, 'Testimony and Epistemic Autonomy' in Jennifer Lackey and Ernest Sosa (eds.), *The Epistemology of Testimony* (Oxford, Oxford University Press, 2006).

ourselves. I will argue that if we trust ourselves epistemically, we cannot consistently fail to trust others epistemically.

Since I have no non-circular reason for thinking I am trustworthy as a whole, I have no non-circular reason to think that as a whole I am more trustworthy than other people are as a whole. But by using powers that I trust, I come to believe that other human beings have the same natural desire for truth and the same general powers and capacities that I have. If I believe that I am generally trustworthy and I accept the principle that I should treat like cases alike, I am rationally committed to thinking that they are generally trustworthy also. I should regard them as generally trustworthy in advance of evidence of their trustworthiness just as I think of myself as trustworthy in advance of the evidence. Since as a conscientious person I trust evidence, I may see that on the evidence some person is not epistemically trustworthy, or not trustworthy in some respect, and if so, my general trust in that person would be defeated. But in so far as I have a general trust in the connection between my natural faculties and desire for truth and success in reaching truth, then I should have trust in the same connection in other people. As long as I see no relevant difference between others and myself, then if I trust myself, I should trust them too.

When I am conscientious I acquire many beliefs about other people. Many other people appear to me to be just as conscientious as I am when I am as conscientious as I can be. At least, many of them are just as conscientious as I am in certain respects or with respect to certain beliefs. Because I place particular trust in myself when I am conscientious, I commit myself to trusting the conscientiously formed beliefs I have about both the general epistemic similarity of other persons to myself, and their own conscientiousness. Because I trust myself when I am conscientious and for the reason that I am conscientious, I must trust others whose conscientiousness I discover when I am being conscientious. I have said that one of the things I do when I am conscientious (but not the only thing I do) is to look for reasons or evidence for my beliefs. I do have plenty of evidence that other people are as conscientious as I am with regard to numerous beliefs. I also have evidence that some people are more conscientious than I am, and, of course, I have evidence that some people are less so.

My commitment to trust my conscientiously formed beliefs about other people means that I cannot consistently expect evidence of the reliability of another person before thinking of them as epistemically trustworthy. In so far as I believe myself to be trustworthy when I am conscientious, and I conscientiously believe that many other people are at least as conscientious as I am in certain respects, I must think of them as epistemically trustworthy in those respects. I am committed to that by the principle that I should think of like cases alike. I have said that a conscientious person trusts evidence in virtue of her trust in conscientiousness, and so a conscientious person might expect evidence of another person's conscientiousness before trusting them. But I want to make two points about that. First, having evidence of another person's conscientiousness is not the same as having evidence of her reliability. We do have evidence that conscientiousness is reliably truth-conducive, so if we have evidence that someone is conscientious, we have indirect evidence that she is reliable. But the more important point from the last section is that we trust evidence in virtue of the fact that we trust conscientiousness, not vice versa, so our trust in the evidence that someone else is conscientious derives from our trust in our own conscientiousness. I have left open the possibility that a conscientious person believes conscientiously without evidence in some cases. If so, she can conscientiously believe that another person is conscientious without evidence of the other's conscientiousness.

So far I have argued that I am committed to thinking of other people as epistemically trustworthy if I think of myself as epistemically trustworthy, but my trust in myself is basic. I must have a general trust in myself and my faculties if I trust the natural desire for truth, and since I am reasonable in believing that other people have the same faculties and the same natural desire, I am reasonable in trusting them and their faculties for the same reason I trust my own. But my trust in others depends upon my beliefs that they are like me and that I should treat like cases alike. My trust in myself does not depend upon those beliefs.

Self-trust is also more basic when I am led by my trust in my own conscientiousness to believe that others are conscientious also, and so the greater trust I have in myself when I am conscientiousness should be extended to those other people whose conscientiousness I discover when I am being conscientious. Trust in my own conscientiousness is basic because my own conscientiousness is probably something that is transparent to my mind, or at least, it is something I can discover through introspection. I would not deny that self-deception is possible, but in general, I know how hard I am trying. In contrast, my reason to believe other people are conscientious depends upon observation of those people and inferences about their inner efforts from their external behavior. So my grounds for believing other people are conscientious is less direct than my grounds for believing that I am conscientious. Nonetheless, it is often reasonable for me to believe that other people are conscientious because it is a belief I form when I am being conscientious. Given that I conscientiously believe they are conscientious, then if I am rationally required to accept the principle that I should treat like cases alike, I am rationally required to trust them for the same reason I trust myself.

Somebody might agree that the paths from self-trust to trust in others succeed in showing that I am committed to thinking of all other people as generally trustworthy, and many other people as just as trustworthy as myself. But it can be argued that it does not follow that I am committed to actually trusting any of these people. I have no obligation to trust everyone I believe to be trustworthy. If I prefer to trust myself and not others, or to trust myself more than others, why shouldn't I do that? Can I reasonably refuse to trust others epistemically?

I think that I cannot do so if I care about truth. If I do not trust others, I must ignore my own evidence that other people are trustworthy; I must ignore the beliefs to which I am led when I am conscientious—when I form beliefs out of a concern for truth. The only way to do that is to care about my own faculties and their outputs more than the truth, to care about my own evidence, not because it leads to the truth, but because it is mine, to care about my own conscientious beliefs, not because I am conscientious and care about truth, but because they are my beliefs. I must regard myself as trustworthy, not because of my conscientiousness or even because of my human faculties, but because I am myself. And that is very implausible. The same problem arises whenever I trust myself more than others when my evidence or the conscientious use of my faculties indicates that they are as reliable or as conscientious as I am. To the extent that I trust myself more than I trust them, my reason is not epistemic. And so I must be valuing my own faculties more than the truth. That is ethical egoism in the realm of the intellect.

Assuming I do not want to be an ethical egoist, I am rationally committed to not only thinking of others as trustworthy, but to actually trusting them on the same grounds as I trust myself. I must have the same attitude of general defeasible trust in all others that I have towards myself, and I must acknowledge that the level of trust that I have in myself when I am conscientious applies to many other people.

4 The *consensus gentium* argument

I have argued that general trust in myself commits me to the position that there is a defeasible presumption in favor of the beliefs of any other person, absent any particular reason I have for trusting or not trusting the person, and absent any reason I may have in advance for believing or disbelieving the proposition he believes. But virtually every real life case of finding out in a way we trust that somebody has a certain belief includes information about the believer that potentially defeats the credibility of the belief. What's more, the content of the belief may be something to which I might assign a low prior probability, given other things I believe, or other psychic states I trust, such as emotions or attitudes. But let's try to imagine a pure case, one in which there is no information that affects the credibility of the belief. For instance, suppose I find out that somebody somewhere of whom I know nothing believes that Poland was invaded by the Tartars in 1279, and suppose that my background knowledge of Poland and the Tartars is so vague that I have no reason to believe or disbelieve in advance, and suppose that neither believing nor disbelieving that Poland was invaded by the Tartars would have any effect on anything else I trust. I submit that I have a reason to believe that Poland was invaded by the Tartars in 1279. Of course, there are no pure cases of this kind. I cannot find out that someone believes a proposition without finding out many other things about the believer of the proposition, and in almost every case the content of the proposition has some bearing on my other beliefs or my emotions or attitudes, which I may trust to one degree or another. So in practice my defeasible reason for believing that Poland was invaded by the Tartars may be defeated easily, either because I have evidence that the believer is untrustworthy, or because I already have a belief I trust that conflicts with the belief about the Tartars, or because the belief would produce dissonance with some non-belief state that I trust. Nonetheless, it is worth noting that once I become aware of the fact that somebody believes that Poland was invaded by the Tartars and I trust my belief that somebody has that belief, I have a defeasible reason to believe it myself. Since I have endorsed weak universalism, I am not claiming that having a defeasible reason to believe p means that I have sufficient reason to adopt the belief p, but the belief of another person counts in favor of the belief. It is a mark in favor of its credibility.

Suppose now that I find out that large numbers of people have the same belief. Maybe I learn that thousands of people believe that Poland was invaded by the Tartars, and again, we need to imagine that I lack any other information about those people or the content of the belief. It seems to me that large number of believers strengthens my defeasible reason for sharing their belief. The degree of trust I should have in their belief increases. Of course, it might turn out that most of these people acquired their belief from one or a few other people, and in fact, most beliefs that are shared by large numbers of people are spread through the community by testimony. So we should say that other things equal, a belief independently acquired by large numbers of people is more trustworthy than the belief of one or a few.

However, the importance of independence should not be exaggerated. If twenty people believe the outcome of one person's addition on the testimony of one who added up the figures, their belief does not count as much as it would if each of them had independently added the figures, but it seems to me that it counts more than the case in which only one person has the belief. That is because the fact that twenty people have the belief is evidence that nineteen people regard the source from which they acquired the belief as trustworthy, and that gives me a defeasible reason to treat the source as trustworthy also. I have a defeasible reason to trust persons whom people I trust trust. If many millions of people share a belief, that gives me a greater defeasible reason to trust the belief than if only one or a few persons believe it, even if the beliefs were not acquired independently. Nonetheless, independence of belief greatly increases the trustworthiness of the belief.

I have argued that trust in agreement by large numbers of other people is justified by self-trust. It is common to treat widespread agreement as a defeasible reason to adopt or maintain a belief, so there is common consent that common consent gives us a reason for belief. This is a ground for belief that is usually unconscious, and even philosophers who are otherwise very careful about identifying and defending their grounds for making an assertion sometimes refer to common agreement without defense.[6] I have offered a defense that arises from consistently applying the attitude of trust in my general epistemic faculties that is both pre-reflective and found upon reflection to be

---

[6] Hume does this in his essay 'On Miracles.' After giving an argument against the reasonableness of belief on testimony that a miracle occurred, he gives an example of something it would be reasonable to believe that has some of the features of a miracle. He postulates that many people testified that darkness fell over the earth for a period of eight days on a date long before the birth of the person making the judgment. There are several features of the situation that Hume thinks increase the reasonableness of believing their testimony. One of the most important is widespread agreement in the testimony.

rationally inescapable. I owe the same attitude to anyone else who has the faculties I trust in myself, which is to say all other human beings.

The belief that common consent gives us a reason to adopt a belief has a long history. Perhaps the most famous case of a *consensus gentium* argument is used to defend the belief in God. We find such an argument in Cicero's dialogue, *On the Nature of the Gods*. Cicero writes:

This belief of ours is not based on any prescription, custom, or law, but it abides as the strong, unanimous conviction of the whole world. We must therefore come to the realization that gods must exist because we have an implanted, or rather an innate, awareness of them. Now when all people naturally agree on something, that belief must be true; so we are to acknowledge that gods exist... This is agreed by virtually everyone—not just philosophers, but also the unlearned. (*The Nature of the Gods*, Book I, 44).

Cicero observes that belief in a deity or deities is virtually universal. Today it is not universal, if it ever was, but it is certainly widespread. In any case, the argument from consent does not require universality of belief. Lack of universality is a problem only to the extent that there are not only large numbers of people who believe in God, but there are also many people who disbelieve in God. Clearly, if the numbers of people who believe in some proposition count, so do the numbers of people who disbelieve that same proposition.

The issue of independence is relevant to Cicero's argument. If millions of people believe in God because they all acquired the belief by testimony from a small number of sources, the vast number of believers does not count as much as the same number of beliefs acquired independently. Most people who believe in God come to believe in the early part of their lives by testimony from their parents and other trusted adults. It is doubtful that the beliefs children get from adults have much more credibility than the beliefs of the adults alone, and I think we should discount the number of children's beliefs as relevant to the *consensus gentium* argument. However, I would not discount the number of theistic beliefs of adults who originally acquired their belief on testimony since there is a defeasible reason to trust their trust in the lack of defeaters for their belief. In any case, there are many millions of beliefs in God that *are* independently acquired. I think we should conclude that the epistemic presumption is in favor of the belief. The fact that another person believes in God gives each of us a defeasible reason to believe. The fact that many millions believe increases the reason, and the fact that many of those millions acquired their belief independently increases the reason further. It is an implication of self-trust that the fact that so many people all over the world at all times have believed in a deity gives each of us a *prima facie* reason to believe in a deity ourselves, a reason that exceeds the reason we would have for believing in God if we were aware of only one or a few believers. Of course, it also follows that the fact that there are many disbelievers counts in favor of disbelief.

Summarizing what I have said, the fact that consistent self-trust leads to trust in others produces a form of the traditional *consensus gentium* argument which we can formulate as follows:

4.1 Consensus gentium *argument from self-trust*

1. Every person must have a general attitude of self-trust in her epistemic faculties as a whole. This trust is both natural and shown to be inescapable by philosophical reflection.
2. The general attitude of epistemic self-trust commits us to a general attitude of epistemic trust in the faculties of all other human beings.
3. So the fact that someone else has a belief gives me a *prima facie* reason to believe it myself.
4. Other things being equal, the fact that many people have a certain belief increases my *prima facie* reason to believe it, and my reason is stronger when the beliefs are acquired independently.
5. The fact that other people believe in God is a *prima facie* reason to believe that God exists, and the fact that many millions of people constituting a strong supermajority believe (or have believed in prior ages) that God exists increases my *prima facie* reason to believe in God myself. Discounting for dependence, there are still many millions of people who independently believe or have believed in past ages in the existence of God.

A parallel argument can be given for atheism since the fact that there are many people who disbelieve in God gives me a *prima facie* reason to disbelieve in God. If there are many more people who believe than disbelieve, the *prima facie* reason for belief is stronger than for disbelief.

The argument I have given here is not the same as traditional *consensus gentium* arguments such as the one I quoted from Cicero. This argument has usually been interpreted as an argument to the best explanation. The idea is that there is a certain datum that needs to be explained: the fact that so many people in so many parts of the world believe in God. The issue is then thought to be whether the best explanation for that datum is the truth of the belief. Various explanations of the datum are then weighed against each other from the standpoint of a neutral arbiter. The arbiter could be a person from another planet. No connection is assumed between the arbiter's trust in the way she goes about evaluating alternative explanations for the datum and the arbiter's trust in the beliefs of the persons evaluated. I hope it is clear that the argument I am proposing is not of this kind. My argument links trust in the beliefs of others with self-trust. Trust in the self commits us to granting *prima facie* credibility to the belief of another, and trust in the credibility of the belief ought to be greater when the belief is widespread.

The reason for belief in God that we get from the belief of other people can be defeated. In particular, it can be defeated by the discovery of lack of conscientiousness on the part of a believer. Given the important place of conscientiousness in self-trust, the argument can be strengthened or weakened, depending upon my conscientious judgment that the people who believe in God are or are not conscientious in their belief. For almost all theistic believers in human history, I have no reason to think that they were especially conscientious or epistemically unconscientious. I am aware of many extremely conscientious people who believe in God, but also many whose belief is no more conscientious than their belief in the likelihood of extra-terrestrial visitors. I am also aware of many conscientious people who disbelieve in God, but the number of conscientious believers seems to me to be significantly greater than the number of conscientious non-believers.

Is there any reason to think that belief in God is over-represented among those who are the least conscientious? Hume notoriously claimed that belief in miracles is more common among 'ignorant and barbarous' peoples.[7] Similarly, some intellectually sophisticated atheists claim that atheism is dominant among intellectually sophisticated persons in Western countries.[8] So some people must think that they can identify a property that defeats the belief that the possessors of the property are trustworthy, although it is unlikely that they think the property defeats the belief that the possessors of the property are conscientious.

The argument I have given here does not claim that there are no defeaters. I am arguing that everyone has a *prima facie* reason to trust all others, a majority of whom believe in God, and that gives us a *prima facie* reason to believe in God. That is a reason that can be defeated by the discovery of the lack of conscientiousness among believers, and it can be strengthened by the discovery of the conscientiousness of believers. An objector might think that when she believes conscientiously she can identify a property of the believer that makes a belief formed out of that property untrustworthy, and that many theists in history have that property. If so, she must think either that this property prevents the believer from being conscientious, or she trusts the truth-conduciveness of that property more than that of conscientiousness. There are many other ways in which aspects of the self one trusts can defeat one's reason for having a certain belief, but my purpose is not to investigate the particular defeaters one could have, but to propose a structure that a reasonable person should use based on self-trust.

The idea of God common among all peoples is exceedingly vague. Common consent clearly cannot support specific theological claims about God, not even the unicity of God, although that attribute has wider acceptance than such traditional attributes as personhood, omnipotence and perfect goodness. What we get from widespread agreement is closer to the 'half glimpse' mentioned by Aristotle than to a clear view of the object. The peoples of the world give different descriptions of the

---

[7] David Hume in Tom L. Beauchamp (ed.), *An Inquiry Concerning Human Understanding* (Oxford, Oxford University Press, 2000), p. 90.

[8] See, for instance, Richard Dawkins, *The God Delusion* (New York, NY, Houghton Mifflin Publishers, 2008), p. 128.

object glimpsed, but they agree that there was a glimpse of something important. Perhaps the vagueness of the idea of God makes the *consensus gentium* argument uninteresting to some people, but I agree with Aristotle that even a half glimpse of something tremendous is more valuable than a complete view of lesser things.

This brings me to my final point. Given that self-trust commits us to trust those who have the qualities we trust in ourselves, disagreement with those we trust is a problem. The popular problem of reasonable disagreement is usually posed in terms of what a reasonable person should do when she is aware of other persons who have a belief that conflicts with her own when those other persons seem to her to be as reasonable as she is herself. The argument I have given here suggests that this problem in its most critical form arises from self-trust because it is self-trust that forces us to trust many of those with whom we disagree. When I am believing conscientiously I come to believe that there are many others who are as conscientious as I am and who therefore deserve the same level of trust I have in myself when I am as conscientious as I can be. In fact, it is not even necessary to accept my argument that the feature of myself in virtue of which I trust myself the most epistemically is epistemic conscientiousness. For any quality I have in virtue of which I trust myself epistemically, whether it is particular intellectual virtues, the best exercise of my reason, or some other epistemically trustworthy property, when I believe in a way that arises from that quality, I will invariably come to believe that there are many other people who have the same trustworthy quality, and who have beliefs that arise from that quality that conflict with some of my own beliefs. I owe them trust because of consistent trust in myself.

My view is that the only way to resolve this problem is to become as self-conscious as we can about the things we trust. Trusting what I trust upon reflection when I am being conscientious is all I can do. Doing so seems to me to be pretty close to what Kant meant by an autonomous agent. But autonomy of intellect, like autonomy of will, should not be confused with self-reliance. Furthermore, intellectual autonomy is something that cannot be universalized. I recognize that different people will end up with different beliefs (and different emotions and values) when they trust the structure of trust in themselves and are conscientious in doing so. But that is to be expected since we are not all the same self.

3

Religious Experience and the Question of Whether Belief in God Requires Evidence

C. Stephen Evans

Reformed epistemologists, most famously Alvin Plantinga, maintain that belief in God can be 'properly basic.' According to Plantinga, this means affirming with Reformed thinkers that 'a believer is entirely rational, entirely within his epistemic rights, in *starting with* belief in God, in accepting it as basic, and in taking it as a premise for argument to other conclusions.'[1] In later works Plantinga goes even further and argues that belief in God that is basic can not only be reasonable and justified, but can even amount to knowledge.[2] At least no one can show that belief in God does not amount to knowledge without showing that the belief in question is false. Plantinga defends an epistemology in which a belief that is true, held with a high enough degree of certitude, and that is the product of cognitive faculties that are designed to achieve truth and that are operating properly in the kind of environment in which they were intended to operate, is one that is known.[3] He then argues that it is highly plausible that if there is a God, these conditions are sometimes fulfilled. The Reformed epistemologist thus presents us with a 'model' as to how one might gain knowledge of God.[4] Plantinga does not claim to have shown that this is actually the way we gain knowledge of God, though he believes that the model or something like it is correct, but he does claim to have shown it is a possible way someone might know about God. Furthermore, he argues that if there is a God, the model or something similar to it is likely to be true.[5]

---

[1] 'Reason and Belief in God' in Alvin Plantinga and Nicholas Wolterstorff (eds.), *Faith and Rationality* (Notre Dame, Indiana, University of Notre Dame Press, 1983), p. 72.

[2] This certainly seems to be strongly implied by chapter 6 of Alvin Plantinga, *Warranted Christian Belief* (New York, Oxford University Press, 2000).

[3] This is a rough summary of the view Plantinga explains on pp. 153–63 in *Warranted Christian Belief*.

[4] The notion of a model is explained by Plantinga on pp. 168–70 in *Warranted Christian Belief*. The initial model he develops, called the 'Aquinas–Calvin model' is supposed to be an account of belief in God. Later in the book he develops what he calls the 'extended' version of this model, which is supposed to be an account of full-fledged Christian belief, not merely theistic belief.

[5] *Warranted Christian Belief*, pp. 169–70.

The account Plantinga offers stresses that although belief in God is not based on evidence, it is not 'groundless.' To the contrary, there are many situations and circumstances, involving various experiences, that evoke belief in God. Plantinga cites several examples. When we 'contemplate a flower' or 'behold the starry heavens' we 'have in us a disposition to believe propositions of the sort *this flower was created by God* or *this vast and intricate universe was created by God.*'[6] Moral experience provides another possibility: 'Upon having done what I know is cheap, or wrong, or wicked, I may feel guilty in God's sight and form the belief *God disapproves of what I have done.*'[7] Strictly speaking, what these grounds make properly basic is not the relatively abstract belief that 'God exists' but more specific and concrete beliefs such as the following: 'God is speaking to me' and 'God disapproves of what I have done.'[8] However, as Plantinga notes, the existence of God follows so directly and obviously from these concrete beliefs that there is no harm in speaking a bit loosely and viewing 'God exists' as itself basic. Even though it is actually inferred, the inferences are so immediate and spontaneous that they hardly count as inferences at all.[9]

The notion of grounds is an important part of Plantinga's response to the 'Great Pumpkin' objection. This well-known objection holds that if it is proper to believe in God without evidence, then belief in just about anything, including absurdities such as the Great Pumpkin, will be proper as well. Plantinga's response is essentially that belief in the Great Pumpkin lacks a proper ground, 'there being no Great Pumpkin and no natural tendency to accept beliefs about the Great Pumpkin.'[10] One might think that the relevant difference Plantinga relies on here is simply that the belief in God's reality is true, since God exists, while belief in the Great Pumpkin is false. That is indeed an important and relevant difference. However, surely, from an epistemic viewpoint, the more important difference is the fact that belief in the Great Pumpkin is groundless, since it is only through the presence or absence of such grounds that one can know that God does exist and the Great Pumpkin does not. Belief in the Great Pumpkin is not natural for human beings, while the widespread, cross-cultural tendency to believe in God suggests that this belief is natural.

Critics of Reformed epistemology have sometimes objected that the claim that belief in God can be proper without evidence rests on an overly narrow, perhaps tendentious sense of 'evidence.'[11] What the Reformed epistemologist really means, maintains the critic, is that belief in God can be reasonable even if it not inferred or

---

[6] Plantinga, 'Reason and Belief in God,' p. 80.

[7] Ibid.

[8] Ibid. 81.

[9] Ibid. 82.

[10] Ibid. 78.

[11] For example, Phillip Quinn argues that the fact that a fact cannot serve as the basis for an argument does not mean that the fact cannot function as evidence. See 'The Foundations of Theism Again: A Rejoinder to Plantinga' in *Rational Faith: Catholic Responses to Reformed Epistemology* (Notre Dame, Indiana, University of Notre Dame Press, 1993), pp. 14–47. See pp. 31–4 in particular. William Alston made a similar point to me in private correspondence.

argued for, and this means that 'evidence' is being used to refer to something like 'a premise that could function as the basis for an argument or inference.' However, the critic goes on to maintain, we often use the term 'evidence' in a broader sense than this. The police detective views things like fingerprints on a weapon left at the crime scene as evidence, even though a fingerprint is obviously not a proposition, and could not function as a premise in an argument. (Though certainly the detective might be able to formulate a proposition about the fingerprint and use that proposition as the basis for an inference.) If we take a broader view of 'evidence' and see whatever makes some truth evident to us as evidence, then it is by no means clear that belief in God is not based on evidence. In fact, the critic might maintain, the very things that Plantinga cites as 'grounds' for belief in God are in fact evidence.

The critic makes an important point. I believe that it is correct that Plantinga has a fairly specific and limited sense of what counts as evidence. It is also correct that in ordinary language the term 'evidence' is often used in this broader sense of 'whatever makes a truth evident' and when used in this way, it is not clear that properly grounded belief in God is not based on evidence. One might conclude from this that Reformed epistemology gives a misleading picture of how knowledge of God is attained. However, I believe that this conclusion would be a mistake. There is an important insight embedded in the Reformed epistemologist's claim that belief in God does not require evidence, and this insight is obscured when we use the term 'evidence' to refer both to something that is functioning as a premise in an argument and something that plays a role in helping us to know a truth in a more direct way.

In his important and unjustly neglected book, *Belief in God*, George Mavrodes has given us an analysis of religious experience that I think helps us see the correctness of the contentions of both the Reformed epistemologist and the critic.[12] In the remainder of this essay, I shall try to summarize that account and show its bearing on the dispute. I shall conclude with some reflections about the epistemic value of some of the traditional theistic arguments.

1 Mavrodes on experience

In *Belief in God* Mavrodes gives an analysis of experience in general before applying this analysis to experience of God. The term 'experience' is notoriously ambiguous, since we commonly use it to refer both to an interior psychological state (as in 'he experienced great sadness') but also to an encounter with a reality independent of a psychological state (as in 'he experienced the Tower of Pisa for the first time'). Mavrodes uses the term in the second sense, as what we might call a success verb, so that a person who claims to experience something that does not exist (as in 'he saw a unicorn behind the

---

[12] George Mavrodes, *Belief in God: A Study in the Epistemology of Religion* (New York, Random House, 1970).

bush') is making a false claim.[13] Mavrodes uses the verb 'experience' as a general term for all the various ways humans encounter the world, such as seeing, hearing, and touching, without attempting to say how many modes of experience may be possible for humans.[14]

Mavrodes does not try to give an account of all the conditions for some individual to have an experience of some object, but he does delineate two conditions that are necessary to have an experience in his sense. The first is that the object experienced must have a causal effect on the subject of the experience. Thus, Mavrodes says, 'a thing that has no effect upon me is not one of the things that I experience, even if I happen, by an odd coincidence, to have an image of that thing in my mind.'[15] Presumably, Mavrodes thinks having such an image of an object would not count as an experience of the object even if, yet more oddly, the image furnished the individual with useful information about the object. (I assume here that the object is not having some causal impact on the subject through some yet-unknown physical power, such as those that parapsychology attempts to study.)

Mavrodes wisely does not try to spell out the nature of the causal chain that must be present for various forms of experience. Hearing, for example, does not necessarily involve only the transmission of sound waves to the ear through air, for digital hearing aids translate those waves into electronic impulses before amplifying and transmitting sound to the ear.[16] Perhaps hearing aids of the future will bypass the ear altogether and transmit sound by directly sending electronic signals to the relevant portions of the brain. So, although the nature of the causal chain is somewhat open, some such chain must be present on his account for an experience to be veridical.

The second condition that must be met for some person N to have an experience of some object x is that 'N makes some appropriate judgment.'[17] Thus, merely receiving the relevant light waves is not sufficient to count as an instance of seeing, and being affected by the relevant sound waves is not sufficient to count as an instance of hearing. I may be in full view of some object, such as a stop sign, but if my attention is entirely focused elsewhere, I may fail to see it. My wife may tell me to take out the garbage, but if I am absorbed in a golf tournament I am watching on television, I may not hear her. In both cases Mavrodes would say I have failed to see and hear because I have not formed any relevant judgment.

It is not clear to me whether Mavrodes thinks the relevant judgment must be one that is explicitly formulated or even fully conscious. However, I am inclined myself to say that neither of these conditions is necessary. We certainly experience many things that we do not formulate explicit judgments about. Moreover, since it is possible later to remember something that one experienced even though one did not consciously take the thing experienced into account at the precise moment one experienced that thing, I am inclined to deny that whatever judgment is necessary must be fully

---

[13] *Belief in God*, p. 51.   [14] Ibid. 50.   [15] Ibid. 52.
[16] Ibid. 57.   [17] Ibid. 52.

conscious. I shall assume therefore that Mavrodes means to allow for cases where the relevant judgment is implicit rather than explicit, and also cases where the relevant judgment is one that the subject may have less than full conscious awareness of.

Mavrodes does say quite clearly that the relevant judgment in question can be mistaken. Thus, (to take an example from my own experience) philosopher Jay Wood and I were running some years ago on a path in the woods, and had an argument about what we saw on the path up ahead of us. Wood maintained that what we were seeing was a deer, while I maintained it was a large dog, an object to be treated with some caution. When we got closer to the object in question, it turned out that we were both mistaken; the object we were experiencing was a bench. Both of us had seen the bench, on Mavrodes' view, but had mistaken the bench for something else, and thus made judgments that were wrong. If, however, we had been so preoccupied with our conversation that neither of us had noticed the bench at all, making no judgment about it at all, this would not count as an experience of the bench.

2 Mediated experiences

An important feature of human experience stressed by Mavrodes is that it is frequently 'mediated.' That is, we experience one thing by means of an experience of another thing. An astronomer may examine the surface of the moon by looking through a reflective telescope. I may hear the voice of my son through a cell phone. In these cases the causal chain is more or less indirect. The light rays from the moon do not come directly to my eye but first impinge on the surface of a mirror, which the astronomer looks at. The sound waves from my son are not sent directly through the air to my ear, but are first converted into digital information, transmitted as electrical packets through various media, and finally reconverted by my phone into sound waves.

Mavrodes considers a proposal by Roderick Chisholm that we should require directness in the causal chain.[18] Chisholm is worried that if we allow mediation, then it will not be possible to see the moon, since the energy we see from the moon was first transmitted from the sun. However, though the light came from the sun, surely when we look at the moon we do not see the sun.

However, Mavrodes argues, very plausibly, that Chisholm's remedy for this problem is too drastic. If we do not allow experiences to be mediated, it will not be possible for the astronomer to see the moon through a reflecting telescope, or for me to hear my son through a cell phone. Sometimes, when we have such a case of mediated experience, the subject of the experience does indeed experience the mediating object. An optical technician who is examining a telescope that happens to be trained on the moon may see the image on the mirror of the telescope, or simply the surface of the mirror, rather than the moon. A cell phone technician may hear the sound produced

[18] Ibid. 54–5.

by the phone's speakers, rather than my son speaking. However, in such cases it does not seem correct that a person must always be experiencing the medium rather than the object that is mediated.[19]

The situation in which a person experiences one thing by way of experiencing another, such as the moon and the telescope mirror surface, Mavrodes describes as one in which the two objects are in 'input alignment.' In the case of the moon and the telescope, Mavrodes says that the telescope image is in 'total input alignment' with the moon, because whenever the image is seen, 'the visual input is also sufficient to allow us to see the moon.'[20] The moon, however, is only in partial input alignment with the image in the mirror, since there are many ways of seeing the moon that do not require or even allow us to see that image.

What is it that allows one person to see an image, and another person, having the same visual input, to see an object such as the moon? Mavrodes proposes that it is the judgment made by the perceiver in such a case.[21] The person who sees the moon through a telescope and thinks he or she is seeing the moon may be correct, and typically is correct, while the person who thinks he or she is perceiving the image of the moon in the mirror may also be correct. We might expand on this answer if we assume that the differences in the judgments made will reflect other differences between the two experiencers, for example, differences in their interests and foci of attention. To alter the example, I hear the voice of my child through the cell phone speaker, because I am interested in hearing what he has to say, while the phone technician hears a distorted pattern of sound from the speaker because he is interested in whether the speaker is working properly.

One might think that the view Mavrodes defends here is too permissive, and that we should admit that we experience an object only when our experience of that object is direct and unmediated. Mavrodes responds to this kind of worry by pointing out how difficult it is to understand what it might mean to say than an experience is direct if we measure directness in terms of the directness of the causal chain that makes an experience possible. For clearly our experiences are mediated even when we are not considering cases of telescopes or cell phones. Sounds waves are propagated through the air and there is a complex causal chain that makes hearing possible. Hence, Mavrodes argues,

The directness of a direct experience is a psychological directness, the immediacy of such an experience is a psychological immediacy. The directness and immediacy do not belong to the process through which the experienced object affects the experiencer. There is no need for directness and immediacy here, and the search for it in this context resembles the project of peeling an onion. It pushes us back from the object to the surface of the object, to the light waves, to the retinal image, to the impulses in the optic nerve, to the brain states. And generally the further back we are pushed the less plausible becomes the suggestion that this is what we really experience.[22]

---

[19] *Belief in God*, p. 58.   [20] Ibid. 60.
[21] Ibid. 62.   [22] Ibid. 65.

This of course has implications for what a person learns by inference and what is learned directly from experience. Mavrodes asks us to imagine a railroad dispatcher who sits in an office and sees on a television screen a freight train being assembled in a yard. It is possible, perhaps, that the dispatcher 'sees the television picture and from that *infers* the existence and properties of the train.'[23] However, Mavrodes maintains that in the case of an experienced dispatcher this would be unusual, and that it is far more likely that the person simply observes the train on the screen, with no inferences required to gain knowledge about the train.[24] Two people who are having the very same causal experiential input may therefore be in very different epistemic circumstances. What one person comes to know by inference, another person in the same circumstances may come to know in a more direct way. To generalize in Mavrodes' own words, 'It will often be the case when a certain entity O is being experienced that, with the same input, it would be possible to experience a different entity from whose existence or properties it would be possible to infer the existence or the properties of O.'[25] However, Mavrodes cautions that we must not think that because a person *might* experience an object without inference the person *must* do so, or that a person who could come to know an object through an inference must do so.[26]

3   Experiencing God

These reflections on experience have rather direct and important implications for religious experience. If we allow for the possibility of mediated experiences of some entity, it seems quite possible for there to be experiences of God, if God is real. For, as Mavrodes points out, if God exists and has the properties traditionally ascribed to God, such as being creator and sustainer of the universe, then God is the ultimate source of whatever energy streams come to us from any object in the created universe.[27] According to traditional theism, the kind of view accepted by traditional Christians, Jews, and Muslims, every piece of matter and energy in the universe has its source in God, not only in the sense that God began the universe, but in the sense that he continuously maintains it in being. This implies, in Mavrodes' terminology, that 'all of the parts of the natural world are in total input alignment with God.'[28] Thus, to use the same examples that Plantinga cites as 'grounds' for belief in God, a person who contemplates a flower or a person who is looking at the 'starry heavens' might indeed be experiencing God through the experience of the flower or the heavens. (Though Plantinga does not claim that such people are necessarily having an experience of God.) Mavrodes concludes that 'whenever anyone is experiencing anything he *might* be experiencing God,' though of course this does not mean 'that whenever anyone is experiencing anything he *is* experiencing God.'[29]

---

[23] Ibid. 65.   [24] Ibid. 66.   [25]Ibid. 66.
[26] Ibid.   [27] Ibid. 69.   [28] Ibid. 69.
[29] Ibid. 69 (emphasis in Mavrodes).

In *Belief in God* Mavrodes goes on to give an illuminating discussion of the kinds of considerations that would be relevant to determining whether an alleged experience of God might be veridical, including an insightful discussion of whether such experiences must be 'verifiable' and how they might actually be verified. Though I find his work here extremely valuable, for my purposes in this essay I shall ignore it. The key point I want to focus on is the possibility that two people who are in the very same circumstances might gain an awareness of God in very different ways, one by direct experience and one by inference.

Let us assume, for example, that God is the creator and sustainer of the flower I am now looking at. The flower naturally has certain properties, and some of those properties might well serve as reliable indicators of God's existence as the flower's creator and sustainer. For example, the flower might have the property of existing contingently rather than necessarily, and this property might be an indicator of the dependence of the flower on God. Or, the flower might exhibit properties such as being beautiful or intricately designed, and these properties might be indicators of God's love of beauty or intelligence. Some people might well infer God's reality from such properties, by way of what philosophers call cosmological or teleological arguments for God's existence, and in such a case we could certainly say that the flower provides putative evidence for God's reality.

However, on Mavrodes' analysis, this is not the only way things could go. Spiritually seasoned observers of the world might experience God through the flower without any kind of inference. Such persons, we might say, are able to see the world as God's handiwork; they are able to 'read' what some theologians have called the 'book of nature,' a manifestation or revelation from God distinct from those particular events and experiences that are inscribed in inspired, revealed writings, such as the Bible for Christians.

4 Are 'grounded' basic beliefs rooted in religious experience?

If Mavrodes' analysis is sound, then I think there is room for at least a partial rapprochement between evidentialist advocates of natural theology and Reformed epistemologists. However, before looking at this partial agreement, I need first to consider the relation between mediated experiences of God in Mavrodes' sense and the grounds of a Plantingean properly basic belief in God. On the surface, it does not seem that all the grounds of properly basic beliefs will be experiences of God in this Mavrodean sense.[30] Plantinga describes his cases as ones in which a person spontaneously forms a belief in God (or, more

---

[30] See Plantinga's discussion of Alston in *Warranted Christian Belief*, pp. 180–4.

accurately, that God is doing or saying something) in particular circumstances, but he does not say that the person in these cases is necessarily having an experience of God.

However, the kind of case Mavrodes describes where one experiences God in a mediated fashion would seem to be at least one kind of ground that fits Plantinga's account, since these experiences would very likely be the result of the exercise of some natural capacity to grasp God in particular situations. Perhaps, in fact, all of the grounds Plantinga has in mind are at least potential ways in which a person could experience God. This is plausible if we regard experience of an object, in a manner inspired by Thomas Reid, as a spontaneous belief elicited in us as a result of contact with some object, with the belief in question being the result of a faculty that is designed to make it possible for us to become aware of the object. However, I will not press this point, and I will content myself with the safer claim that experiences of God of the sort that Mavrodes explores as a possibility would at least be one type of ground for properly basic beliefs. In the discussion that follows, I shall initially limit my attention to this particular kind of ground.

In these cases where the grounds of belief in God consist in or at least include a mediated experience of God, there does seem to be a clear sense in which the ground could be described as evidence for God's reality. This is so for two reasons. First, as noted above, there is a broader, non-propositional sense of 'evidence' as that which makes truth evident, and the experience would certainly seem to be evidence in this sense. Secondly, drawing on Mavrodes' account, though such a mediated experience can lead to knowledge of God that is psychologically direct, for others the very same experience could be the basis for an inference to God's reality. Hence there is a sense in which the critic of Reformed epistemology makes a helpful point, at least with respect to one type of ground, calling our attention to the ways in which the grounds of properly basic beliefs can be regarded as evidence.

However, again relying on Mavrodes, the Reformed epistemologist still has a useful point to make as well. For there is an important difference between coming to know an entity through direct experience and inferring the existence of an entity. If we take 'evidence' in the broad sense described above, this difference is obscured, and this can lead to confusion. If one does not distinguish this broad sense of 'evidence' from the narrower sense in which evidence must consist of propositions believed that can serve as the basis for inference, then the person who has a properly basic belief in God may mistakenly think that, in order for her belief in God to be reasonable, she must be able to cite her evidence or use it to develop an argument. Or such a person might think that there is something second-rate or second-best about her belief if she cannot do this, even if the belief is not completely unreasonable or unjustified. Hence, it seems important that we also recognize that there is a sense of 'evidence' in which such properly basic beliefs, while grounded, are not based on evidence.

5 Theistic arguments as articulations of natural signs of God

In the remainder of this essay, I shall try to do two things. First, I want to use the insights developed above to advance a general thesis, of a somewhat speculative nature, about the strengths and limitations of classical arguments for God's existence. I hope that this thesis will to some degree further reconcile evidentialist natural theology with Reformed epistemology. In the last section I will try to illustrate this thesis about theistic arguments by looking more specifically at one such argument, a version of a moral argument.

I begin with a look at some of the classical arguments for God's existence, focusing on cosmological, teleological, and moral arguments. (I shall ignore the ontological argument.) These arguments are perennial subjects for philosophical reflection, and their status itself constitutes a kind of philosophical puzzle. On the one hand, many philosophers have given criticisms of these arguments, and even claimed to refute them in a decisive manner, at least for the past 350 years. However, despite being frequently refuted or even dismissed, the arguments continue to be advanced, and other philosophers find them sound and even convincing. Perhaps even more surprisingly, some of the philosophers who are usually given credit for having offered powerful refutations continue to find something powerful in the arguments. In David Hume's *Dialogues Concerning Natural Religion*, widely regarded as containing one of the most devastating critiques of the argument from design, Hume puts the following words in the mouth of the character Philo, usually viewed as the character who is closest to Hume's own view: 'A purpose, an intention, or design strikes everywhere the most careless, the most stupid thinker; and no man can be so hardened in absurd systems, as at all times to reject it.'[31]

Immanuel Kant, also widely recognized as a decisive critic of the argument, gives similar witness to the force of this experience of purposive order:

Reason, constantly upheld by this ever-increasing evidence, which, though empirical, is yet so powerful, cannot be so depressed through doubts suggested by subtle and abstruse speculation, that it is not at once aroused from the indecision of all melancholy reflection, as from a dream, by one glance at the wonders of nature and the majesty of the universe.[32]

Why should this be so? Why should it be the case that arguments that are subject to well-known and widely-accepted criticisms nonetheless still remain attractive and even seem to have a kind of force, even for those who reject them? Here is my suggestion. Though Mavrodes is right to claim that in theory any part of the created order could

---

[31] Hume's *Dialogues*, p. 214.

[32] Immanuel Kant, *Critique of Pure Reason*, trans. Norman Kemp Smith (New York, St Martins Press, 1965), p. 520.

mediate an experiential awareness, in reality certain parts of the created order seem especially likely to point to God's reality. The contingency of the natural world, its character as a manifestation of design and purposiveness, and the experience of moral obligation seem to function especially well as 'natural signs' that point to God.[33] If there is a God, and God wishes humans to be aware of him, it seems plausible that he would place such pointers or signs in the world, as well as give human persons a natural tendency or disposition to read or experience these signs as pointing to his reality.

These natural signs have two interesting characteristics. One is that they are pervasive in human experience, easy to grasp and, in fact, hard to ignore. I call this the 'Wide Accessibility Principle' in *Natural Signs and Knowledge of God*.[34] The Wide Accessibility Principle implies that natural signs for God will require no special degree of learning or expertise to notice. The principle also implies that the natural signs for God will be present in many cultures and times. These are, I believe, characteristics we would expect to be present in genuine natural signs for God's reality, assuming God wants all humans to have the opportunity to know about him.

The second characteristic is that, despite the pervasive character of the signs and their ubiquity, they are far from constituting what I would call coercive proofs of God's reality. The signs may point to God, but they do not do so conclusively. Those who wish to explain them and interpret them in other ways are free to do so. I call this the 'Easy Resistibility Principle.'[35] And we can easily understand why God might want any natural signs he has implanted in human experience to have this characteristic as well. At least that is so if we assume that God wishes to have a relation with humans in which humans freely chose to serve him, motivated by love. Since God is all-powerful, it is not hard to see how, if God's reality were too obvious, human persons might serve him out of fear or for the sake of some kind of external or extrinsic reward God could provide, rather than out of love. It seems plausible that a God who wants a free and loving response from his creatures would also allow them the space to ignore him and shut him out of their lives.[36]

My suggestion about the theistic arguments is that they are best thought of as inferences that take as their starting points some of the natural signs God has placed in human experience to point to himself. When these natural signs simply function as signs, then they may well be grounds of properly basic beliefs. In some cases, at least, these natural signs may function as mediators of God's reality, actually allowing

---

[33] This suggestion is developed in detail with respect to cosmological, teleological, and moral arguments in my *Natural Signs and Knowledge of God: A New Look at Theistic Arguments* (Oxford, Oxford University Press, 2010).

[34] See chapter one of Ibid. 12–17.

[35] See Ibid. 15–17.

[36] One might think, following some arguments of John Schellenberg, that God might make knowledge of himself not only widely available, but universal for everyone who does not willfully resist it. For an argument that Schellenberg is wrong and defense of the Wide Accessibility Principle and Easy Resistibility Principle, see chapter six of *Natural Signs and Knowledge of God*, pp. 159–69.

some individuals to experience God directly. In these kinds of cases the Reformed epistemologist is right to say that the belief in God that is grounded in these signs may be properly basic and not based on any kind of inference or argument. Note that the differences between these two cases may lie solely within the individual who is experiencing or inferring God. The causal relation to God may be precisely the same in both cases, but in the one case the person simply 'reads' the sign spontaneously and perceives God, while in the other case the individual perceives the sign and infers God's reality.

The difference between a case in which there is a direct perception of God and a case where an explicit, conscious process of inference occurs is clear enough. But of course there are more difficult cases. Could an inference be unconscious or 'tacit?' If so, how would such an inference differ from a case of direct perception? Such questions are difficult to answer, both because our ordinary psychological concepts of 'inference' and 'perception' may not be sharp and fine-grained enough to allow us to make fine distinctions, and also because our introspective powers may not be adequate to the task. However, the fact that there may be cases in which it is hard to tell whether a process of inference has occurred or not does not show that there are not clear cases where a distinction between an inference and a perception can be drawn. My claim is simply that it may be possible for an individual to become aware of God in a psychologically direct manner, even though the awareness is mediated by a natural sign.

However, although an argument is not *required* for a natural sign to point someone to God, that does not mean that the natural sign cannot be used as the starting point for an argument. The very same feature that functions as a mediator for a direct awareness of God may also function as an evidential indicator for God's reality, a basis for inference in which one sees something in the natural world as best explained by God's activity. The classical theistic arguments can be viewed as attempts to develop the natural signs in just this manner. So far as I can see, we have no a priori reason to think that developing these natural signs into arguments is necessarily better or worse than having them function in the more direct way. Rather, I believe that each type of use of the signs has characteristic advantages and disadvantages, and probably different people will find themselves drawn to one approach or the other for a variety of reasons. I suspect that for many the two approaches will be complementary, and each will to some degree shore up weaknesses in the other.

Let us consider first the case of someone who has a more immediate, direct awareness of God. Let us take again the case where I examine the flower and I am struck by the beauty and design it seems to manifest and naturally see it as the work of God. Knowing, as I do, that apparent perceptions are not always veridical, it is possible that I may on some occasions wonder whether it is right for me to experience the flower in this way. Perhaps I have read Dawkins and have come to wonder whether the design and purposiveness I directly perceive in the flower as God's handiwork is not a kind of illusion. One way of interpreting this worry is that it is a concern that the theory of evolution is a defeater for experiencing the flower as the work of God, evidence that the experience is not genuine or is being misinterpreted or misunderstood.[37] In such a situation, where a person is worried that he or she has a defeater for an experience of God, some version of the argument from design might be helpful, particularly newer versions of the argument that accept the theory of evolution and try to show that the evolutionary process itself points to design.[38]

On the other hand, a person who bases belief on an argument may be helped by having his or her attention drawn to the experience upon which the argument draws. Many objections to theistic arguments, such as the argument from design, amount to showing that the evidence for God in question is not conclusive or coercive in nature. There are, for example, alternative explanations for design, or perhaps arguments that the design that is perceived is only apparent design, and that other explanations than divine activity can be offered. The person who is troubled by such objections may be helped in a twofold way by thinking about the natural sign that is the foundation of the argument. First, the person may realize that the fact that alternative explanations are possible does not mean those explanations are plausible; the fact that it is possible to explain some evidence in a different way simply means the evidence is not deductive and therefore not conclusive in nature. It does not mean that the evidence does not have genuine force as pointing towards a particular explanation. Second, the person may be helped by being encouraged to focus on the experience in question, or even to repeat the experience or put himself or herself in a position to do so. In other words, it is helpful to realize that the evidential force (in the broader sense of evidence) of the sign is not exhausted by its use in an inference, and to experience the 'push' that experience provides again.

6 The moral argument as example

In conclusion, I want to take a closer look at one particular natural sign of God's reality: moral obligations. Moral arguments for God's existence are, I believe, among the more powerful and convincing arguments for ordinary persons, even if they have not always been the most popular among professional philosophers.[39] Recently, philosophers such as Robert Adams and Philip Quinn have defended a divine command theory of moral obligations, in which genuine moral obligations are dependent on divine commands, and I believe that their work has at least showed that this is a viable account of moral obligations.[40] In what follows I shall assume the correctness of a divine command

---

[37] For an argument that evolutionary theory is not a defeater for the perception of God through the natural sign of 'beneficial order' see *Natural Signs and Knowledge of God*, chapter four, pp. 89–98.

[38] For an example of such an argument, see Richard Swinburne, *Is There a God?* (Oxford, Oxford University Press, 1996), pp. 48–68.

[39] As evidence for this I would cite the amazing popularity of C. S. Lewis's *Mere Christianity*, which begins with a form of the moral argument for God. It seems very likely to me that this book is by far the most successful piece of apologetics written in the last 100 years.

[40] See Robert Adams, *Finite and Infinite Goods* (Oxford, Oxford University Press, 1999), and Philip Quinn, 'Divine Command Theory' in Hugh La Follette (ed.), *The Blackwell Guide to Ethical Theory* (Oxford, Blackwell, 2000), pp. 53–73. Divine command theories of obligations come in different forms, and not all

account of moral obligations. However, the assumption is made only for simplicity of exposition, since it is very easy to understand how, if a divine command theory of obligation is true, moral obligations could be natural signs of God. However, I argue in *Natural Signs and Knowledge of God* that moral obligations can be natural signs of God even if a divine command account of moral obligations is not correct.[41]

If moral obligations are identical with God's commands or call on individuals or expectations for people, then it is not surprising that some people should find moral obligations to be mediators of God's reality.[42] For in that case it would be literally true that a person who is aware of a moral obligation is aware of God's claim or call or command to that person. It is not surprising then that some people find themselves with a properly basic belief in God that is grounded in experiences of moral obligation. I might find myself tempted to suppress some income on my tax return, and suddenly find myself thinking, 'God wants me to be honest and not lie about this.' Or, in a case where I have actually violated my moral duty, I may find myself thinking, 'I have failed to live up to God's expectations; I have disappointed God.' No argument or inference is necessary.

However, although no argument is necessary, it is quite possible for one to be given. Here is a simple version of a moral argument:

1. There are real moral obligations.
2. Without God's commands there could be no moral obligations.
3. There must be a God who issues commands.[43]

Reflection on such an argument might be helpful for some individuals in some situations. Again, this seems especially likely to be the case when I am in a situation where I have acquired some reason to doubt my moral experience. Perhaps I have read an 'error theorist' who argues forcefully that moral obligations are a kind of illusion. In that case I might well profit from thinking about premise one of the argument. What reasons do I have for thinking that moral obligations are genuine and not illusory? What would be the consequences of taking all such obligations to be illusory?

---

versions posit an identity between divine commands and moral obligations. Alternatives include the view that God's commands create moral obligations causally or that moral obligations supervene on God's commands. For simplicity of exposition in this paper I shall assume the identity version of the theory. This is actually the version I favor. See my *Kierkegaard's Ethic of Love: Divine Commands and Moral Obligations* (Oxford, Oxford University Press, 2004).

[41] See chapter five of *Natural Signs and Knowledge of God*, particularly pp. 138–42.

[42] One could also speak of moral obligations as being created by God's commands or as supervening on God's commands, rather than being identical to those commands. For simplicity of exposition I shall assume identity, but the points made are consistent with the other ways of understanding a divine command theory of moral obligation.

[43] As noted above, this may appear to assume the correctness of a divine command theory of moral obligation. However, in reality this is not the case. All that is needed for this argument is some account of how moral obligations are dependent on God, and a divine command theory is only one alternative. In reality, a version of this argument can be formulated even if it is not the case that all moral obligations depend on God; all that is required is that some obligations that humans are aware of depend on God.

Or, perhaps my doubts about my moral experience are occasioned by someone who argues that God is not necessary as the basis for moral obligations. We can explain such obligations in some other way, as the result of evolution, or as a social bargain or contract human beings have made with one another. In that case, I may well profit from reflection on the second premise of the argument. Can evolution really explain genuine moral obligations, or can it only explain why humans might feel obligations? Could a social bargain or contract really provide the authority to account for my obligations to people whom I do not know and who could not benefit me in any way?[44]

I conclude that although this natural sign that points to God can be the ground of properly basic beliefs that are not rooted in inference or argument, in many cases reflection on such an argument could be helpful in strengthening the belief. Perhaps for some people, the argument will be essential; without it, they will be prone to dismiss the experience of obligations as illusory or indecisive.

However, to focus solely on the argument would also be a mistake. For in the end the argument does not exhaust the force of the sign. If moral obligations are divine commands, and God has given us a natural tendency to perceive him through our experience of obligation, then there will be a kind of force in this experience that is not completely captured by the argument. This is why, I believe, even people who may be inclined to reject the argument may still feel the force of the sign. Imagine someone, for example, who accepts an evolutionary account of moral obligations as a kind of error theory and thinks that the argument is unsound because premise one is false. Such a person may still find himself/herself in a situation where the person senses an obligation to perform a particular action, and might find it natural to think of himself/herself as responsible or accountable to someone. Such a person is experiencing a kind of tension between a theory the individual holds and his or her experience, and it is even possible in some cases that he might come to doubt the theory and reconsider his beliefs.

My conclusion is as follows: Mavrodes' account of religious experience helps us to see the value of both Reformed epistemology and evidentialist arguments. The Reformed Epistemologist is right to argue that belief in God can be properly basic and not based on inference. However, this may not be true for everyone; some people may need arguments. And even those for whom belief is basic may find arguments helpful. However, it is also important to recognize that the force of the natural signs that ground our properly basic beliefs is not exhausted by arguments. Such signs may lead to justified beliefs in God that are, like perceptual beliefs, direct and immediate.

---

[44] In *Kierkegaard's Ethic of Love* I argue in chapters 10 through 12 that none of these accounts of moral obligation are adequate. The same points are argued in a different way in chapter five of *Natural Signs and Knowledge of God*.

4

Phenomenal Conservatism and Evidentialism in Religious Epistemology

Chris Tucker

Phenomenal conservatism, as I discuss it in this chapter, is a theory of evidence possession. It holds that if it seems to a subject that P, then the subject thereby possesses evidence which supports P. In this chapter I apply phenomenal conservatism to religious belief with the aim of securing two theses. First, phenomenal conservatism is better suited than is proper functionalism to explain how a particular type of religious belief formation can lead to non-inferentially justified religious beliefs. Second, phenomenal conservatism makes evidence so easy to obtain that the truth of evidentialism wouldn't be much of an obstacle to justified religious belief. In Section 1, I explicate the evidentialist principle that will be the focus of this paper, and in Section 2, I explicate phenomenal conservatism and explain what it means for it to seem that P. The third and fourth sections secure the two main conclusions of the paper, respectively. Given how easy it is to acquire evidence according to phenomenal conservatism, it is natural to object that the principle is absurdly permissive. In Section 5, I argue that this objection fails.

1 Evidentialism

My main goal in this section is to clarify the sort of evidentialism that will be the focus of this paper (though I consider a very different form of evidentialism in Section 4.3). I begin with this task because it provides a convenient way to introduce a number of key terms that will be important in the rest of the paper.

Evidentialism, in religious epistemology, holds that religious beliefs must satisfy some evidential requirement if they are to have some epistemic status, such as justification or knowledge. I focus on a version of evidentialism which applies to any domain not merely the religious one. It holds that a subject has a certain type of justification for a proposition just in case she has undefeated evidence for it; however, it does not further demand that the evidence be inferential (i.e. believing the premises of a good argument). To arrive at a more precise understanding of this evidentialism, we need to clarify the type of justification at issue by making two distinctions.

The first distinction is between doxastic and propositional justification. *Doxastic justification*, which Earl Conee and Richard Feldman call 'well-foundedness,' is a property of *beliefs*.[1] *Propositional justification*, on the other hand, is a property that a *proposition* has relative to a subject. Suppose that some thing X (e.g. a belief or an experience) provides propositional justification for P. It is common to hold that X provides doxastic justification for one's belief in P only if that belief is *based on* X.[2]

An important result of the preceding characterizations is that one can have propositional justification for P even though her belief that P fails to be doxastically justified.[3] Suppose, for example, that a lawyer believes that his client is innocent, he has powerful evidence that his client is innocent, but he bases this belief, not on his powerful evidence, but on the testimony of a magic 8-ball. The lawyer's powerful evidence propositionally justifies for him the proposition that his client is innocent; however, since his belief in the client's innocence isn't based on this evidence, this evidence doesn't doxastically justify his belief that his client is innocent. In this paper, I talk primarily about *propositional* justification.

The second distinction concerns two types of propositional justification, *prima facie* and *ultima facie* (propositional) justification. One has an *ultima facie justification* for P just in case it is rational to believe P. One has *prima facie justification* for P just in case she has *ultima facie* justification for P in the absence of relevant defeaters. A *defeater* is something that prevents *prima facie* justification from constituting *ultima facie* justification. We can illustrate these concepts with the following example.

Suppose Mary has some evidence E1 which supports the claim that Marty will moonwalk at tonight's talent show. This evidence might include her knowledge that Marty claims he will do the moonwalk, that his act is called the 'Magical Moonwalk' and that he has been practicing the moonwalk for months. In such a case, she would have *prima facie* justification for the claim that Marty will moonwalk tonight. If there are no relevant defeaters, then some small portion of Mary's total evidence, namely E1, would provide her with *ultima facie* justification.

---

[1] *Evidentialism* (New York, Oxford University Press, 2004), p. 93.

[2] Cf. Michael Bergmann, *Justification without Awareness: A Defense of Epistemic Externalism* (New York, Oxford University Press, 2006), pp. 4–5 and Juan Comesaña, 'Evidentialist Reliabilism' (*Nous* forthcoming), section 2. The basing relation is an important but poorly understood relation. Epistemologists generally hold that a belief B is based on another mental state M only if M non-deviantly causes B (e.g. Richard Swinburne, *Epistemic Justification* (Oxford, Oxford University Press, 2001), p. 129). It is highly controversial, however, as to what makes the relevant type of causation 'non-deviant' and what further requirement, if any, should be imposed on the basing relation.

[3] The above characterizations are silent on whether one can have doxastic justification without propositional justification.

Yet suppose that Mary has some evidence E2 that even more strongly supports the conclusion that Marty will *not* moonwalk at the competition. For example, she might know that he was just seriously injured in a car accident and, to make matters worse, his favorite moonwalking shoes were just stolen. In this example, the *prima facie* justification provided by Mary's evidence, E1, would be defeated by her competing evidence, E2. Although she would have *prima facie* justification for P, she would fail to have *ultima facie* justification for P.

Although I discuss both *prima facie* and *ultima facie* justification, I focus on a version of evidentialism that most directly concerns the latter. Its basic idea is that *all* of a person's evidence and *only* a person's evidence determines whether she has *ultima facie* justification for P. More precisely:

Evidentialism about Propositional Justification: S has ultima facie propositional justification for P just in case (i) S has some evidence E1 that supports[4] P, and (ii) S does not have any more inclusive body of evidence E2 that fails to support P.[5]

Although this evidentialism does not explicitly mention *prima facie* justification or defeaters, it is still very relevant to those topics. The first condition is tantamount to the claim that one has *prima facie* justification for P just in case she has evidence for it. The second condition is often called a 'no defeater condition' because it is tantamount to the claim that a subject's *prima facie* justification is defeated just in case she has some more inclusive body of evidence which fails to support P. In slogan form, this evidentialism says that a proposition is *ultima facie* justified for a subject just in case the subject has undefeated evidence for it. Unless I indicate otherwise, when I henceforth say 'justification' and 'evidentialism' I will mean '*ultima facie* propositional justification' and 'Evidentialism about Propositional Justification' respectively.

---

[4] Others use different terminology to refer to this support relation. Richard Swinburne calls this relation 'epistemic probability' in his *Epistemic Justification* and his 'Evidentialism,' in Charles Taliaferro, Paul Draper, and Philip L. Quin (eds.), *A Companion to Philosophy of Religion*, 2nd edn (Malden, Blackwell Publishing Ltd, 2010), pp. 681–8. Conee and Feldman use the term 'fit.' There is little agreement about what it takes for support. Swinburne holds that evidential support is a type of logical probability in his *Epistemic Justification* and 'Evidentialism.' Conee and Feldman hold that it is deeply connected to best explanation in their 'Evidence,' in Quentin Smith (ed), *Epistemology: New Essays* (Oxford, Oxford University Press, 2008), pp. 97–8. Alvin Plantinga holds that it is deeply connected to proper function in his *Warrant and Proper Function* (Oxford, Oxford University Press, 1993), p. 168. I won't defend a complete account of support, but in the next section I do object to Plantinga's account.

[5] Although it is worded very differently, my evidentialism is roughly equivalent to that of Conee and Feldman, the main difference being that their evidentialist thesis covers degrees of justification and mine doesn't (*Evidentialism*, p. 83). Swinburne's evidentialism is intended to be equivalent to Conee and Feldman's, but it isn't ('Evidentialism,' p. 681). Their evidentialism concerns propositional justification and his concerns doxastic justification; Conee and Feldman don't address doxastic justification, or well-foundedness, until p. 93. In addition, Swinburne's version of evidentialism is obviously false, as it fails to have a no defeater condition, i.e. a counterpart to (ii) (or, alternatively, his evidentialism implausibly demands that one base a belief on one's *total* evidence).

2 Phenomenal conservatism

I introduced, in the previous section, one of the two main characters in this paper. My goal in this section is to introduce the second main character, namely phenomenal conservatism. In 2.1, I provide a general introduction to the view. In Section 2.2, I distinguish seemings from sensations, because this oft-missed distinction is needed to properly assess the merits of phenomenal conservatism (eg see Section 3 below).

2.1 Phenomenal conservatism: the basic idea

Phenomenal conservatism is traditionally construed as a view about propositional justification: if it seems to S that P, then in the absence of defeaters, S has propositional justification for P.[6] Since this volume concerns the role of evidence in rational religious belief, I will construe it as a thesis about evidence possession:

Phenomenal Conservatism: if it seems to S that P, then S thereby has evidence which supports P.

When I say that some evidence *supports* P, I will mean that the evidence for P is strong enough to provide P with propositional justification in the absence of defeaters. Hence, the phenomenal conservative thesis about justification follows from this thesis about evidence possession.

Phenomenal Conservatism is compatible both with evidentialism and its denial. Recall that evidentialism holds that one has justification for P just in case one possesses undefeated evidence for P. Phenomenal conservatism is compatible with evidentialism because the latter is silent concerning when one possesses (undefeated) evidence for P. In other words, it is no contradiction to hold both that undefeated evidence is necessary and sufficient for justification (i.e. endorse evidentialism) and that seemings always provide evidence (i.e. endorse phenomenal conservatism). Phenomenal conservatism is compatible with the *denial* of evidentialism because it doesn't entail that evidence is necessary for justification. In other words, it is no contradiction to hold that seemings suffice for evidence (i.e. endorse phenomenal conservatism), but then deny that evidence is required for justification (i.e. deny evidentialism).

As I have construed it, phenomenal conservatism says that I have evidence for P if it seems to me that P. But what is a seeming? A seeming that P is merely a certain kind of

---

[6] I defend this type of phenomenal conservatism under the label 'dogmatism' in my 'Why Open Minded People Should Endorse Dogmatism' (2010), *Philosophical Perspectives* 24, pp. 529–45. Huemer defends it in his *Skepticism and the Veil of Perception* (Lanham, Rowman & Littlefield Publishers, Inc, 2001) and 'Compassionate Phenomenal Conservatism' (2007), *Philosophy and Phenomenological Research* 74, pp. 30–55. Conee defends the view, but he uses the term 'seeming evidentialism' and it isn't clear whether he actually endorses it. See Conee and Feldman's *Evidentialism*, pp. 11–36. Criticisms of phenomenal conservatism include Roger White's 'Problems for Dogmatism' (2006). *Philosophical Studies*, 131, pp. 525–57; Crispin Wright's 'The Perils of Dogmatism' in Susana Nuccetelli and Gary Seay (eds.), *Themes from G. E. Moore: New Essays in Epistemology and Ethics* (Oxford, Oxford University Press, 2008); pp. 119–20 of Peter Markie, 'Epistemically Appropriate Perceptual Belief' (2006), *Nous* 40, pp. 118–42 and pp. 356–7 of his 'The Mystery of Perceptual Justification' (2005), *Philosophical Studies* 126, pp. 347–73.

experience with propositional content. What distinguishes seemings from other experiences is their peculiar phenomenal character, which Huemer calls 'forcefulness,' though I prefer the term 'assertiveness.'[7] William Tollhurst says that seemings 'have the feel of truth, the feel of a state whose content reveals how things really are.'[8] The phenomenology of a seeming makes it feel as though the seeming is 'recommending' its propositional content as true or 'assuring' us of the content's truth. All sorts of propositions might seem true in this sense. Right now it seems to me that there is a desk in front of me, that $2 + 2 = 4$, that I have a slight headache, and that phenomenal conservatism is true.

In everyday speech, I might say, 'Well, it seems to me that the Republican candidates have the most political experience,' and I might simply mean that I *believe* that the Republican candidates have the most experience. As I use the term, however, a seeming that P is *not* a belief that P. Nor does 'it seems to me that P' entail 'I believe that P.' A proposition might seem necessarily true even though I know it leads to paradox and so disbelieve it. Or a table may seem to be red even though I know it is really white and illuminated by red lights. Nor is a seeming that P an inclination or disposition to believe P. A perceptual seeming that the cheese is old and moldy *explains* why I am inclined to have a belief with that content. I do think that my use of 'seeming' has some currency in every day speech, but my characterization of this term is at least partly stipulative (cf. Huemer (2007), pp. 30–1).

Seemings count as non-inferential evidence. E is (some of) S's *non-inferential* evidence for P only if E is one or more of S's non-doxastic mental states (e.g. an experience). E is (some of) S's *inferential evidence* for P only if E is one or more of S's beliefs.[9] Since a seeming that P is an experience and not a belief, it counts as non-inferential evidence for P. A justified belief in the premises of a good argument for P counts as inferential evidence for P.

2.2 Seemings vs. sensations

It is commonly assumed that a sensation is a special kind of seeming,[10] but I argue that this is incorrect. Since the distinction between seemings and sensations will be important in the next section, I need to make this distinction at least somewhat clear. Sensations, like seemings, are experiences, and it is plausible that at least some of them have

---

[7] *Skepticism and the Veil of Perception*, pp. 77–9.

[8] See his 'Seemings' (1998), *American Philosophical Quarterly* 35, 293–302, pp. 298–9.

[9] I talk here and elsewhere as though a subject's evidence is some *mental state* rather than, say, the propositional content of her mental states. I talk this way because it is convenient. For an introduction to the ontology of evidence, see John Turri, 'The Ontology of Epistemic Reasons' (2009), *Nous* 43, pp. 490–512. Swinburne suggests that 'an evidentialist should construe someone's evidence as encompassing no more than the *content* of their basic beliefs' (see his 'Evidentialism', p. 681, emphasis mine). This suggestion is surprising since he considers himself an evidentialist and, in his earlier work, he holds that the subject's evidence is not the propositional content of certain mental states, but the mental states themselves (*Epistemic Justification*, p. 152).

[10] See, e.g. Tolhurst's 'Seemings,' p. 300 and Huemer's *Skepticism and the Veil of Perception*, pp. 58–79.

content. I have a visual sensation when I look at my dog. It is the mental 'picture' or visual image of a little white creature wearing a blue halter. I have an auditory sensation when I hear my dog barking. It is the mental 'sound' of the bark, a mental phenomenon that causes me great irritation. At the very least, there are also tactile, olfactory, gustatory and perhaps even proprioceptive sensations.

Sensations and seemings, in my view, are distinct kinds of experiences. There are a variety of considerations that make this view at least plausible. First, there are introspective considerations. Alvin Plantinga remarks:

> Upon being appeared to a familiar way, I may form the belief that I perceive a branch of a peculiarly jagged shape. Here there is, of course, sensuous experience; but there is a sort of nonsensous experience involved as well, an experience distinct from that sensuous experience but nonetheless connected with the formation of the belief in question. That belief has a certain felt attractiveness or naturalness, a sort of perceived fittingness; it feels like the *right* belief in the circumstances.[11]

Plantinga suggests that typically when we have a sensation, such as a visual image, it is accompanied by some nonsensuous experience, which is 'a certain felt attractiveness or naturalness, a sort of perceived fittingness.' What I want to suggest (whether Plantinga would agree or not) is that Plantinga's nonsensuous experience just is a seeming that the branch has a particularly jagged shape. What we ordinarily think of as a perceptual experience, in my view, is really a composite of a seeming and its accompanying sensuous experience, or sensation.

A thought experiment confirms the testimony of introspection. Right now I have a visual image in my mind, one that represents a desk's being in front of me, but the content of this image is far too rich for me to describe fully. My powers of imagination nonetheless could be so powerful that I could imagine a picture that is phenomenally just like the one that is now in front of my mind.[12] Both the perceptual and imagined 'pictures' that a desk is in front of me have the same phenomenology; however, only the perceptual picture accompanies a seeming that there is a desk in front of me. When I have a visual image of a desk's being in front of me, it *seems* that there is a desk in front of me. When I have an imagined image of a desk's being in front of me, it does *not* seem that there is a desk in front of me. (But nor does it necessarily seem that there is not a desk in front of me either.) Since the sensation and imagination are phenomenally identical and the imagination isn't itself a seeming (i.e. it doesn't come with assertiveness), the sensation isn't itself a seeming.[13]

---

[11] *Warrant and Proper Function*, pp. 91–2, emphasis original.

[12] If a mental picture gets its representational content in part by how it is caused (if such things even have content), then the imagined picture will not have the same content as the one that is, in fact, caused by a desk and a computer. Yet the two pictures would still 'look' the same despite having different contents.

[13] Cf. Huemer's *Skepticism and the Veil of Perception*, p. 77.

If seemings and sensations really are distinct,[14] you might expect to find one without the other, and this is precisely what we find. A priori intuitions are plausible examples of seemings that are not accompanied by a sensation. More controversially, there are even perceptual seemings which fail to be accompanied by any sensation. The phenomenology of proprioception doesn't seem as rich as that of, say, vision or audition, and perhaps this is because it typically involves only proprioceptive seemings and not proprioceptive sensations, if there are such things.[15] Or consider the phenomena of blindsight. Blindsighted patients apparently lack visual imagery in a certain region of their visual field, but they nonetheless show remarkable sensitivity to the region corresponding to their 'blindspot.' This sensitivity may be explained by the presence of (reliable) seemings despite the absence of some corresponding sensation.[16]

There also seem to be some sensations which fail to be accompanied by seemings. Some patients with visual associative agnosia apparently know what keys are, have very detailed visual imagery of a key, and nonetheless fail to identify something as a key. Plausibly, the problem is that these patients fail to have the seemings (e.g. the seeming that this object is a key) which would allow them to identify keys as such.[17] The above thought experiment is also relevant here. The imagined image from the thought experiment presumably fails to be a sensation because it was caused by my hypothetical powerful imagination, not my perceptual faculties. Yet it is sensation-like insofar as it is phenomenally identical with the sensation that I am currently having, and despite being sensation-like, it isn't accompanied by a seeming that its content is true.

3 Phenomenal conservatism vs. proper functionalism

Plantinga, following Calvin, holds that some people form non-inferentially warranted Christian beliefs in light of the 'glories of nature.'[18] My admiration of a beautiful sunset, for example, might in some sense trigger the belief that God exists and loves me, and Plantinga holds that a belief formed in this way very well may be warranted. *Warrant* is the property enough of which makes true belief knowledge, and it is generally assumed that justification is required for warrant. My goal in this section is not to argue that this method of belief formation genuinely produces warrant or justification; I will simply assume that it does (or at least that it can) produce justification. Rather, my goal is to argue that

---

[14] Strictly speaking, I don't need the claim that seemings and sensations are *always* distinct kinds of experiences. Suppose you think that a sensation can be a seeming if it has the property I called 'assertiveness.' You still could explain everything I want to explain if you hold the following claims: (i) one can have a sensation without having a corresponding seeming; (ii) one can have a seeming without having a corresponding sensation; and (iii) one can have a sensation (e.g. of a sunset) and yet have a seeming with some unrelated content (e.g. that God loves me). Once (i)–(iii) are accepted, I simply find it easier to talk as though seemings and sensations are always distinct.

[15] Cf. Huemer's *Skepticism and the Veil of Perception*, p. 67.

[16] See my 'Why Open-Minded People Should Endorse Dogmatism,' section 1.

[17] Ibid.

[18] *Warranted Christian Belief* (Oxford, Oxford University Press, 2000), pp. 172–9.

phenomenal conservatism is better suited than is proper functionalism to explain how it can produce such justification. I will argue, in 3.1, that any such explanation should satisfy a certain criterion. In 3.2, I show that the proper functionalist explanation fails to satisfy this criterion and, in 3.3, that phenomenal conservatism is to be preferred.

3.1 An important criterion

Suppose that, in response to his witnessing a particularly marvelous sunset, someone believes that God loves him. Witnessing a particularly marvelous sunset involves at the very least a visual image of the sunset, but perhaps it also involves a feeling of admiration or awe as well. It strikes me as implausible that the visual image of the sunset, by itself or when combined solely with the feeling of awe, can be evidence for the claim that God loves one. Bear with me while I (attempt to) elicit this intuition.

Consider:

(1) My belief that my students hate Keystone Light beer can evidentially support a belief in Gödel's (First Incompleteness) Theorem.

This claim says that the beer proposition can support Gödel's Theorem all by itself, but that seems absurd. Of course, the beer proposition might support Gödel's Theorem when conjoined with other beliefs (e.g. the belief that if the beer proposition is true, then so is Gödel's Theorem).[19] Presumably, 1 seems absurd because my belief about Keystone Light doesn't have the right content to be evidence for Gödel's Theorem. In any event, it is widely held that 1 is counterintuitive. Some accounts of evidential support are committed to the truth of 1, and even the proponents of these views often concede that this commitment is a significant cost of their views.[20]

Now consider the claim that:

(2) My sensation and admiration of a sunset can evidentially support a belief in Gödel's Theorem.

2 seems just as counterintuitive as 1. The sensation and admiration of a sunset, whether taken jointly or individually, are evidentially irrelevant to whether Gödel's Theorem is true. Of course, the sunset sensation (and the awe) might support a belief in Gödel's Theorem when conjoined with other experiences or beliefs (e.g. the belief that if one has a sensation of a sunset, then Gödel's Theorem is true). Presumably, the sensation and admiration of a sunset, by themselves, are evidentially irrelevant to Gödel's Theorem because they don't have the right content to be evidence for Gödel's Theorem.

---

[19] *Objection*: If the theorem is true, then it is necessarily true. If it is necessarily true, then every proposition entails it (because there is no world where some proposition is true and the theorem is false). So the beer proposition evidentially supports Gödel's theorem after all. *Reply*: Yes, every proposition entails every necessary truth, but this does not reveal that every proposition supports every necessary truth; rather, it reveals that entailment does not suffice for evidential support.

[20] See, e.g., Comesaña's 'Reliabilist Evidentialism,' sec. 8.2.

Now that we have 1 and 2 in the back of our minds, consider again:

(3) My sensation and admiration of a sunset can evidentially support a belief that God loves one.

The sensation and admiration of a sunset, whether taken jointly or individually, seem evidentially irrelevant to the claim that God loves one. Of course, the sunset sensation might support the idea that God loves one when conjoined with other experiences or beliefs (e.g. the belief that one's ability to appreciate a sunset is best explained by the existence of a loving God). Presumably, the sensation and awe of the sunset seem irrelevant to whether God loves one because they don't have the right content to be evidence for the existence of a God who loves one.

The falsity of 3 reveals an important criterion. If a theory of justification is to allow the glories of nature to play a role in the justification of religious belief, it needs to do so without allowing the visual image or admiration of the sunset to play an *evidential* role. That is, a theory of justification needs to respect the fact that the visual image and admiration of the sunset, by themselves, are evidentially irrelevant to whether God loves one. Unfortunately, proper function accounts of evidence, such as those of Plantinga,[21] Bergmann,[22] and Richard Otte[23] fail to respect this fact.

3.2 The proper functionalist explanation

Proper functionalists about justification tend to hold that evidentialism is false because evidence isn't *necessary* for justification.[24] Nonetheless, they tend to hold that having evidence for P is *sufficient* for *prima facie* justification. They can allow that evidence is sufficient for *prima facie* justification because they understand evidence in terms of proper function. Plantinga's account of evidential support is complicated,[25] but the complications won't affect the following discussion.[26] Hence, we can focus on this relatively simple

Proper Function Account of Evidence: S's mental state M evidentially supports P just in case it is proper function for S to believe P on the basis of M.

The basic idea of this account, according to Bergmann, is that 'the fittingness of a doxastic response to evidence is contingent upon the *proper function* of the cognitive faculties in question.'[27] Since evidence is understood in terms of proper function, M might be evidence for believing P for some possible creatures but not others.[28]

---

[21] *Warrant and Proper Function*, p. 168.

[22] *Justification without Awareness*, p. 130.

[23] 'A Theistic Conception of Probability' (1987), *Faith and Philosophy*, 4, 427–47.

[24] See, e.g., Bergmann's *Justification without Awareness*, pp. 63–4.

[25] *Warrant and Proper Function*, p. 168.

[26] Besides greater complication, Plantinga's account is restricted only to when one belief supports another, but in conversation, he said he would be happy to generalize his account to when any mental state supports a belief.

[27] *Justification without Awareness*, p. 168.

[28] Ibid. 118–21.

When this proper function account of evidence is applied to the case at hand, it allows a visual image of a sunset (perhaps in combination with a feeling of admiration) to support the claim that God loves one. Plantinga supposes that we have a faculty, the *sensus divinitatis*, which is designed to form religious beliefs.[29] This faculty takes our visual image (and admiration of) the sunset as inputs and then produces belief that God loves one or some other religious belief as an output. Here is the basic picture:

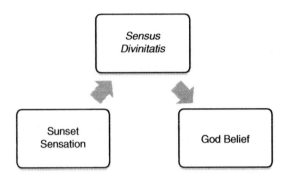

Since humans are designed to have a *sensus divinitatis* that functions this way, it is proper function for them to believe certain religious beliefs on the basis of the visual image and/or admiration of the sunset. Given the Proper Function Account of Evidence, it follows that the visual image and admiration of the sunset support the claim that God loves one, which violates the criterion from the previous sub-section.

3.3 The superiority of phenomenal conservatism's explanation

One may think that phenomenal conservatism fares little better at explaining how an appreciation of the glories of nature contributes to the justification of religious beliefs. She might reason as follows. (i) When one has a visual image of a sunset, it is natural to suppose that this image has the content *that there is a sunset*; however, (ii) it would be bizarre to suppose that the image has the content *that God loves me*. Hence, (iii) it seems to the subject that there is a sunset, but it doesn't seem that God loves one. (iv) Since one wouldn't have a seeming that God loves one, it is doubtful that phenomenal conservatism can explain how an appreciation of the glories of nature can justify a belief that God loves one.

The problem with this objection is the transition from (ii) to (iii). This transition apparently assumes that the content of a seeming must be identical to or closely resemble the content of the sensation, but these two states are distinct and their contents can differ widely (see above, Section 2.2). The phenomenal conservative can explain the justificatory power of this type of religious belief formation simply by

---

[29] See, e.g., *Warranted Christian Belief*, pp. 173–5.

re-describing the role of the *sensus divinitatis*. If in response to the visual image of the sunset it produces a belief that God loves one directly and without the mediation of, say, a seeming that God loves one, then the phenomenal conservative should say that the subject lacks evidence for the belief (unless, of course, he has evidence for this belief in some other way). Yet, in response to a visual image of a beautiful sunset, the *sensus divinitatis* might be designed to produce a seeming about God, his love, power, etc. The re-described picture is:

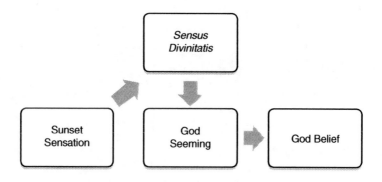

On this picture,[30] an appreciation of the glories of nature leads to a justified non-inferential belief that God loves one, not because the appreciation itself provides good evidence for that claim, but because it triggers an evidentially relevant seeming. Although it doesn't seem plausible that a sunset sensation can provide evidence for God's loving one, even proper functionalists will grant that a seeming that God loves one can or does provide evidence for God's loving one.

The phenomenal conservative explains how an appreciation of the glories of nature can contribute non-inferential evidence for religious beliefs by re-describing the *sensus divinitatis*: it takes an appreciation of a sunset as an input and produces, not a belief, but a seeming that God loves one. The proper functionalist can accept the same description of the *sensus divinitatis*. She could then say that we are designed to accept religious beliefs, not on the basis of the visual image itself, but on the basis of the seemings triggered by the visual images. Given this re-description, the Proper Function Account of Evidence no longer has the unsavory implication that the visual image of the sunset supports the claim that God loves one. For it would be proper function to believe that God loves one on the basis of the relevant seeming, not the visual image. So, one might think, the proper functionalist fares no worse than the phenomenal conservative.

The proposed response merely pushes the problem back. If the proper functionalist accepts my re-description of the *sensus divinitatis*, she avoids the counterintuitive

---

[30] This picture doesn't represent a faculty that mediates the transition between the God seeming and the God belief, but the existence of such a faculty would not affect my arguments in the paper.

implication that the sunset sensation supports the claim that God loves one in the *actual world*. But design plans are flexible. Even if *sensus divinitatis* is designed to produce religious seemings, it could have been designed to produce religious beliefs instead—if not for us, then for some other possible creature. The proper functionalist is still stuck with the counterintuitive consequence that the visual image of a sunset, by itself, *could* support the claim that God loves one.[31]

I have been arguing that phenomenal conservatism is better suited than is proper functionalism to explain how the glories of nature can lead to a justified religious belief. The basic idea of this argument is that the phenomenal conservative relies on a more plausible theory of evidence than does proper functionalism. This claim is supported by two intuitions. The first is that a sensation of a sunset, by itself (or in conjunction with a feeling of awe), cannot provide evidence for the claim that God loves one. I recognize that die-hard proper functionalists may not share this intuition, but I expect it to be widely-shared anyhow. The second intuition is that a seeming that God loves one can be evidence for the claim that God loves one. Even those who reject phenomenal conservatism concede that the second intuition is at least plausible.

4 Phenomenal conservatism and evidentialism

I promised in the introduction that I would argue for two main conclusions. In the previous section, I secured the first, that phenomenal conservatism is better suited than is proper functionalism to explain how an appreciation of the glories of nature can lead to justified religious belief. In this section, I secure the second, that if phenomenal conservatism is true, then it is so easy to acquire evidence that it doesn't really matter whether evidentialism is true. The second thesis, more precisely, is that, when conjoined with phenomenal conservatism, evidentialism allows cognitively unsophisticated subjects to have justified religious beliefs, and it allows them to have such beliefs even if they lack access to experts in the religious community who can provide persuasive arguments for those beliefs. Evidentialism holds that undefeated evidence suffices for justification. In 4.1, I argue that phenomenal conservatism makes it easy to have evidence for one's religious beliefs, and, in 4.2, I argue that it makes it easy to have *undefeated* evidence for religious beliefs. In 4.3, I consider whether a disparate type of evidentialism would be a significant obstacle to epistemically valuable religious belief even if phenomenal conservatism were true.

4.1 Given phenomenal conservatism, evidence is cheap

Recall that evidentialism, as we discussed it in Section 1, is the claim that one has (propositional) justification to believe P just in case one has some evidence E that

---

[31] For additional counterexamples to the proper function account of evidence and externalist accounts more generally, see my 'Evidential Support: What it is, Why it Matters, and Why Externalist Accounts Fail' (manuscript).

supports P and does not have any more inclusive body of evidence which fails to support P. Whether this evidentialism imposes a significant constraint on justified religious belief depends on how easy it is to acquire evidence. If evidence for religious beliefs were something that only the intellectually elite could acquire, then evidentialism would be a significant constraint on justified religious belief. Yet if even cognitively unsophisticated subjects can acquire evidence for their religious beliefs and do so independently of expert testimony, the potential truth of evidentialism isn't nearly as interesting.

Phenomenal conservatism says that a subject has evidence for P if it seems that P. Religious claims can seem true to cognitively unsophisticated subjects just as easily as they can seem true (false) to the intellectually elite. Given phenomenal conservatism, even cognitively unsophisticated subjects can have evidence for their religious convictions and they can have this evidence independently of expert testimony. Of the people who have religious convictions, I suspect that they often hold at least some of their convictions because they seem true. Phenomenal conservatism entails that those subjects have non-inferential evidence for (some of) their religious convictions, and presumably this non-inferential evidence is usually independent of expert testimony. Given plausible empirical claims, phenomenal conservatism entails that many people who have religious beliefs are such that they have testimony-independent, non-inferential evidence for at least some of their religious beliefs.

Even if someone grants these empirical claims, she may have the following concern.

Yes, if someone has religious experiences or seemings with religious content, then they could acquire evidence easily and evidentialism wouldn't impose a significant burden on those subjects. But what about those subjects who fail to have significant religious experiences of any sort? Wouldn't evidentialism impose a significant constraint on their religious beliefs?[32]

Suppose Barry is a subject who fails to have the seemings that would count as religious experiences. Either Barry has access to undefeated non-inferential testimonial evidence for his religious beliefs or he doesn't. If he does have such access,[33] then he can get evidence for his religious beliefs easily and evidentialism does not pose a significant obstacle to his having justified religious beliefs. If he doesn't have such access, then Barry may have a justified religious belief only if he has inferential evidence for it, and this may be a significant obstacle to his having justified religious beliefs. It does not follow, however, that this obstacle is posed *by evidentialism*. Suppose proper functionalism is true. It is plausible that our design plan allows us to form religious beliefs in only three ways: on the basis of religious experiences; on the basis of testimony; or on the basis of some sort of argument. Proper functionalism, given the above assumption about our design plan,

---

[32] Thanks to Sam Newlands for raising this concern.

[33] The phenomenal conservative might say that, when testimony gives us non-inferential evidence to believe the content of what was said, it is because the testimony triggers a seeming that the relevant content is true. Of course, testimony doesn't always have this effect. Sometimes someone tells us P, and it seems to us that the testifier is lying or is incompetent in the relevant subject matter.

would hold that Barry has a justified religious belief only if he has a good argument for it. A similar point could be made using most other non-evidentialisms.

Given phenomenal conservatism, subjects with religious seemings (however cognitively unsophisticated these subjects may be) can acquire evidence easily and independently of testimony. Those subjects who don't have religious seemings may need inferential evidence to have justified religious beliefs, and this may be a significant obstacle.[34] Yet this obstacle arises, not from evidentialism, but from some plausible thesis concerning which epistemic abilities (or sources of evidence) we actually have. Phenomenal conservatism may fail to make it easy for everyone to acquire evidence, but it doesn't follow that *evidentialism* imposes any significant obstacles to justified religious beliefs.

4.2 Given phenomenal conservatism, defeating defeaters is easy

Phenomenal conservatism makes it easy to have evidence for religious beliefs, at least for a wide range of subjects, including cognitively unsophisticated subjects who lack access to expert testimony. This point is crucial to showing that, given phenomenal conservatism, evidentialism doesn't impose a significant hurdle to justified religious belief. Yet it doesn't quite do the job by itself. Recall that evidentialists hold that one has propositional justification to believe P only if the subject doesn't have any relevant defeaters (i.e. the subject doesn't have any more inclusive body of evidence that fails to support P). One may concede that phenomenal conservatism makes it is easy to have evidence, but nonetheless insist that evidentialism is a significant hurdle because satisfying the no defeater condition can be a significant achievement. Stephen Wykstra, for example, argues (i) that an awareness of religious disagreement[35] constitutes a defeater for one's non-inferential religious beliefs and (ii) that this defeater can be defeated only if the subject has relevant *inferential* evidence.[36]

Wykstra holds that even if we have non-inferential evidence for some propositions, these propositions may 'come to need inferential evidence because our basic [i.e. non-inferential] faculties give us, as it were, conflicting signals about their truth.'[37] He asks us to suppose 'that my mother tells me one thing [P] and my father the contrary [~P].'[38] Wykstra's position is roughly as follows. He has non-inferential evidence for P in virtue of his mother's testimony; however, this evidence is defeated by his evidence for ~P which he has in virtue of his father's testimony. In light of his father's contrary testimony, he needs some *inferential* evidence to have a justified belief that P. Presumably, this inferential evidence must be further evidence for P or evidence that his

---

[34] I say that needing inferential evidence *may* be a significant obstacle because, given phenomenal conservatism, inferential evidence can come cheaply (see Section 4.3 below).

[35] By 'religious disagreement' I have in mind not only incompatible religious beliefs, but also experiences which (allegedly) support incompatible religious beliefs.

[36] 'Toward a Sensible Evidentialism: On the Notion of "Needing Evidence"' in William L. Rowe and William J. Wainwright (eds.), *Philosophy of Religion: Selected Readings*, 3rd edn (Oxford, Oxford University Press, 1998).

[37] Ibid. 490.

[38] Ibid.

mother's testimony is more trustworthy than his father's. Likewise, in light of the contrary testimony of other religious traditions, religious believers need some inferential evidence to have justified religious beliefs.[39] Presumably, this inferential evidence must be further evidence for the truth of those religious beliefs or evidence that the subject's religious experiences are more trustworthy than those had within other religious traditions.

The problem with Wykstra's position here is his assumption that the additional evidence must be inferential: he says nothing in favor of this assumption, and his own analogy suggests that it is false. Suppose his mother says there is a cat in the next room and his father says there isn't. His brother then comes along and provides independent testimony that there is a cat in the room. The evidence provided by his brother's testimony is non-inferential by Wykstra's lights, and it seems sufficient to make Wykstra's total evidence support P rather than ~P, which suffices for propositional justification according to evidentialism. If it isn't clear yet that Wykstra would have justification, we can suppose that Wykstra acquires even stronger non-inferential evidence when he goes into the room and sees the cat for himself. With this further non-inferential evidence, Wykstra clearly has justification for believing that there is a cat in the next room, despite his father's contrary testimony. More generally, if one's non-inferential evidence is counterbalanced by contrary evidence, that tie can be broken by further non-inferential evidence.

Suppose that, for some subject, the non-inferential evidence provided by her religious experiences is initially counterbalanced by her awareness of religious disagreement. After thinking carefully about the matter, it might seem to her that her religious experiences are more reliable than those of competing religious traditions. In such a case, phenomenal conservatism says that she would have acquired non-inferential evidence for regarding her religious experiences as more reliable than those had within rival traditions. This additional evidence should be enough to break the tie and make her overall evidence support her religious beliefs.

Or suppose that after thinking carefully about the matter, it seems even more obvious to her that the relevant feature of her religious tradition is true. Given the plausible assumption that stronger seemings provide better evidence, this increase in the seeming's strength improves the subject's evidence for her religious tradition. This improvement in her evidence should be enough to break the tie and make her total evidence support her religious beliefs.[40]

---

[39]   I have attributed to Wykstra the view that each individual religious believer needs inferential evidence for her religious beliefs. This may sound like a misinterpretation because, on p. 488, Wykstra insists that individual theists need not possess inferential evidence as long as it is 'available to the theistic community.' If he holds on to that claim, he must give up the above analogical argument. It is no good to Wykstra if there is some evidence 'available to the community' that his mother's testimony is more reliable: if he is to have a justified belief that P, he needs to possess that evidence.

[40]   Plantinga makes a similar point without relying on phenomenal conservatism in his 'Pluralism: A Defense of Religious Exclusivism' in Thomas D. Senor (ed.), *Rationality of Belief and the Plurality of Faith* (Ithaca, Cornell University Press, 1995).

Assuming that seemings really do provide genuine evidence, it is hard to see what more Wykstra would want. Of course, one may doubt that seemings do or at least always provide evidence. Or, more bluntly, one might insist that phenomenal conservatism provides an absurdly permissive account of evidence. I consider an objection along these lines in Section 5. Yet, *assuming* the truth of phenomenal conservatism, defeating the defeater posed by religious disagreement does *not* require acquiring inferential evidence of some sort.

We considered whether evidentialism would pose a significant hurdle to justified religious belief because satisfying the no defeater condition often will involve acquiring relevant inferential evidence. Yet given phenomenal conservatism, satisfying the no defeater condition is easy and doesn't require inferential evidence. Since phenomenal conservatism makes it easy to acquire evidence for religious beliefs and easy to satisfy the no defeater condition, it makes it easy to have justification whether or not evidentialism is true—at least it makes it easy for many subjects. If a subject fails to have the relevant seemings, then it may be hard for her to have justified religious beliefs. This difficulty, however, would not be posed by evidentialism; it would be posed by some plausible thesis concerning what epistemic abilities or sources of evidence a subject actually has. Hence, we have established the main point of this section, namely that, given phenomenal conservatism, evidentialism is not a significant hurdle to justified religious belief.

4.3 Wykstra's evidentialism

Even if phenomenal conservatism would make evidentialism insignificant *as it was defined above*, one might wonder whether there is some other plausible evidentialism that would remain significant even given phenomenal conservatism. In fact, Wykstra seems to think that he has identified such a view:

Wykstra's Evidentialism: S's religious belief that P is warranted only if there is inferential evidence available to S's religious community that P is true.[41]

Wykstra's Evidentialism is different in five respects from evidentialism, as it was defined in Section 1. First, Wykstra's Evidentialism is restricted only to the religious domain, not any domain whatsoever. Second, it concerns warrant, not (*ultima facie*) justification. Third, it lays down only a necessary condition on warrant, not a necessary and sufficient one. Fourth, it requires *inferential* evidence, whereas the earlier evidentialism simply required evidence, whether inferential or non-inferential. Finally, and perhaps most significantly, Wykstra's evidentialism holds that *someone else*'s evidence might be relevant to whether *my* religious beliefs are warranted. My religious beliefs might be

---

[41] 'Toward a Sensible Evidentialism,' p. 488. Wykstra talks about what it takes to be 'free of deep epistemic defectiveness' rather than what it takes to have warrant. I don't really know what deep epistemic defectiveness is unless it is failing to have warrant or something in the neighborhood. I, therefore, treat Wykstra's evidentialism as a thesis about warrant.

warranted not because *I* have non-inferential evidence for them, but because someone else in my religious community has evidence for them. According to the evidentialism from Section 1, it is *my and only my* evidence that matters to the justification of my religious beliefs; what evidence *anyone else* has for my religious beliefs is totally irrelevant.

Given phenomenal conservatism, Wykstra's Evidentialism, as stated, wouldn't pose much of an obstacle to warranted religious beliefs. Suppose I endorse the following argument: if torturing for fun is morally wrong, then God exists; torturing for fun is morally wrong; therefore, God exists. Also suppose that my only evidence for the premises is that they seem true. In such a case, I would have *inferential* evidence that God exists, so this belief would satisfy Wykstra's Evidentialism. But this inferential evidence came so cheaply that Wykstra's Evidentialism doesn't seem to be a significant obstacle to warranted religious beliefs. I suspect that Wykstra did not intend for his evidentialism to be satisfied by just any inferential evidence, but I'm not sure what restriction he might have in mind (except perhaps the vague restriction that the argument should be more like those employed in natural theology). We don't need to sort out these interpretive matters here. Regardless of how broadly he wants to construe 'inferential evidence,' Wykstra's Evidentialism is dubious.

Wykstra supports his evidentialism with an analogy. We ordinary folk seem justified in believing in electrons in part because we (justifiably) take scientists to have excellent *inferential* evidence for this claim. Yet our belief would fail to have warrant if the scientists really didn't have such evidence. Wykstra allows that I can have a *justified* belief in electrons even if the experts failed to have good inferential evidence for their existence.[42] He contends, however, that the experts must have inferential evidence for me (and for them) to have a *warranted* belief in electrons. Likewise, Wykstra says, even if neither the experts in my religious community nor I need inferential evidence for my religious beliefs to be *justified*, the experts (or someone else in the religious community) must have inferential evidence for my religious beliefs to be *warranted*.

There is an obvious disanalogy between electron-beliefs and religious beliefs: we do not take ourselves to have (testimony-independent) non-inferential access to electrons, but (some) religious practitioners do take themselves to have such access to religious matters. This disanalogy provides a principled reason for saying that a warranted belief in electrons requires the experts to have inferential evidence for claims about electrons, but then denying that 'if theistic belief is to be free of deep epistemic defectiveness, it is essential that an evidential case be available to the theistic community.'[43]

For a belief to be warranted, we require that it have an appropriate causal history, but— and this is important—the standards for appropriateness vary according to how the belief is formed. Most of us believe in electrons on the basis of some expert testimony, so it is plausible that our belief is warranted only if the expert's belief is warranted. Since we

---

[42] 'Toward a Sensible Evidentialism,' pp. 485–6.   [43] Ibid. 488.

assume that scientists warrantedly believe that electrons exist only if they have inferential evidence for this claim, it is plausible that our belief in electrons is warranted only if scientists have inferential evidence for this claim.

Suppose, on the other hand, that we believe that dogs exist on the basis of it perceptually seeming that way. Insofar as this belief is based on an experience (e.g. a perceptual seeming) what matters is that the experience is caused in an appropriate way (e.g. by a properly functioning visual faculty), not that the experts have inferential evidence for those beliefs. Wykstra agrees that our perceptual beliefs can be warranted even if there is no relevant inferential evidence that is available to community. If we were to discover that no such inferential case exists, 'we would not consider our confidence that dogs exist to be in big doxastic trouble.'[44] What Wykstra fails to see, however, is that a parallel point holds for certain religious beliefs.

Some religious beliefs might be analogous to belief in electrons in that they are based on expert testimony. We might hold, then, that those religious beliefs are warranted only if the experts in the community have some inferential evidence that those beliefs are true. Yet, at least some religious beliefs are analogous to our perceptual beliefs: they are based on certain experiences (e.g. seemings), and insofar as they are based on those experiences what matters is that the experiences are caused in an appropriate way (e.g. by a properly functioning *sensus divinitatis*), not that the experts have inferential evidence for those beliefs.

I have argued that, if phenomenal conservatism is true, then the evidentialism from Section 1 fails to be significant constraint on *justified* religious belief. We considered whether Wykstra's Evidentialism might nonetheless pose a significant constraint on *warranted* religious beliefs, but his evidentialism is dubious. Insofar as our religious beliefs are based on religious experiences, we should hold that those beliefs are warranted only if those experiences are caused in some appropriate way. Since the availability of inferential evidence is irrelevant to whether these experiences are caused appropriately, we should deny that a religious belief is warranted only if there is some inferential evidence that is available to the subject's religious community.

5 Is phenomenal conservatism too permissive?

I suspect that, at this point in the paper, many readers are thinking, 'Sure, maybe it's the case that *were* phenomenal conservatism true, evidentialism wouldn't impose a significant requirement on justified religious beliefs. But who cares? Phenomenal conservatism makes it absurdly easy to acquire evidence!' This worry is only amplified when you consider two additional facts. First, phenomenal conservatism allows seemings to provide evidence for their content *no matter how they are caused*—even if they are caused by wishful thinking, paranoia, cognitive malfunction, etc. Second, it is widely assumed,

---

[44] Ibid. 485.

even by non-evidentialists, that evidence for P suffices for *prima facie* propositional justification for P (see Section 3.2 above). Since I think people will be even more worried by how cheap phenomenal conservatism makes *prima facie* justification than they are about how cheap it makes evidence, I will respond most directly to the worry that phenomenal conservatism makes *prima facie* justification absurdly cheap.

There are perhaps many ways in which one could press this worry, but I will focus on Peter Markie's way of pressing it.[45] Consider:

HEAVEN: After my physical death, I will undergo a bodily resurrection and then live a happy and meaningful life for all of eternity.

Suppose that HEAVEN seems true to Wishing Willy simply because he deeply desires and hopes it to be true and that he believes HEAVEN on the basis of this seeming. Markie considers it absurd to say that this wishfully-produced seeming provides Willy with *prima facie* propositional justification for HEAVEN.

The putative problem for phenomenal conservatism is not that it licenses every form of wishful thinking. It can allow that my wishfully-produced belief that P lacks even *prima facie* justification when my wanting P to be true causes that belief directly (and without the causal mediation of a seeming that P). Nor is the problem that phenomenal conservatism approves of wishfully-produced beliefs as they are typically formed. In most cases of wishful thinking, people have some reason to suspect that they are thinking wishfully and so have at least partial defeaters for their wishfully-produced beliefs. In the ordinary case, then, it is unclear whether phenomenal conservatism allows wishful thinking to provide *ultima facie* justification. The alleged problem, though, is that phenomenal conservatism allows a wishfully-produced seeming to produce *prima facie* justification when it can't.

This objection notices an important fact about Willy's belief in HEAVEN: even if we stipulate that Willy has no relevant defeaters, his belief is clearly defective. If phenomenal conservatism is worth taking seriously, it needs some plausible explanation for why Willy's belief seems (and is) defective. The natural strategy for the phenomenal conservative is to distinguish between *prima facie* propositional justification, which Willy's belief has according to PC, and some other epistemic status which Willy's belief does not have. This strategy, if employed properly, would allow the phenomenal conservative to say that Willy's belief seems intuitively bad, not because it fails to have even *prima facie* justification (because it does have that property), but because it lacks this other epistemic status. This is precisely the strategy that I will pursue.

---

[45] 'Mystery of Perceptual Justification,' p. 356–7 and 'Epistemically Appropriate Perceptual Belief,' pp. 119–20. Alvin Goldman explicitly endorses Markie's objection in his 'Immediate Justification and Process Reliabilism' in Quentin Smith (ed.), *Epistemology: New Essays* (Oxford, Oxford University Press, 2008), sec 4. Similar objections appear in Michael Bergmann's 'Externalist Justification and the Role of Appearances' (manuscript) and Susanna Siegel's 'Cognitive Penetrability and Perceptual Justification', *Nous* (forthcoming).

My version of this strategy relies on a certain way of distinguishing between non-inferential justification and non-inferential warrant, where warrant is the property enough of which makes true belief knowledge. The proponent of phenomenal conservatism, it seems to me, should say that non-inferential justification is the property a proposition has when believing it is an appropriate response to an experience, whether that experience is caused appropriately or not. Justification is a necessary condition on warrant (or so I assume for the sake of this paper), so non-inferential warrant requires one's belief to be an appropriate response to experience; however, non-inferential warrant additionally requires that the experience be caused in some appropriate way.

One virtue of this way of distinguishing between non-inferential justification and warrant is its ability to explain the appeal of the new evil demon objection to reliabilism.[46] Suppose there is a mental duplicate of you. This person will have all the same beliefs and experiences as you,[47] and these beliefs and experiences will be organized in the same way as yours. If you believe that you are sitting in front of a computer on the basis of its perceptually seeming that you are sitting in front of a computer, the duplicate believes that he is sitting in front of the computer on the basis of its perceptually seeming that he is so situated.

Unfortunately, your duplicate is the victim of an evil demon's systematic deception. While your perceptual beliefs are mostly true, those of your duplicate are mostly false. Your perceptual seemings and beliefs are formed in a reliable way; your duplicate's are not. Certain versions of reliabilism entail that you have considerably more non-inferential justification than your duplicate; however, there is a widespread intuition that both you and your duplicate have exactly the same degree of non-inferential justification. Even some reliabilists try to identify versions of reliabilism that can accommodate this intuition.[48]

How does the above distinction explain the appeal of the new evil demon objection? Although a demon victim's experiences are caused in an *in*appropriate way, namely by the machinations of some demon, they still can provide non-inferential justification for believing ordinary perceptual claims. No one claims, of course, that these demon-caused experiences can make one's ordinary perceptual beliefs warranted. Intuitively, demon-caused experiences can't make a belief warranted even though they can make a belief justified. Why is this so? The proposed distinction between

---

[46] Stewart Cohen presses this objection in his 'Justification and Truth' (1984), *Philosophical Studies* 46, pp. 279–95.

[47] Strictly speaking, it is likely impossible for there to be a duplicate with exactly the same beliefs and experiences as you. It is generally acknowledged that a duplicate's beliefs and experiences would have the same phenomenal character as yours, but they will sometimes have a different content. Take indexical beliefs, for example: your belief 'I am a philosopher' has a different content than your duplicate's belief that 'I am a philosopher.' These differences are generally ignored, as they make little difference to the force of the new evil demon objection.

[48] See, e.g., Comesaña's 'Reliabilist Evidentialism' and David Henderson and Terry Horgan, 'Transglobal Reliabilism' (2006), *Croatian Journal of Philosophy* 17, pp. 171–95.

non-inferential justification and warrant provides an appealing answer: the demon victim's beliefs are justified because they are appropriate responses to her seemings, but they aren't warranted because her seemings, unbeknownst to her, were caused in an inappropriate way.

When combined with phenomenal conservatism, this way of distinguishing between non-inferential justification and warrant holds that Willy's belief is justified (because it is an appropriate response to his seeming that HEAVEN is true) but not warranted (because the seeming is caused by wishful thinking). The intuitive badness of Willy's belief is explained by the belief's failing to have any warrant at all. I find this result intuitively satisfactory, but perhaps others will insist that there is some relevant difference between demon-produced seemings, on the one hand, and wishfully-produced seemings, on the other.

It is natural to suggest there is a relevant difference because Willy is *responsible* for his inappropriately caused seeming and the demon victim isn't. In reply, it is easy to imagine a demon victim case in which the subject *is* responsible for her demon-caused experiences. Perhaps Weirdo had always wanted to be a demon-victim, and he paid, even begged a demon to make all his perceptual experiences delusional, such that he would never remember having told the demon to do so. Thus, Weirdo would be responsible for his delusional experiences because of some *past* actions; however, he *now* has reason to believe neither that his experiences are demon-induced, nor that he is responsible for their being demon-induced. In such a case, it still seems that those perceptual experiences would non-inferentially justify Weirdo's perceptual beliefs.

If perceptual experiences can provide non-inferential justification when, unbeknownst to the subject they are demon-caused *and* he is responsible for them being demon-caused, why can't a seeming that P produce non-inferential justification when, unbeknownst to the subject, that seeming was produced by wishful thinking *and* that subject is responsible for that wishful thinking? There don't seem to be any such reasons; therefore, being produced by wishful thinking does not prevent a seeming from providing justification for some claim. More generally, we should affirm that the cause of a seeming, by itself, has no bearing on the ability of that seeming to provide non-inferential justification (or evidence), even though it has much to do with the ability of that seeming to produce non-inferential warrant.[49]

6 Conclusion

If you've read this far, you've traveled a long road, so let me remind you of where you've been. The main goal of this paper was to apply phenomenal conservatism to religious belief with the aim of establishing two main theses. The first was that phenomenal conservatism is better suited than is proper functionalism to explain

---

[49] I defend my reply to Markie's objection at greater length in my 'Why Open-Minded People Should Endorse Dogmatism,' sec. 6.

how an appreciation of the glories of nature leads to justified religious beliefs. I argued that the phenomenal conservative's explanation was superior because only it avoided the counterintuitive claim that a visual image of a sunset can evidentially support the claim that God loves one (Section 3). The second thesis was that, if phenomenal conservatism is true, then a certain type of evidentialism fails to provide a significant obstacle to justified religious belief. I argued that, since phenomenal conservatism makes evidence so cheap, it makes it easy to acquire justified religious beliefs for a wide range of subjects, including cognitively unsophisticated ones with no access to expert testimony (Sections 4.1–2). This discussion naturally raised two questions: is there some other type of evidentialism that would pose a significant obstacle to epistemically valuable religious belief even if phenomenal conservatism were true? And does phenomenal conservatism make it *too* easy to acquire evidence? To partially answer the first question, we considered Wykstra's Evidentialism about warranted religious belief, but his evidentialism was dubious and it wasn't even clear that it would pose such an obstacle (Section 4.3). To partially answer the second question, we considered whether phenomenal conservatism was too permissive because it allows seemings to provide evidence and *prima facie* justification no matter how they are caused. After considering an analogy with the new evil demon objection to reliabilism, we concluded that inappropriately-caused seemings might provide *prima facie* justification (and evidence), even though they can't provide warrant (Section 5).[50]

[50] Thanks to the many people who made helpful comments on this paper, including Charity Anderson, Alex Arnold, Erik Baldwin, Thomas P. Flint, Adam Green, Michael Huemer, Mark Murphy, Jeremy Neill, James M. Nelson, Samuel Newlands, Alvin Plantinga, Michael Rea, Alan Rhoda, Jeffrey Snapper, Jerry Walls, Liu Zhe, and especially Ron Belgau who made the diagrams for this paper. The Center for Philosophy of Religion at the University of Notre Dame provided the financial support which made writing this paper possible. It goes without saying that I am very grateful for the Center's support.

PART II

The Relation of Beliefs to Evidence

5

Theistic Proofs, Person Relativity, and the Rationality of Religious Belief

William J. Wainwright

The present essay focuses on an objection to religious belief which claims that agnosticism is more admirable than the faith of a Christian whose strength of conviction exceeds what the evidence warrants since the latter sins against reason while the former does not. It is argued that this objection is mistaken because it assumes a faulty conception of the proper role of reason in religion. The first section examines the purposes for which proofs have historically been used in the major religious traditions and offers a defense of their value. The second extends the suggestion that proofs are 'person-relative' in a new direction, and the third argues that the concept of a rational religious belief that emerges from the discussions of the first two sections is essentially untouched by the objection that agnosticism is preferable to religious faith.

I

Historically, proofs of God's existence and other theologically significant matters have served a number of different purposes. Proofs have sometimes been used to establish common ground. One of the primary aims of Thomas Aquinas's *Summa Contra Gentiles*, for example, was to convince Muslims of the truth of the Christian faith. In this context, proofs of God's existence, omnipotence, and the like were employed to articulate a common ground 'upon which additional, more specifically Christian, arguments could be built.' Again, the pioneering Jesuit missionary, Roberto de Nobili, employed a version of Aquinas's theistic proofs to establish a 'point of contact' between (primarily theistic) Hindus and Christians, 'and thereby make the Hindus more receptive to the Christian message.'[1]

---

[1] John Clayton, 'Religions, Reasons, and Gods' (1987), *Religious Studies* 23, pp. 12–13.

Theistic proofs have also been used *within* a tradition to resolve intramural disputes. For example, Udayana was a devotee of Siva, and one of the most important philosophical theologians of the Nyaya-Vaisesika tradition. His theistic proofs were directed towards Buddhists but also toward Mimamsakas who were Hindu, and therefore shared allegiance to a common body of scriptures (most notably, the Vedas). In that context, the function of his arguments was to convince Mimamsakas that their atheistic interpretation of the Vedas was mistaken. Again, Al Ghazali deployed the Kalam cosmological argument against the 'philosophers' (preeminently Avicenna and Averroes) to show that their interpretation of the Quran's doctrine of creation was heretical.[2]

In addition to these uses, theistic proofs can be employed in devotional contexts, and, when they are, their aim is rather different. Anselm's *Proslogion*, for instance, is cast in the form of a prayer to God by someone who strives 'to raise his mind to the contemplation of God and... understand what he [already] believes.'[3] Udayana's *Nyayakusumanjali* is also instructive. The arguments in that work have three avowed purposes—to persuade unbelievers and to strengthen the faith of those who already believe, but, most importantly, to offer a loving gift to God. In the end, it doesn't greatly matter to Udayana whether his arguments succeed in accomplishing his first two goals 'so long as they are acceptable as a gift to the Lord Siva, so that 'the Guru of Indra's Guru... may be pleased by [his] presenting [them] as an offering at his footstool.'[4]

What these examples suggest is that theistic arguments have not always, or even usually, been addressed to those who deny that God exists, is omnipotent, omniscient, perfectly good, and the like. Nevertheless, they have sometimes been addressed to nonbelievers. Anselm's *Monologion*, for instance, was not only addressed to his fellow monks but also to the 'ignorant' who don't believe, and whom he hoped to persuade, through reason alone, that God exists, is the source of all goods and himself the Good that alone truly satisfies. And, as noted earlier, Udayana's arguments were addressed not only to his co-religionists and to God but also to Buddhists who denied that God exists and that the world has been created. Moreover, the rise of widespread nonbelief over the past 350 years has not surprisingly led to a more frequent use of positive apologetics. Christian apologists, for example, have offered 'proofs' of God's existence and providential care, the reliability of scripture, and other central claims of the Christian faith in an attempt to convince nonbelievers.

---

[2] The philosophers taught that the created world was eternal, and that relevant passages of the Quran should be interpreted so as to accommodate this fact. Al Ghazali responded by attempting to show that the world must have a beginning. The importance of the dispute was this. In the Aristotelian framework that the philosophers were employing, eternity and necessity were co-implicative. That God eternally generates the universe therefore entails that he necessarily does so. 'Necessity excludes will' however, and a God without will isn't a person and, hence, isn't the God of theism (John Clayton, 'Piety and Proofs' (1990), *Religious Studies* 26, p. 26).

[3] Marilyn McCord Adams, 'Praying the *Proslogion*: Anselm's Theological Method' in Thomas D. Senor (ed.), *The Rationality of Belief and the Plurality of Faith* (Ithaca, NY, Cornell University Press, 1995), p. 14. For more on the use of theistic arguments see my 'Religious Experience, Theological Argument, and the Relevance of Rhetoric' (2005), *Faith and Philosophy* 22, pp. 391–412.

[4] Clayton, 'Piety and Proofs,' p. 38.

Other Christians view this enterprise with suspicion, however. Nicholas Wolterstorff, Alvin Plantinga, and other Reformed epistemologists, for example, believe that positive apologetics is deeply misguided.[5] Why do they think this? For at least two reasons. First, they suspect that the nonbeliever's demand for evidence is no more than a rationalization concealing 'the real source of [his or her] unbelief,' namely, 'a sinful desire not to acknowledge God.' If it is, then the provision of proofs and evidence is irrelevant because it doesn't address the nonbeliever's real problem.[6] Second, evidentially based theistic beliefs can only be 'held . . . tentatively, weakly, with less than full commitment,' and are therefore religiously inadequate (Mavrodes 1983, p. 214).

George Mavrodes rightly finds these reasons unpersuasive. Reformed epistemologists *are* willing to engage in *negative* apologetics, defusing objections to the truth of theistic claims and to the rationality of believing them. Yet what justifies their doing so? If it is appropriate to reject the nonbelievers' demand for evidence on the ground that the real source of their nonbelief is their sinful desire not to acknowledge God, then why shouldn't it be equally appropriate to reject their demand for solutions to their objections for the same reason? Conversely, if *negative* apologetics can sometimes be useful (as Wolterstorff and other Reformed epistemologists think), then why insist that *positive* apologetics[7] can never be useful? Of course both positive and negative apologetics may be unsuccessful. 'The possibility of failure is not peculiar to the apologist,' however. For 'unbelievers can, and often do, resist *non*apologetic endeavors to bring them into the faith' (Mavrodes 1983, p. 201, my emphasis).

Mavrodes responds to the Reformed epistemologists' second point in two ways. Wolterstorff, Plantinga, and like minded Christian philosophers think that theistic beliefs should be held basically.[8] But basic beliefs, too, can be held weakly.[9] That one's belief in God is basic 'does not at all guarantee that the basic belief is held strongly, or with "trustful certitude" . . . or anything of the sort.' And while there may be 'a natural human tendency . . . to hold one's "life-orienting" beliefs, whether religious or otherwise, strongly,'[10] this is just as likely to be true of *evidentially based* life-orienting beliefs as of life-orienting beliefs that one holds basically. It is simply not evident, then, that

---

[5] This stance is not peculiar to Reformed theologians or even to Christians. Advaitins, for instance, believe that while reason can be successfully employed to defuse objections to Advaita Vedanta, it cannot be used to establish the central features of their interpretation of reality.

[6] George I. Mavrodes, 'Jerusalem and Athens Revisited,' in Alvin Plantinga and Nicholas Wolterstorff (eds.), *Faith and Rationality: Reason and Belief in God* (Notre Dame, IN, University of Notre Dame Press, 1983), p. 200. Henceforth Mavrodes 1983.

[7] Making the evidence which many Reformed epistemologists think that nonbelievers have 'still more insistent, more explicit, and so on' (Mavrodes 1983, p. 201).

[8] A basic belief is one that is not based on other beliefs. Perceptual beliefs, memory beliefs, and some simple logical and mathematical beliefs are standard examples.

[9] For example, my memorial belief that I had shredded wheat for breakfast last Wednesday is basic but not very firm.

[10] Yet strong in what sense? Relatively free from doubt? Central to one's life? Hard to dislodge? (The third may be a consequence of the second.) I suspect that Mavrodes' claim is true only if 'strong' is taken in the second or third sense.

evidentially based theistic beliefs are more likely to be held weakly or tentatively or half-heartedly than theistic beliefs one holds in the basic way (Mavrodes 1983, pp. 214–15).

Whether or not evidentially based theistic beliefs *can* be held strongly or wholeheart-edly may be irrelevant, though. For Wolterstorff and Plantinga seem to think that if a believer bases her beliefs on evidence she *ought* to hold them no more strongly than the evidence warrants. If this is true, and the objective evidence is as weak as they think, then she ought to hold her religious beliefs tentatively whether she in fact does so or not. The problem is, however, that if a belief based on *weak* evidence should itself be weak, then it would seem that a belief based on *'no evidence at all'*—such as properly basic theistic beliefs—'should be accorded *zero* degree of belief.' Of course Wolterstorff and Plantinga may 'favor some modified version of [the doctrine that the strength of one's belief should be proportional to the strength of one's evidence] to the effect that beliefs that are *held on the basis of evidence* should have their strength proportional to the evidence. But if we can [as they necessarily must] reject the full blooded doctrine of proportionality, why should we not also reject *this* version?' (Mavrodes 1983, p. 216, my emphases).

Wolterstorff and other Reformed epistemologists seem to think that it is enough if one's beliefs are deontologically rational—such that in holding them one violates no epistemic duties.[11] But deontological rationality is no guarantee of truth, however.[12] If one's aim is *truth*, it isn't sufficient that in forming one's belief one violates no epistemic duties; it is also necessary that one's belief forming processes be successfully aimed at truth. 'So a person may want some procedure to add to [deontological] rationality, a procedure which will improve his chances of truth by guiding him among the alternatives which [deontological] rationality leaves open' (Mavrodes 1983, p. 211). And this may very well include the collection and assessment of evidence. For it is, at least initially, as plausible to say that God has created us with a natural disposition to form theistic beliefs on the basis of evidence as to say (with the Reformed epistemol-ogists) that we have been created with a natural disposition to believe in him *sans phrase*.

Yet suppose we grant that positive arguments for theism can sometimes play a useful role both in the search for truth and in discussions with nonbelievers. What makes an argument of this sort a *good* one? Mavrodes address this question in 'On the Very Strongest Arguments.'[13]

---

[11] This helps explain, by the way, why Reformed epistemologists think that it is sometimes necessary for believers to engage in negative apologetics. If one is presented with a reason that suggests that her religious beliefs are false or irrationally held, it may be incumbent on her to defuse them. Failure to do so may violate an epistemic duty to abandon beliefs one has good reason to think false or irrationally held. It should be noted, however, that this admission is compatible with the recognition that, even if they are sound, one's arguments may not convince one's critics. Responses to the nonbeliever's objections may be adequate even when they aren't, strictly speaking, successful instances of negative *apologetics*.

[12] Eighteenth century scientists who advocated the phlogiston theory of combustion before better alternative theories were available were deontologically rational, for example. Their belief was nonetheless false.

[13] George I. Mavrodes, 'On the Very Strongest Arguments' in Eugene Thomas Long (ed.), *Prospects for Natural Theology* (Washington, DC: The Catholic University of America Press, 1992). Henceforth Mavrodes 1992.

Alvin Plantinga and Richard Swinburne articulate similar versions of a widely held view. Plantinga has suggested that a good argument is not only valid but 'draws its premises from the stock of propositions accepted by nearly every sane man, or perhaps nearly every rational man.' Swinburne thinks that a good argument is a valid argument 'whose premises are known to be true by those who dispute about the conclusion.' Both Plantinga and Swinburne are thus implicitly assuming that *universality* is an important good-making characteristic of arguments, and this isn't implausible. For 'an argument that had this property would' provide 'an epistemic good for a whole lot of people ... It would provide them with a way of knowing something that they did not know before (or, at least, that they might not have known before).' Call arguments which exhibit this property 'compelling' (Mavrodes 1992, pp. 81–2). How might 'compelling' be defined?

First Attempt: (C1) An argument is compelling if and only if it is sound and everyone accepts it.

This obviously won't do, however, since no interesting or important arguments satisfy 'the condition in (C1).' For there are too 'many ways in which a person might fail to accept an argument—by failing to understand it, for example, or by never having heard of it or thought of it' (Mavrodes 1992, pp. 83–4). So if (C1) captures the good-making property of universality, no significant arguments exhibit it. But if this is true, and *good* arguments possess this property, then no significant arguments are good ones. Since this seems absurd, it would be best to try again.

Second Attempt: (C2) An argument is compelling if and only if it is sound and everyone who understands it accepts it.

But now consider two arguments—Gödel's proof of the incompleteness of arithmetic and a valid proof of God's existence with all true premises which is not accepted by everyone who understands it. Both arguments are sound. Yet while nearly everyone who understands Gödel's proof accepts it, relatively few people understand it, and the number of those who would understand the argument if it were presented to them, while larger, is still quite small. The second argument, however, may be understood by many more 'of whom about half accept it' and there may be a much larger number 'who could understand it if they studied it, again with an acceptance rate of about one half' (Mavrodes 1992, pp. 84–5). Both arguments are sound but only the first is compelling in the sense of (C2). So if (C2) captures the property of universality, the first argument alone exhibits it. And this is paradoxical. For the second argument may extend the knowledge of many more people because it is more 'accessible' or easily understood than the first. Accessibility is thus important if a nearer approach to real universality is our goal. So let's try once more.

Third Attempt: (C3) An argument is compelling if and only if it is sound and everyone who understands it accepts it and everyone who studies it understands it.

Gödel's proof isn't compelling in this sense but the proof that there is no largest prime number may be. And arguments which meet the conditions of the third definition have an important virtue. 'For they could have a universal epistemic effect. "Could have," however, is not the same as "does have" or "will have" ... For there could be an argument that satisfied the condition in (C3) but was nevertheless "unattractive" in the sense that it did not attract many people to study it' (Mavrodes 1992, pp. 86–8).

Mavrodes may be right about this but more important, I think, is that while few if any interesting philosophical arguments, *including those for and against theism*, meet the second condition of the third definition, some of them may extend more people's knowledge of important truths than arguments which meet all three of (C3)'s conditions.

The foregoing reflections may be inconclusive. Nevertheless, they strongly suggest that some arguments which fail to meet Plantinga's and Swinburne's rigorous standards may have greater universality than many which do. So if universality really is our goal, then those standards should probably be relaxed.

It may be a mistake to place too much weight on the value of universality, however. For the 'strength' of an argument is also important. Strength, though, 'is more a matter of quality than quantity.' Strong arguments are arguments which 'establish' or 'demonstrate' or 'prove' their conclusions—'they make their conclusions secure.' And arguments that fall far short of universality may possess 'maximal epistemic security' (Mavrodes 1992, pp. 88–9). This can be true, for example, when a non-circular argument validly proceeds from premises I know to be true but others don't even though they may understand them or would understand them if they were to study them. For what could be more secure *for me* than a valid non-circular argument which proceeds from premises which I know to be true? And what this suggests is that arguments are 'person-relative' in the sense that a good argument for one person may not be a good argument for another. We will explore the implications of this important suggestion in the next section.

II

Mavrodes introduced the notion of a proof's person-relativity in his book *Belief in God*.[14] He began by distinguishing two sorts of 'propositional concepts.'[15] Subjective propositional concepts 'have psychological implications or content.' Examples are 'believed,' 'doubted' and the like. Objective propositional concepts 'have no psychological [implications or] content.' 'Important examples' are the terms 'truth' and 'falsity.' Propositions incorporating subjective psychological concepts are person-relative. A proposition can be believed by me, for example, without being believed by you, or doubted by you without

---

[14] George I. Mavrodes, *Belief in God: A Study in the Epistemology of Religion* (New York, Random House, 1970). Henceforth Mavrodes 1970.

[15] 'A propositional term is one that can reasonably fill the blank' in a sentence of the 'form "*p* ... is —"' where *p* ranges over proposition (Mavrodes 1970, p. 36).

being doubted by me. Propositions incorporating only objective propositional concepts are not person-relative. A proposition can't be true for me and not true for you, although you may, of course, not recognize its truth. An important consequence of these definitions is that the concept of knowledge is also person-relative. Because a necessary (though not sufficient) condition of A's knowing *p* is that A believes *p*, if the latter is person-relative, then so too is the former (Mavrodes 1970, pp. 36–7, 39–40).

How does this bear on the notion of proof? To answer this question, Mavrodes further distinguished between an argument's soundness, its 'cogency' and its 'convincingness': 'An argument is cogent for a certain person N if and only if (1) it is sound and (2) N knows it to be sound' (Mavrodes 1970, p. 32). 'An argument is convincing for N if and only if (1) it is cogent for N and (2) N knows that each of its premises is true, without having to infer any of them from its conclusion or from any other . . . statements that he knows only by an inference from that conclusion' (Mavrodes 1970, p. 34).

Soundness isn't person-relative.[16] But cogency and convincingness are since their definitions contain subjective propositional concepts. Because we ordinarily reserve the word 'proof' for cogent or convincing arguments, the concept of proof, too, is person-relative.

While I think there is something profoundly right about Mavrodes' contention, it does raise two questions.

The first is this: Philosophy has traditionally made claims on universal assent. Philosophers have believed that at least *some* arguments and *some* claims *ought* to be accepted by *all* rational or properly disposed subjects. In their view, a proof, properly so-called, is an argument which all rational or properly disposed subjects *ought* to find cogent or convincing whether they in fact do so or not. Call arguments which meet this condition 'probative.' We may grant that cogency and convincingness are person-relative. It is less clear that probativeness is. For the concept of probativeness incorporates an epistemic ought, and epistemic oughts, like moral oughts and truth, aren't obviously person-relative. If I morally ought to do x, then anyone in my situation ought to do x. Similarly, if I ought to believe *p* or accept *a* (where *p* and *a* take propositions and arguments as values, respectively), then anyone in my situation ought to believe *p* or accept *a*. Note that the fact that A ought to believe *p* or accept *a* doesn't imply that A does believe *p* or accept *a*. Subjective propositional concepts like believe and accept are indeed part of the content of the epistemic ought in the sense that, in unpacking the latter, we introduce hypothetical or counter factual conditionals which include them (for example, 'if anyone were in my situation, she should believe *p*'). But unlike Mavrodes' standard examples of 'mixed concepts' (knowledge, proof)[17] the application of the relevant concepts ('ought to believe,' 'ought to accept') to a subject

---

[16] For the soundness of an argument is a function of the truth of its premises and its validity, and 'truth' and 'validity' aren't subjective propositional concepts.

[17] 'Knowledge' is a mixed concept because it includes both objective and subjective elements. 'A knows *p*,' for example, entails that *p* is true and that A believes *p*.

doesn't ascribe a psychological state to that subject, and so isn't person-relative in Mavrodes' sense.

The second, and perhaps more interesting question, though, is this: What exactly *accounts* for the person-relativity of proofs? In some cases, differences of education, intelligence, or training. A trained physicist, for example, may know certain truths in physics, or be able to follow certain scientific demonstrations, which the untrained lay person doesn't (and perhaps can't) know or follow. Again, since what a person knows is partly determined by his or her temporal and spatial location, one person may know things which others do not. Thus, I may know that it is now raining on Milwaukee's east side although my cousin in Arizona does not. Or again, I may be privy to information which isn't available to others. The culprit may have confessed to me, for instance, but to no one else. Or God may have revealed something to Israel which he didn't reveal to other nations. There are other, more interesting, sources of person-relativity, however. It is plausible to suppose that a good argument is a sound noncircular argument which accomplishes its purpose. Yet as we saw in Section I, these purposes vary. Theistic proofs, for example, may be used to convince non-believers, to strengthen the faithful, as instruments of contemplation, or as offerings to God. A good argument for one person may not be a good argument for another if the latter doesn't share the former's purposes. If an argument is designed to establish common ground, for instance, or to further the project of contemplation, or as an offering to God, it may be of little or no interest or use to a person who doesn't share these aims—*even if the argument is sound and noncircular*. Thus, while Plantinga's version of the ontological proof is, arguably, sound and non-circular, and can play a useful role in furthering one's understanding of God, it has little value if one's aim is to convince nonbelievers since the latter can (and usually do) reject one or more of its premises.[18] Moreover, even if one sees no flaws in an argument, one may dismiss it from one's mind, give it little or no weight in one's practical or theoretical deliberations, or treat it as at most an interesting intellectual curiosity. William James thought that we regard something as real only when we have use for it,[19] and something similar may be true here. Arguments are taken seriously only when they seem to us to have some bearing on how we should think or act or feel. Whether or not they appear to us to have that

[18] For example, philosophically sophisticated contemporary nonbelievers typically reject the argument's possibility premise (that God's existence is possible).

[19] 'In the relative sense, then, the sense in which we contrast reality with unreality, and in which one thing is said to have more reality than another, and to be more believed, reality means simply relation to our emotional and active life. This is the only sense the word ever has in the mouths of practical men. In this sense, whatever excites and stimulates our interest is real' (William James, *Principles of Psychology*, vol. 2, (Cambridge, Harvard University Press, 1981), p. 924). Again, 'the *fons et origo* of all reality from the absolute or practical point of view, is thus subjective, is ourselves . . . A whole system may be real if it only hangs to our Ego by one immediately stinging term.' We feel 'our own present reality with absolutely coercive force' and ascribe an all but equal degree of reality, first to whatever things we lay hold on with a sense of personal need, and second, to whatever further things continuously belong with these . . . The world of living realities . . . is thus anchored in the Ego, considered as an active and emotional term' (Ibid. 925–6).

bearing depends importantly on our purposes. An argument may thus fail to be a good argument for someone because she doesn't have the interests and concerns needed for her to take the argument seriously.

There is an even more important source of the person-relativity of arguments, however. Not all good arguments are sound deductive or inductive arguments. For conclusions are sometimes warranted even though they aren't entailed by one's premises and can't be derived from the evidence by inductive extrapolation (by generalizing from the character of a fair sample, for example, or by inferring that an event will occur because similar events have occurred under similar conditions in the past). Cumulative case arguments or inferences to the best explanation are examples.[20] Moreover, sound deductive or inductive arguments themselves are often embedded in cumulative case arguments. Modal versions of the ontological argument and Samuel Clarke's cosmological argument are cases in point. Both arguments seem to me to be sound, for I believe that their premises are true and entail their conclusions.[21] In practice, however, these proofs are no more than *parts* of larger arguments in which they are embedded. These larger arguments include reasons supporting the proofs' premises and responses to the more telling objections to them and to the proofs' claims to validity and non-circularity. For in the final analysis, our assessment of the proofs will express our best judgment of the cumulative force of *all* the considerations bearing on their overall adequacy.

One of the simplest versions of the modal ontological argument, for instance, has three premises:

(1) What is possibly necessary is necessarily necessary,
(2) If God exists, he necessarily exists, and
(3) It is logically possible that God exists.

(1) is an axiom in the strongest systems of modal logic. (2) and (3) are controversial, however, and need support. For example, (2) might be supported by claiming that God is maximally perfect and that it is better or more splendid to exist and be God in all possible worlds than to exist and be God in only some of them. (3) might be supported by showing that attempts to derive a contradiction from the concept of God are unsuccessful, and by defending the claim that the idea of God isn't artificially constructed or 'cooked up' but instead natural, deeply rooted in humanity's religious consciousness.[22] And of course claims like these may in turn require further support. Our assessment of the modal ontological argument's adequacy will thus ultimately

---

[20] See my *Philosophy of Religion*, 2nd edn (Belmont, CA, Wadsworth, 1998), pp. 178–87.

[21] More accurately, I believe that some modal arguments, and a suitably qualified version of Clarke's argument, are sound. See ibid., chapter 2.

[22] The idea here is that notions which are deeply rooted in human consciousness, and which we spontaneously believe to be possible, are antecedently more likely to be coherent than artificially constructed concepts whose implications haven't been thoroughly explored.

depend on our sense of the comparative weights of all the conflicting considerations bearing on the proof's soundness and non-circularity.

Several things make universal agreement as to a proof's overall adequacy unlikely, however. In the first place, our assessment of the premises and of the reasons offered in their support may be unavoidably affected by our experiences and by what William James called our 'willing' or 'passional' nature—our temperament, needs, concerns, hopes, fears, passions, and deepest intuitions. For example, our assessment of 'It is logically possible that God exists' may be partly determined by our having or not having had apparent experiences of the divine, by the strength of our need for a larger meaning, or by our hunger for God or lack of it. Other things being equal, a person who has enjoyed an apparent experience of God, or who hungers after him, is more likely to find God's possibility intuitively obvious than someone who lacks these experiences or feels no need for God.

In the second, a person's assessment of the strength of the claims offered in support of the premises is often a function of his or her evaluation of the comparative plausibility of comprehensive explanatory systems which include these claims as parts. That God is maximally perfect and that maximal perfection involves necessary existence, and that the idea of God is a natural product of human religious consciousness, are both parts of classical western theism, for example. Disagreements over a proof's adequacy can thus ultimately involve a clash of world views, and world views are supported by cumulative case arguments.

Third, our final assessment of the comparative weight of the numerous considerations bearing upon the adequacy of the ontological proof, or any other interesting philosophical argument, is a paradigm example of informal reasoning. In assessing an inference to the best explanation, for example, we have to decide which hypotheses should be taken seriously and which dismissed as non-starters, what evidence is relevant and what isn't, the comparative weights to be placed on various kinds of evidence, and so on. We must also make judgments of prior probability. Some hypotheses and opinions are legitimately dismissed without argument but those we can't dismiss must be assigned a certain antecedent probability. Moreover, each of us approaches arguments with his 'own view concerning' the likelihood of the conclusion 'prior to the evidence; this view will result from the character of his mind . . . If he is indisposed to believe he will explain away very strong evidence; if he is disposed' to believe he may be willing to 'accept very weak evidence.'[23]

Finally, and perhaps most important, each reasoner must make an assessment of the argument's overall force, determine how strongly an argument's 'antecedents' (its premises and the considerations bearing on them) support its conclusion.

There are no mechanical decision procedures for making these assessments. Judgment is called for and, in the last analysis, each of us must form her own best judgment concerning

---

[23] John Henry Newman, 'Love the Safeguard of Faith against Superstition' in *Fifteen Sermons Preached before the University of Oxford* (Oxford, 1843); reprint (Westminster, MD, Christian Classics, 1966), p. 226.

these matters. Our judgments, however, are irredeemably personal since, when all is said and done, each of us can only view the various pieces of evidence 'in the medium of [her] primary mental experiences, under the aspects which they spontaneously present to [her], and with the aid of [her] best' efforts to do justice to them.[24]

Assessments of interesting and existentially significant philosophical arguments thus invariably reflect our personal histories. They also reflect our passional nature. Nor is this necessarily a bad thing. As I have argued elsewhere,[25] certain dispositions of the heart may be needed to reason rightly about value laden subject matters. That certain dispositions and attitudes are needed to reason rightly about moral matters, for example, is a commonplace in classical Chinese and western moral philosophy. Thus Plato thought that 'no man who is not naturally inclined and akin to justice and all other forms of excellence, even though he be quick at learning and remembering this or that . . . will ever attain the truth that is attainable about virtue.'[26] And Aristotle believed that the first premises of moral reasoning are general propositions about what is good for people in general, or for certain kinds of people, or for people in certain circumstances. General propositions of this kind are partial articulations of the good life. Men and women whose natures have been warped by bad education or circumstances, however, will have a perverted sense of the good (identifying it with the life of pleasure, say, or the life of worldly honor). These people (as Plato says) have a 'lie in their soul,' and are therefore incapable of reasoning correctly about moral matters. A properly cultivated emotional nature is thus essential to sound ethical reasoning.

Now classical Christian theism identified God with Goodness itself. If this identification is correct, it is not surprising that the proper dispositions and feelings should also be thought to be necessary to reason correctly about God.

Moreover, the relevance of my remarks is even more general than my application of them to classical ethics and Christian theism might suggest. The most obvious instances of the thesis that basic disputes reflect different passionally inflected assessments of more or less the same body of evidence is furnished by conflicts over comprehensive world views. Some of these world views are religious but many are not. It is at least arguable, however, that all comprehensive world views integrally incorporate values. If they do, and values can't be grasped in the absence of the right feelings and attitudes, then appropriate dispositions of the heart will be needed to discern the truth of a world view. Wrong dispositions, on the other hand, will result in false judgments and intellectual blindness.

Yet if this is correct, then arguments are person-relative in an even deeper sense than those discussed earlier. Since an argument's cogency and convincingness can depend

[24] John Henry Newman, *An Essay in Aid of a Grammar of Assent* (London, 1870); reprint (Notre Dame, IN, University of Notre Dame Press, 1979), p. 318.

[25] William J. Wainwright, *Reason and the Heart: A Prolegomenon to a Critique of Passional Reason* (Ithaca, NY, Cornell University Press, 1995).

[26] *Plato's Epistles*, trans. with critical essays and notes by Glen R. Morrow (Indianapolis, IN, Bobbs-Merrill, 1962), pp. 240–1.

on the state of one's heart, and the states of people's hearts vary, an argument which is cogent or convincing for one person may not be cogent or convincing for another.

Some of these arguments may nonetheless be probative, however. Proofs are relative to persons *because* they differ in education, training, and intelligence, *because* they differ in their spatio-temporal location or the information available to them, or *because* they differ in purpose or the state of their hearts. Many of these differences are epistemically innocent. Variations in education, training, and intelligence, or in spatio-temporal location or the available information, are examples. Other differences are less obviously so. It is arguable, for instance, that *all* men and women *ought* to exhibit the dispositions and motions of the heart needed to reason rightly about moral matters and the things of religion, or to share certain purposes. If they should, then any person–relativity derived from variations in purpose or in dispositions of the heart ought not to exist; and (other things being equal) proofs whose cogency and convincingness depend upon having the right dispositions or sharing the right purposes *should* be cogent and convincing to everyone who can understand them. They are therefore probative in the sense defined earlier whether everyone or even most people accept them or not.

III

Consider the following 'perverse' combinations:

(1) *p* and it is not rational to believe *p*
(2) *p* and it is rational to believe not-*p*
(3) not-*p* and it is rational to believe *p*

It seems possible that one prove, or have strong evidence for, both conjuncts in one or more of these conjunctions.[27] In cases of this sort, rationality and truth pull apart. What, then, should one do? Mavrodes has said that 'if push comes to shove, . . . I would opt for truth over rationality every time,' that 'would be the right way to choose, the way one ought to choose.'[28] If so, this has an interesting consequence. Suppose that the Christian God exists but that the evidence for his existence is no stronger than that against it. (Many Christians believe this. Kierkegaard, as sometimes interpreted, is an example.) If this is correct, then, while agnostics may be more rational than Christians, a Christian faith which believes in the absence of adequate evidence is better than agnosticism.

---

[27] For example, one might have strong (but not conclusive) evidence for 'God exists' and so rationally believe that God exists, while also having good reasons for thinking that at least some atheists, too, are rational. (That is, while the evidence may seem to one to favor 'God exists' one may think that it isn't strong enough to brand atheists as nonrational.) If one does, then one has a good reason for believing Mavrodes' second conjunction. Or again, one might think that while God probably doesn't exist, there are good pragmatic reasons for believing that he does. If one does, one implicitly endorses the third conjunction.

[28] George I. Mavrodes, 'Rationality and Religious Belief—A Perverse Question' in C. F. Delaney (ed.), *Rationality and Religious Belief* (Notre Dame, IN, University of Notre Dame Press, 1979), p. 33.

John Schellenberg denies this.[29] Faith can be admirable.[30] For loyalty,[31] courage, humility, and other virtues may be needed to maintain one's belief in the face of strong intellectual challenges to it. Agnosticism can be at least *equally* admirable, however, because precisely the same virtues may be needed to persevere in one's agnosticism when (as many agnostics would) one would very much like to believe. Loyalty and courage are necessary to preserve one's allegiance to the truth (as one sees it, namely, that the arguments for and against theism are more or less evenly balanced). And humility is needed to acknowledge and accept one's own lack of knowledge. And, indeed, agnosticism is even *more* admirable than faith when the believer's confidence exceeds what the evidence would warrant, as it so often does. It is more admirable because Christians of this sort typically claim to *know* 'the great things of the gospel' attributing their faith to the gracious instigation of the Holy Spirit and nonbelief to sin. The trouble is that the epistemic stance of these believers *undermines* their claim to warrant, and so, given that warrant is what transforms belief into knowledge, their claim to know that what they believe is true. For the very attitudes and virtues needed to maintain their faith in the face of skeptical onslaughts militate against their fairly considering objections to their belief and hence undercuts its warrant.[32]

---

[29] John L. Schellenberg, "'Breaking Down the Walls that Divide:" Virtue and Warrant, Belief and Nonbelief' (2004), *Faith and Philosophy* 21, pp. 195–213. Henceforth Schellenberg.

[30] But, as we shall see in a moment, Schellenberg's professed admiration of faith seems a bit disingenuous. For, in his view, the person of faith *isn't* loyal to the truth because her assessment of the evidence and responses to objections aren't genuinely fair or honest. Compare, in this connection, Socrates's discussion of courage in the *Protagoras*: 'Courage' in the defense of false values isn't *true* courage. While a 'courageous' defense of false values may be admirable from a limited point of view, it *isn't* admirable (and hence can't be regarded as truly courageous) when viewed from a wider perspective. Schellenberg's view is like this. Traditional faith has some admirable features but isn't admirable all things considered.

[31] To what one believes to be the truth, or to a person (namely, God) whom one believes to exist (?).

[32] Schellenberg thinks I overstate his case and insists that, in fact, his claims are more limited. For, in the first place, he is only concerned with situations in which 'love and loyalty toward God may challenge one's willingness to accept the truth, whatever it may be' and is not 'making some more general pronouncements about rationality.' Moreover, he doesn't deny that the believer's loyalty is 'admirable all things considered. For *her* loyalty is to God, and [he doesn't] compare the admirableness of this with that of loyalty to the truth. (For all [he has said] they might come out even . . . What [he *does* say] is that the believer's loyalty to God can get in the way of what is required for knowledge of God (whatever the value of the latter might be).' (Correspondence, quoted with permission.) Strictly speaking, what Schellenberg says is correct. Even so, the *general tone* of his remarks in both the article under discussion and in other recent work strongly suggests that he thinks that the virtuous agnostic *is*, on the whole, more admirable than a person whose primary loyalty is to God. (For if he doesn't, why should he recommend the virtuous agnostic's stance as he rather clearly does?) Schellenberg's charge, in essence, is that a person who loves God more than the truth will be tempted to fudge the evidence by either ignoring the evidence against his beliefs or failing to give it its due weight. If God is a lover of truth, however (or, more strongly, *is* the truth as much of the tradition maintains), then a genuine love of God *cannot* conflict with a love of the truth. Only a defective or misplaced or idolatrous love of God could lead one to mishandle the evidence. Part of the problem, it seems to me, is Schellenberg's assumption that '*in so far as truth is one's goal* (as it must be where a knowledge claim is made) one should seek . . . neutrality' (ibid.). If this is true, then (because loyalty tends to militate against neutrality), there is an obvious tension between loyalty to God and a love of truth. Schellenberg's assumption seems to me dubious, however. A love of truth entails intellectual fair mindedness but doesn't clearly entail neutrality. More on this below.

Furthermore, their attribution of nonbelief to sin is as questionable as their claim to knowledge for, on the face of it, some nonbelief is non-culpable, involving no obvious violation of one's moral or epistemic duties. Some atheists and agnostics, for example, would dearly like to believe, and reluctantly arrive at their conclusion after a long, and apparently honest and conscientious, examination of the evidence. Nor is what Schellenberg calls 'sophisticated Calvinism' significantly more plausible. Sophisticated Calvinists contend that our sin or the sin of others has vitiated our epistemic faculties, producing in nonbelievers 'a misguided exercise of [doxastic] virtue.' Yet this is as implausible as the claim that nonbelief is always culpable. For 'cognitive dullness... would have to involve something like a lack of thoroughness or penetration in investigating; and moral disorder... would have to involve something like carelessness or distraction by self-centered motives' and there is no empirical evidence that either is involved in the cogitations of all reflective atheists and agnostics.

Finally, the Calvinists' claims are not only implausible, they are morally and spiritually suspect. For the humility and charity valorized by *all* Christians militate against attributing sinfulness to apparently virtuous nonbelievers when all the empirical evidence is against it. So in so far as the Christian 'observes genuine goodness in many of them (even in the way their nonbelief is formed or maintained)'—and she should, she should not 'go along with... the Calvinist position' (Schellenberg: 208, 210–11).

It isn't clear that the Christian should be convinced by this. For, arguably, what our own sin, or the sin of others who have helped form our epistemic faculties, impairs is our ability to appreciate 'the great things of the gospel'; we lack a perception of their spiritual beauty or splendor. And this skews our investigations by adversely affecting our weightings (of the evidence), attentions, and assessments of the evidence's overall force. Its doing so would be apparent neither to honest nonbelievers, however, nor to 'neutral' observers because both lack this perception. The fact that many instances of nonbelief *seem* virtuous to nonbelievers is thus only to be expected.[33] Furthermore, the Calvinian Christian can consistently say of at least *some* apparently virtuous

---

[33] Schellenberg suggests that I mistakenly assume 'that the nonbelievers lack the relevant dispositions of the heart...—that they don't feel the gospel message to be beautiful. And this seems just false... (at least as a generalization). A clear counter example is provided by those nonbelievers who are former *believers*, and whose Christian belief was stripped away while they still very keenly felt its content to be beautiful.' (Correspondence) I have two things to say about this. In the first place, I have never claimed that appropriate dispositions of the heart are *sufficient* to ensure that one weighs the evidence as one should because the due operation of those dispositions may be impeded by other dispositions or by mistaken views of rationality, and the like. So even if the agnostic *does* have the relevant dispositions, it won't follow that he will weigh the evidence properly. In the second, that one has *had* the relevant dispositions and feelings does not entail that one *still* has them. That I loved Cynthia, for example, vividly and fondly recall what loving her was like, and even wish that I still loved her does not entail that I *now* love her (i.e., continue to experience the relevant emotion). Similarly here. I strongly suspect that what the Christian who has lost his faith retains is typically a simulacrum of the passions and 'intuitions' he formerly enjoyed. (Note, too, Edwards's claim that a sense of the gospel's true beauty is inextricably bound up with the conviction of its *truth*, of the *reality* of the great things it adumbrates [which, by the way, was not only a Puritan commonplace but a commonplace of the Christian spiritual tradition as a whole]. If a sense of the gospel's 'true beauty' *does* involve this, then Christians who have lost their faith clearly *don't* retain it.)

nonbelievers that while (1) their noetic faculties are impaired by sin, (2) their epistemic and nonepistemic goodness *as a whole* surpasses her own, and even admit that (3) they may be closer to God than she is. The Calvinian view is thus consistent with both genuine love and genuine humility.[34]

Schellenberg's charge, at bottom, is that the Christian whose strength of conviction exceeds what the evidence warrants typically sins against reason because his loyalty to God interferes with his loyalty to truth. Schellenberg's *conception* of reason seems to me faulty, however.

Notice, first, that intellectual fair mindedness is not the same as neutrality. A fair minded inquirer 'seeks out evidence and pays attention to criticism and counter claims . . . supports his judgment with recognizable good reasons,' is 'open to the possibility that he might be wrong' and 'revises and rejects his beliefs in the light of new information.'[35] Neutrality, however, involves bracketing, or prescinding from, one's interests and predilections, feelings and emotions, desires and wishes, and 'divinations' and hunches.

Schellenberg seems to identify a *fair* treatment of the evidence with a *neutral* treatment of it but while rationality *does* entail fair mindedness, it *doesn't* clearly entail neutrality.[36]

Rationality may entail a wholehearted love of truth. Yet as James points out, a passion for truth can take two quite different forms depending on whether an inquirer privileges the injunction to seek truth or, on the contrary, privileges the injunction to avoid error. 'Believe truth! Shun Error!—these . . . are two materially different laws; and by choosing between them we may end by coloring differently our whole intellectual life. We may regard the chase for truth as paramount, and the avoidance of error as secondary; or we may, on the other hand, treat the avoidance of error as more imperative, and let truth take its chance.'[37] Note that the latter is much more likely to lead to a self-conscious cultivation of 'neutrality' than the former.

Moreover, neutrality, understood as bracketing, or prescinding from, what James calls our 'willing' or 'passional' nature, is reasonable only upon the assumption that that nature isn't truth oriented—an assumption which Jonathan Edwards, John Henry Newman, James, and I deny. For one thing, neutrality (as distinct from fair mindedness) is simply out of place in ethical and aesthetic inquiry. There is no reason to

---

[34] For more on this possibility see my 'Competing Religious Claims' in William E. Mann (ed.), *The Blackwell Guide to the Philosophy of Religion* (Oxford, Blackwell, 2004), p. 240.

[35] Louis P. Pojman, *Religious Belief and the Will* (London and New York, Routledge & Kegan Paul, 1986), pp. 198, 203.

[36] Fair mindedness *may* require us to imaginatively place ourselves in the shoes of our intellectual opponents, seeing things as they do and thus seeing or appreciating just *why* they assign the evidence the weight that they do. (It may, in other words, require something like John Keats's 'negative capability.') Need this involve bracketing one's own point of view, however, or abstracting from one's intellectual and emotional proclivities? Did Milton, for example, or Dostoevsky bracket their Christian points of view when they constructed their rounded and convincing pictures of Satan and Ivan, respectively? I, for one, doubt it.

[37] William James, 'The Will to Believe' in *The Will to Believe and other Essays on Popular Philosophy* (New York, Dover, 1956), p. 18. Need we privilege one over the other? James, at least, thinks that we must since in some cases the truth is unlikely to reveal itself to those who are unwilling to run the risk of error.

think that a person who refuses to allow herself to be influenced by her moral and aesthetic proclivities, sentiments, and feelings is more likely to arrive at the truth about moral and aesthetic matters than someone who doesn't or, indeed, is even *as* likely to do so. And in fact the contrary seems to be true.[38] Yet as I indicated in Section II, not only comprehensive world views but *all* existentially freighted hypotheses imply or incorporate values. If they do, then what I have just said about moral and aesthetic inquiry will *also* be true of religious inquiry—*including the inquiries of the agnostic*— namely, that it is guided by the assumptions, interests, predilections, sentiments, and feelings of the inquirer.[39]

Schellenberg insists that there is a significant difference between a 'virtuous' believer and a virtuous agnostic, however. For the former's commitment to a substantive metaphysical assertion (namely, that God exists) adversely affects the way he handles the evidence. The latter, on the other hand, is not committed to substantive claims but only to finding the truth. And this does not (and presumably cannot) do so.

But this is questionable on at least two counts. First, one's weighting of evidence is (largely?) a function of one's picture of the way things are, one's hunches about what the world is (and isn't) like, and these pictures and hunches invariably involve metaphysical claims. By bracketing controversial metaphysical assumptions like theism, Schellenberg's agnostic forms her weightings against a background which is, effectually, naturalistic. Her judgments are thus *not*, in fact, metaphysically neutral. Second, a commitment to Schellenberg's enlightenment conception of rationality as (among other things) 'neutral,' is itself a controversial commitment. For why should one assume that neutrality (as distinguished from fair mindedness) is essential to either deontological rationality or warrant? One can legitimately do so, I think, only if one identifies *proper* weightings of the relevant evidence with those of a person who has no stake in the matter, no intellectual proclivities, 'divinations' or hunches.[40] To do so, however, begs the question against views of reason like Newman's, James's, or mine.[41]

---

[38] Note that being *influenced* by one's moral and aesthetic sentiments is not the same as noticing that one *has* them, and then treating that fact as evidence. A person who does the latter is, in principle, no different from someone who *hasn't* had them but, noting that others have, adds that fact to her evidence base. By contrast, an inquirer who allows herself to be *influenced* by her own moral and aesthetic sentiments and feelings does *not* allow herself to be influenced by those of others (except, of course, in those cases in which she has been persuaded to make them fully her own). Indeed, doing so would then be incoherent since the feelings and sentiments which would then influence her would pull her in contrary directions.

[39] Note that this does *not* imply (nor do James or Newman or Edwards think it does) an uncritical endorsement of just any prompting of one's passional nature. One may have (or at least should have) reasons to distrust a desire or sentiment or predilection and, when one does, one must critically examine them. (See my *Reason and the Heart*, pp. 140–7.)

[40] Or more accurately, on Schellenberg's view, while the inquirer may in fact *have* a stake in the matter, interests, hunches, and the like, she should set those aside, temporarily identifying her stance with that of a person who does *not* have them.

[41] Commenting on these claims, Schellenberg says that 'it is hard to see how *any* non-question-begging assessment of theism, . . . can avoid "bracketing controversial metaphysical assumptions like theism." . . . [I]t is [also] hard to see how the background to the agnostic's musings must be "effectively naturalistic." If she really is an *agnostic* won't this . . . be because she finds that neither theism nor naturalism . . . is fully defensible? And

There is a further problem as well. If Schellenberg is right, it is doubtful that a philosopher can claim to know *any* substantive and existentially important proposition—that our wills are or are not free, for example, or that morality is or isn't objective, that physicalism is or isn't true, or that democracy is or is not the best form of government. For strong convictions that one and not the other of one or more of these alternatives is more likely to be true, shape and guide most philosophical inquiry into the relevant issues. Now, as far as I can see, Schellenberg must respond to this observation in one of three ways.

(1) He can reject my characterization of the philosophical inquiries in question by asserting that impartial (neutral) reason *does* support one member of at least some of these disjunctions more strongly than it supports the other. Yet this would be a mistake, I think. William James's 'The Dilemma of Determinism' is instructive in this regard for, if James is right, our moral proclivities and sentiments play a major role in determining whether or not we find the case for free will convincing.[42] And similar claims can be made about other highly fraught metaphysical and ethical issues.

(2) Alternatively, Schellenberg could argue that because 'objective' or 'impartial' reason *can't* settle these matters, philosophers *don't* know that we do or do not possess incompatibilist free will, for example, and should therefore adopt an agnostic attitude toward the claim that we do. But this implies that most philosophers are not entitled to assert many things which seem to them, on balance, to be clearly true. This is not only counter-intuitive but rests on views of reason which cannot be supported without begging the question against alternative conceptions, like Newman's or James's, or mine.

(3) Finally, Schellenberg *might* concede that controversial philosophical claims *can* sometimes be rationally held (or belief in them be rationally justified), and that

---

might she not be remaining open to *all* the possibilities here, making *no* assumptions that bring her down on one side or the other?' (Correspondence, last two emphases mine.) Schellenberg's first claim seems to miss my point, however, namely, that the agnostic alternative is *equally* question begging. If theism or James's generic religious hypothesis or some similar religious hypothesis is true, then (as Edwards, Newman, James, and I argue) it is probable that one will miss the force of the evidence for it if one approaches the evidence 'neutrally.' So to insist that one *should* approach the evidence neutrally begs the question against these hypotheses. Schellenberg's second point *is* well taken. There is still a problem, however. If the agnostic prescinds from *all* world views, *all* conceptions of the general nature of things, what guides her assessments of the prior probabilities of the hypotheses she considers, the relevance of various evidence-candidates and their weights, and the evidence's overall force? We surely don't, and indeed can't, make these judgments in a vacuum. Like everyone else, then, the agnostic must form her assessments against *some* background. So what will her background be like? It will presumably include those propositions which are generally agreed upon among all parties to the dispute but will not include propositions that are at issue between them. It will therefore include well attested propositions of science and common sense and will *not* include the claims of religion. Naturalism, however, just *is* the view that the world of science and common sense is the only world there is. The background picture against which the agnostic forms her assessments is thus effectually naturalistic.

[42] William James, 'The Dilemma of Determinism' in *The Will to Believe and other Essays on Popular Philosophy*.

therefore some philosophers may be entitled to assert them even though they aren't *known* by those philosophers to be true. 'A is rationally entitled to assert *p*' can be interpreted in at least two ways, however: as (a) 'A violates no epistemic duties in believing *p*,' or as (b) 'A's belief that *p* is produced by epistemic processes sufficiently like those that would be operating in an ideal (human?) inquirer in A's circumstances.' The first option isn't open to Schellenberg for, in his view, the philosophers in question *are* violating an epistemic duty since they allow their predilections, hunches, and the like to impair their neutrality. Yet if Schellenberg adopts the second option, then[43] the difference between rationally or justifiably believing *p* and knowing *p* is so small that the claim that, while these philosophers may justifiably believe *p*, they don't know *p*, becomes innocuous.[44]

If the argument of this section is correct, then, Schellenberg has not shown that the principled agnostic is more admirable than the man or woman of faith whose strength of conviction exceeds what would be warranted by an 'objective' or 'impartial' view of the evidence. Our discussion also casts doubt on the claim that rationality and truth might come apart, however. For while '*enlightenment*' rationality and truth can come apart, it isn't clear that truth and a reason which is informed by appropriate dispositions of the heart can do so. If it can't, and *right* reason is a passionally inflected reason, then the choice between reason and truth is spurious.

---

[43] Given an externalist epistemology, at least.

[44] Or more accurately, there is little or no difference *if* we are justified in assuming that the conclusions that would be reached by an optimally rational epistemic agent in the circumstances in question would accurately track the truth.

6

Hiddenness, Evidence, and Idolatry

E. J. Coffman and Jeff Cervantez

1 Introduction

In some of the most important recent work in religious epistemology, Paul Moser develops a multifaceted reply to a prominent attack on belief in God—what we'll call the *Hiddenness Argument*.[1] This paper raises a number of worries about Moser's novel treatment of the Hiddenness Argument. After laying out the version of the argument Moser most explicitly engages, we explain the four main elements of Moser's reply and argue that it stands or falls with two pieces in particular—what we call the *Purposively Available Evidence Argument* and the *Cognitive Idolatry Argument*. We then show that the Cognitive Idolatry Argument fails, leaving the Purposively Available Evidence Argument as Moser's only potentially viable objection to the Hiddenness Argument. We conclude that Moser's treatment of the Hiddenness Argument depends crucially on some controversial epistemological claims about certain of our moral beliefs, and is thus considerably more vulnerable than many have recognized.

2 The Hiddenness Argument and Moser's multifaceted reply

2.1 The Hiddenness Argument

In the following passages, Moser articulates the version of the Hiddenness Argument he means to engage:

How could a perfectly loving God, who reportedly aims to communicate with people, *fail* to be manifested in such a way that removes all reasonable human doubt about God's reality? Many people, including many philosophers, deny that this is possible. [. . .] We might have thought, at

---

[1] See his 'Cognitive Idolatry and Divine Hiding' in D. Howard-Snyder and P. Moser (eds), *Divine Hiddenness: New Essays* (New York, Cambridge University Press, 2002); 'Divine Hiddenness Does Not Justify Atheism' in M. Peterson and R. VanArragon (eds), *Contemporary Debates in Philosophy of Religion* (Malden, MA, Blackwell Publishing, 2004); and *The Elusive God: Reorienting Religious Epistemology* (New York, Cambridge University Press, 2008). All undated citations are to *The Elusive God*.

least initially, that a perfectly loving God's existence, if real, would be beyond reasonable doubt for all cognitively normal adult humans. God's existence, however, is not beyond reasonable doubt according to many cognitively normal adult humans. So, according to these people, we may reasonably deny that God exists or at least reasonably refrain from believing that God exists. (p. 106) Some philosophers ... have objected that God's alleged self-revelation is too unclear, at best, to merit reasonable acknowledgement. Surely, their objection goes, God would owe us more miraculous signs and wonders, whatever God's redemptive aims. Why doesn't God entertain us, once and for all, with a *decisive* revelation of God's awesome power? After all, it wouldn't cost God anything, and it may vanquish nagging doubts about God's reality. As a result, we're told, a truly loving God would surely use strikingly miraculous self-revelation to free us from our doubts. This, however, hasn't happened. God's redemptive purposes, many people will thus object, wouldn't exonerate God from the charge of excess restraint in self-revelation. (p. 128)

It'll be helpful to have a more formal statement of the Hiddenness Argument on hand. Letting *spectator evidence* mean evidence for God's existence you can acquire without thereby being called by God to submit to a morally transformative relationship with him (p. 128), here's the statement of the Hiddenness Argument we'll start with:

The Hiddenness Argument

1. If God existed, then every cognitively normal adult human would be (epistemically) justified in believing that God exists.
2. A cognitively normal adult human would be justified in believing that God exists only if she had adequate spectator evidence that God exists.
3. So: If God existed, every cognitively normal adult human would have adequate spectator evidence that God exists.
4. Some cognitively normal adult humans lack adequate spectator evidence that God exists.

C. So: God doesn't exist.

Premise 2 suggests the general view that epistemic justification requires adequate evidence. Actually, that's controversial: there's vigorous debate in mainstream epistemology over the merits of such requirements.[2] The point to see here is that, given his own approach to epistemic justification, Moser will accept whatever general evidentialist assumptions lie behind the argument:

Belief that God exists would be *evidentially* arbitrary and thus *cognitively* irrational in the absence of supporting evidence, even if it's *true* that God exists. [...] The requirement of adequate evidence for cognitively rational belief is impeccable, if its notion of adequate evidence is suitably broad and free of unduly narrow empiricist, rationalist, and deductivist strictures. (p. 33)

Moser will thus have to aim his attacks elsewhere than the argument's underlying evidentialism about epistemic justification.

---

[2] For a recent discussion, see chapters 3 and 5 of M. Bergmann, *Justification without Awareness* (Oxford, Oxford University Press, 2006).

By our count, Moser presents four main interrelated objections to the Hiddenness Argument. In the remainder of this section, we'll argue that one of these objections is a nonstarter, and that a different objection collapses into a third. This will leave two potentially viable objections to the Hiddenness Argument: the Purposively Available Evidence Argument and the Cognitive Idolatry Argument.

2.2 Against 2: the Spirit of God Argument

What we'll call the *Spirit of God Argument* targets premise 2. Moser presses this objection in the following passage:

[T]he intervening personal Spirit of God would be the best source, including the most direct source, to confirm God's authoritative reality . . . Indeed, given God's being inherently personal, God's intervening personal Spirit would be the only *directly self-authenticating* source of firsthand veridical evidence of God's reality, since *the genuinely experienced presence* of God's intervening personal Spirit, via conscience, would constitute the firsthand veridical evidence in question, and only God's Spirit could provide this evidence. [. . .] In picking something other than God's intervening Spirit as the direct source for veridically confirming God's reality, we could always plausibly ask this: what is the cognitively reliable connection between *that other thing* and *God's reality*? This question will leave a vast opening to doubt, even in a cognitively serious manner, the authenticity of the supposed veridical witness to God's reality. So, with unsurpassable authority and in agreement with God's character of perfect love, God's intervening Spirit directly witnesses to, and thus confirms, God's reality *directly* for willingly receptive people at God's chosen time. In thus witnessing with personal intervention in human conscience, the personal source of divine veridical personal evidence becomes the veridical evidence itself. This kind of *cognitive inspiration* yields firsthand foundational (that is, noninferential) evidence and knowledge of God's reality. (pp. 149–50)

A close inspection of this argument will reveal that whatever apparent power it enjoys stems from a 'de dicto/de re' confusion. Letting *God's Spirit* mean 'the irreducibly personal power behind volitional transformation of humans toward God's moral character' (p. 144), we restate Moser's argument as follows:

The Spirit of God Argument

1. You (a cognitively normal adult human, let's suppose) couldn't doubt whether there's a 'cognitively reliable relation' between your experiencing (via conscience) the presence of God's Spirit and [God exists].[3]
2. For anything *other* than your experience of the presence of God's Spirit, you could doubt whether there's a cognitively reliable relation between it and [God exists].
3. So: Your experiencing the presence of God's Spirit would be the best kind of evidence for God's existence.

---

[3] Here and elsewhere, '[P]' abbreviates 'the proposition that P.'

4. If your experience of the presence of God's Spirit would be the best kind of evidence for God's existence, then a cognitively normal adult human could have adequate ('belief-justifying') evidence for God's existence that's not spectator evidence.[4]

C. So: A cognitively normal adult human could be justified in believing that God exists absent adequate spectator evidence for God's existence.

We begin by noting that there are de dicto and de re readings of 1 and 2. On the de dicto reading, 1 seems clearly true but 2 is clearly false. On this reading, 1 amounts to this:

- You couldn't doubt whether there's a cognitively reliable relation between [You experience the presence of God's Spirit] and [God exists].

Since [You experience the presence of God's Spirit] clearly entails [God exists], this de dicto reading of 1 is quite plausible. But the same can't be said for the de dicto reading of 2:

- For anything *other* than [You experience the presence of God's Spirit], you could doubt whether there's a cognitively reliable relation between it and [God exists].

Consider any clearly valid argument for God's existence that doesn't employ [You experience the presence of God's Spirit]. Since such an argument's premises clearly entail [God exists], you couldn't doubt whether there's a cognitively reliable relation between those premises and [God exists]. So the premises of any clearly valid argument for God's existence (that doesn't employ [You experience the presence of God's Spirit]) would seem to be a counterexample to the de dicto reading of 2.

Unfortunately, the de re reading is no more promising, for it fails at the first step:

- You couldn't doubt of what's in fact an experienced (via conscience) presence of God's Spirit that there's a cognitively reliable relation between it and [God exists].

Even if we often do experience the presence of God's Spirit via conscience, a cognitively normal adult human could quite easily doubt whether what's in fact such an experience really is such an experience. Such a thinker could thus doubt whether there's a cognitively reliable relation between that experience and [God exists]. Since both available readings of the Spirit of God Argument involve at least one dubious premise, that argument doesn't successfully rebut its target. We submit that the Hiddenness Argument emerges unscathed from this attack.

---

[4] We're granting Moser's claim that '[o]ur willingly experiencing God's intervening personal Spirit, as a foundation of firsthand knowledge of God's reality, figures centrally in an ongoing struggle between our destructively selfish wills and the life-giving will of a perfectly loving God' (p. 152). If that's right, then (presumably) an experienced presence of God's Spirit wouldn't be spectator evidence (i.e., evidence for God's existence you can acquire without being called to a morally transformative relationship with God).

2.3 Against 2: the Transformative Gift Argument

According to Moser (§2.8), it's possible that a cognitively normal adult human, S, justifiedly infer that God exists from propositions like these:

P1. I (= S) am willingly taking part in a process of conviction, forgiveness, and transformation by God (in Moser's [pp. 134–5] shorthand: 'I (= S) have received the transformative gift').

P2. If I (= S) am willingly taking part in such a process, then God exists.

Now, if S can justifiedly infer God's existence from P1 and P2, then S's beliefs in P1 and P2—plus the 'justifiers' of those beliefs—constitute adequate evidence that God exists. But such adequate evidence wouldn't be spectator evidence for God's existence. Presumably, S holds justified beliefs in P1 and P2 only if S has been called by God to submit to a morally transformative relationship with him. So premise 2 of the Hiddenness Argument is false: A cognitively normal adult human could justifiedly believe that God exists absent adequate spectator evidence for God's existence. We'll call this the *Transformative Gift Argument*.

Taken by itself, this objection turns out to be dialectically deficient. Absent additional argumentation, it's an unsatisfactory reply to premise 2 of the Hiddenness Argument. But the problem lies elsewhere than you might initially think.

You might think that beliefs in P1 and P2, *even if* justified, couldn't yield a justified belief that God exists: P1 so obviously entails God's existence, after all. Well, what's true is this. In a context where God's existence is in question, it would of course be dialectically inappropriate to present something like P1 in support of God's existence. But as many epistemologists have recently argued,[5] the fact that it would be dialectically improper across a wide range of contexts to offer (e.g.) P1 and P2 on behalf of God's existence is perfectly compatible with your holding beliefs in those propositions that justify your belief that God exists. More generally, something can justify you in believing P without being such that you could employ it in a dialectically proper argument for P. So the dialectical deficiency we detect here isn't just Moser's suggestion that, in principle, beliefs in P1 and P2 could justify you in believing that God exists.

Nevertheless, when isolated from other argumentation, this objection to premise 2 of the Hiddenness Argument *is* dialectically deficient. For as Moser makes clear, his claim that P1 could be justified for you depends on the thought that you could have adequate nonspectator—or, as he often puts it, *purposively available*—evidence to believe P1:

---

[5] See M. Bergmann, 'Epistemic Circularity: Malignant and Benign' (2004), *Philosophy and Phenomenological Research*, 69, pp. 709–27; J. Pryor, 'What's Wrong with Moore's Argument?' (2004), *Philosophical Issues*, 14, pp. 349–78; P. Markie, 'Easy Knowledge' (2005), *Philosophy and Phenomenological Research*, 70, pp. 406–16; A. Hazlett, 'Epistemic Conceptions of Begging the Question' (2006), *Erkenntnis*, 65, pp. 343–63; R. White, 'Problems for Dogmatism' (2006), *Philosophical Studies*, 131, pp. 525–57.

In keeping with perfectly authoritative firsthand evidence of divine reality, as opposed to spectator evidence, premise [P1] above is irreducibly first-person, self-implicating, and self-involving. It rests on undefeated authoritative evidence of divine reality that is inherently and directly firsthand and purposively available . . . In particular, the evidence involves my evident willing reception of an authoritative call in conscience to volitional fellowship with the One worthy of worship. (p. 138)

Moser here invokes adequate *nonspectator* evidence for God's existence—constituted in part by an experienced 'will-challenging' call from God—to support his claim that a thinker could be justified in believing P1 above. A key premise of the Transformative Gift Argument thus depends on the claim that there can be adequate ('belief-justifying') nonspectator evidence for God's existence.[6] So, when construed as a freestanding objection to premise 2 of the Hiddenness Argument (which implies, recall, that there *can't* be adequate nonspectator evidence for God's existence), the Transformative Gift Argument is dialectically improper.

Let's turn, then, to where the real action is: Moser's novel argument for the possibility of adequate nonspectator (or, purposively available) evidence for God's existence.

2.4 Against 2: the Purposively Available Evidence Argument

What we call the Purposively Available Evidence Argument aims to establish surprising substantive requirements on adequate evidence for God's existence by way of reflection on certain of God's central attributes. (In this way, Moser's distinctive theistic evidentialism is rooted firmly in theistic metaphysics.) Here's a helpful summary statement of his argument:

Conclusive evidence of God's existence would be purposively available to humans, given God's purpose to engage humans in terms of what they truly need and thus to avoid trivializing (evidence of) divine reality as a matter of casual human speculation. The relevant evidence of God's existence would thus be available to humans in keeping with God's vital purpose in making it available, and this purpose would reflect God's morally perfect character. In particular, God would have a significant, morally relevant purpose regarding how humans are to receive the evidence, and this purpose would set requirements for human reception of the evidence. A central divine purpose, characteristic of a perfectly loving God, would aim noncoercively but authoritatively to transform human purposes to agree with divine purposes, including a goal of divine-human fellowship in perfect love. God would aim, accordingly, to have us willingly attend to the relevant evidence in such a way that it would emerge saliently for what it is intended to be: an evident authoritative call to volitional fellowship with God. (p. 23)

---

[6] It *almost* goes without saying that the Transformative Gift Argument must include the claim that you could *justifiedly* believe (something like) P1: A justified belief in P2 plus an *un*justified belief in P1 wouldn't qualify as adequate evidence that God exists. But, as Moser seems to recognize (p. 138), any justified belief in P1 will depend for its justification on adequate nonspectator evidence. Hence our charge in the main text: The claim that a person could justifiedly believe P1 presupposes there could be adequate nonspectator evidence that God exists.

Because we'll soon revise it in light of objections, it'll be useful to put Moser's argument somewhat more formally here:

The Purposively Available Evidence Argument

1. If God existed, then one of his main aims for you would be that you freely submit to a morally transformative relationship with him.

2. If one of God's main aims for you were that you freely submit to such a relationship with him, then your having adequate evidence for his existence would involve your receiving 'an evident authoritative call to volitional fellowship with God'—where such a call 'would include intended conviction of [your] waywardness and noncoercive nudging of [your] will toward divine-human fellowship in perfect love' (p. 136).

3. If your having adequate evidence for God's existence involved your receiving 'an evident authoritative call to volitional fellowship with God,' then you would have adequate nonspectator (purposively available) evidence that God exists.

C. So: If God existed, then your having adequate evidence for God's existence would involve your having adequate nonspectator evidence that God exists.

The Hiddenness Argument's proponent has supposed (at her second premise) that *even if* God existed, every cognitively normal adult human justified in believing God exists would need to have adequate spectator evidence that God exists. But if the above argument succeeds, any such thinker justified in such belief would have adequate nonspectator evidence for God's existence. And if that's right, then the aforementioned key supposition of the Hiddenness Argument is doubtful. For it's doubtful that, if God existed, *every* thinker justified in believing God exists would need to have *two different kinds* of adequate evidence for God's existence.

While we do think that a revised version of Moser's Purposively Available Evidence Argument may well threaten the Hiddenness Argument, we're convinced that the above version doesn't. For there are counterexamples to its second premise, ones that even Moser himself should accept. To see this, consider the following plausible things Moser has to say about testimonial evidence for, and testimonial justification and knowledge of, theistic belief:

The second-best kind of veridical evidence [of God's reality], after firsthand acquaintance with God's intervening personal Spirit, comes from firsthand acquaintance with people transparently in volitional fellowship with, and thus led by, God's intervening Spirit. They can personally, saliently, and veridically manifest the reality of God's loving character to others, even if somewhat indirectly. Thus Paul writes: '... thanks be to God, who in Christ always leads us in triumph, and through us spreads the fragrance of the *knowledge of him* everywhere' (2 Cor. 2:14, RSV, italics added). [...] Paul regarded the Corinthian Christians themselves, in virtue of their volitionally transformed lives, as a 'letter of recommendation' confirming the veracity of Paul's message of the reality of God's powerful redemptive love in Jesus. [...] God's intervening personal Spirit, according to Paul's pneumatic epistemology, changes a willingly receptive person's heart (or, volitional center) to make that person a living sign, even breathing and speaking evidence, of the reality of God's powerful transforming love. (p. 151)

Against the backdrop of these considerations, a counterexample to the second premise of Moser's Purposively Available Evidence Argument emerges.

Suppose one of Paul's Corinthian Christians, Ann, tells one of her fellow citizens, Bob, who presently lacks evidence for God's existence, some important things about God. Presumably, Ann could do this without thereby conveying to Bob 'an evident authoritative call to volitional fellowship with God.' Assuming this scenario could be filled out so that it meets a plausible sufficient condition for testimonial justification, Ann's testimony renders Bob justified in believing that God exists. Supposing now (with Moser) that some or other species of Evidentialism about epistemic justification is correct, it follows that this testimonial exchange has resulted in Bob's gaining adequate evidence that God exists. Finally, we can suppose that one of God's main aims for (even) Bob is that he freely submit to a morally transformative relationship with God. The upshot is this: *Even if* one of God's main aims for you is that you freely submit to a morally transformative relationship with him, you might still gain adequate evidence for his existence without (yet) receiving 'conviction of [your] waywardness and noncoercive nudging of [your] will toward divine-human fellowship.' As it currently stands, then, premise 2 of Moser's Purposively Available Evidence Argument is false.

It's worth noting that the above counterexample can be developed in a slightly different way that some might find more persuasive. Moving a little more slowly and cautiously, let's suppose only that the testimonial exchange between Ann and Bob renders Bob justified in believing that Ann is herself justified in believing that God exists. Bob then combines his justified 'second-order' belief about Ann with (i) a justified belief in a plausible sufficient condition for testimonial justification *and* (ii) a justified belief about the circumstances of the exchange, justifiedly concluding that *he* is now justified in believing that God exists (via Ann's testimony). Finally, provided that having justification to believe you have justification to believe P suffices for your actually having justification to believe P,[7] Bob is now justified in believing that God exists—all without (yet) receiving 'conviction of [his] waywardness and noncoercive nudging of [his] will toward divine-human fellowship' by God, who (still) wants (even) Bob to freely submit to a morally transformative relationship with him. We now have an additional counterexample to the second premise of Moser's Purposively Available Evidence Argument.

By our lights, then, the version of the Purposively Available Evidence Argument Moser most explicitly suggests fails. As we've indicated, though, there's a revised version that sidesteps the above counterexamples while still connecting with the Hiddenness Argument. To get such a version, replace the 'would' in 2's consequent

---

[7] For recent defense of this 'JJp → Jp' principle, see J. Gibbons, 'Access Externalism' (2006), *Mind*, 115, pp. 19–39; White, 'Problems for Dogmatism,' p. 539.

with a 'might,' thereby protecting 2 from the testimonial counterexamples just described. That change yields the following:

Revised Purposively Available Evidence Argument

1. If God existed, then one of his main aims for you would be that you freely submit to a morally transformative relationship with him.
2. If one of God's main aims for you were that you freely submit to such a relationship with him, then your having adequate evidence for his existence *might* involve your receiving 'an evident authoritative call to volitional fellowship with God.'
3. If your having adequate evidence for God's existence involved your receiving 'an evident authoritative call to volitional fellowship with God,' then you would have adequate nonspectator evidence for God's existence.

C. So: If God existed, then your having adequate evidence for God's existence *might* involve your having adequate nonspectator evidence that God exists.

The Hiddenness Argument's proponent, recall, has supposed that *even if* God existed, every cognitively normal adult human justified in believing God exists would need to have adequate spectator evidence that God exists. But if the above argument succeeds, some such thinker justified in such belief might have adequate nonspectator evidence for God's existence. And if that's right, then the aforementioned key supposition of the Hiddenness Argument is doubtful. For it's doubtful that, if God existed, *some* thinker justified in believing God exists would need to have *two different kinds* of adequate evidence for God's existence.

We reckon the above revised argument one of Moser's two potentially successful objections to the Hiddenness Argument. The other is what Moser calls the *Divine Purposes Reply*—which, we'll now argue, depends crucially on one of its pieces in particular, what we call the Cognitive Idolatry Argument.

2.5 Against 1: the Divine Purposes Reply

In the following passages, Moser sets out one large portion of this reply—which, unlike the preceding objections focusing on the Hiddenness Argument's second premise, attacks the first premise:

A sound approach to the problem of divine hiding includes the *Divine Purposes Reply*: God would restrain divine manifestations, at least for a time, to at least some humans in order to enhance satisfaction of God's own diverse perfectly authoritative and loving purposes regarding humans. The Divine Purposes Reply allows that the amount and kind of God's self-revelation can vary among people, even *if* there is a common minimal self-revelation purposively available on God's terms to all people. The variation in divine self-manifestation would result from God's purposes, or intentions, regarding recipients of divine revelation. If these purposes are perfectly morally righteous and loving, then God can be perfectly morally righteous and loving in giving varied self-revelation, even elusive varied self-revelation, to humans. The myth of a cognitively promiscuous, bland, uniform, predictable, or convenient God regarding divine self-manifesta-tion should thus die easily. (pp. 110–11)

Conceivably, God hides on occasion from some people for various perfectly loving divine purposes. At least the following arise: (a) to teach people to yearn for, and thus eventually to value wholeheartedly and above all else, personal volitional fellowship with God, (b) to strengthen grateful trust in God even when times look altogether bleak, (c) to remove human complacency toward God and God's redemptive purposes, (d) to shatter destructively prideful human self-reliance, and (e) to prevent people who aren't ready for fellowship with God from explicitly rejecting God. This list is by no means exhaustive; nor should we assume that an exhaustible list is available to humans. Even so, we can readily imagine that in some cases of divine hiding, some people would apprehend the ultimate emptiness of life without God's presence, and thus heighten their attentiveness to matters regarding God. A perfectly loving God could use this consideration for the good of at least some humans. (p. 107)

We of course agree with Moser that it would be unreasonable to judge *comprehensive-ness* an adequacy constraint on this kind of reply to the Hiddenness Argument's first premise. Nevertheless, we'll now argue that an additional (to those listed above) element of Moser's Divine Purposes Reply is essential to this reply. Without the indicated element—the Cognitive Idolatry Argument—the Divine Purposes Reply won't seriously threaten the Hiddenness Argument.

Notably, we think Moser would have a hard time disabling the forthcoming argument that the Divine Purposes Reply depends crucially on the Cognitive Idolatry Argument. To motivate his own Divine Purposes Reply, Moser defends the Hidden-ness Argument's first premise from two prominent alternative objections—what he calls the *Freedom Response* and the *Proper-Motivation Response*. Essentially, the argument we're about to present just turns Moser's main objection to those alternative responses against the large portion of his own Divine Purposes Reply set forth in the above passages.

We begin our argument by noting that Moser draws a distinction between two different kinds of knowledge of God: (*i*) propositional knowledge that God exists *and* (*ii*) so called *filial knowledge* of God, which is '*reconciling* personal knowledge whereby we enter, if imperfectly, into a (volitional) *child–parent* relationship involving volitional fellowship with God as our perfectly loving Father' (p. 96). Clearly, while filial knowledge of God entails propositional knowledge that God exists, the latter doesn't return the favor: 'One can know that God exists... but hate God.'[8]

The distinction between propositional and filial knowledge of God yields two different kinds of divine hiddenness, two different ways God can be hidden from a person. One way God can be hidden from you is your lacking adequate evidence that he exists—and so, your lacking propositional knowledge that he exists (assuming, with Moser for present purposes, some brand of Evidentialism about epistemic justification, and that propositional knowledge requires such justification). We'll call this *divine*

---

[8]   Moser, 'Divine Hiddenness Does Not Justify Atheism,' p. 49.

epistemic hiddenness. Passages like the following indicate that this is the kind of divine hiddenness Moser is primarily concerned with:

Let's say that God's existence is concealed, hidden, or *incognito* for a person at a time if and only if at that time God's existence fails to be not only obvious but also *beyond cognitively reasonable doubt* for that person. (p. 1)

A second way God can be hidden from us—a way that we humans often hide from each other, for various good purposes—is God's refusing to 'be servile toward us or always at our beck and call,' refusing to be 'obsequious or fawning' (pp. 107–8). We'll call this *divine relational hiddenness.*

Now the Hiddenness Argument's first premise concerns (what we're calling) divine *epistemic* hiddenness: The argument's proponent there claims that God's existence is incompatible with some cognitively normal adult human's lacking justification to believe God exists. The large portion of Moser's Divine Purposes Reply set out in the above quotations suggests that divine *epistemic* hiddenness is what (in part) enables God to achieve those cited goals (a)–(e). But, to turn Moser's limited defense of the Hiddenness Argument against that large portion of his own preferred reply to the argument:

The mere fact of less obscurity in God's self-revelation wouldn't seem to challenge contrite, humble, and passionate seeking after God. God could readily promote such seeking, with no added difficulty, in an environment of less obscure divine revelation. (p. 110)

We couldn't agree more. What's arguably true is that divine *relational* hiddenness can be an effective partial enabler of God's achieving goals like (a)–(e) above. But—as Moser, along with everyone else, should concede—divine relational hiddenness doesn't require divine epistemic hiddenness: You can be justified in believing God exists but not (yet) be in an 'appropriate *child–parent* relationship with God.'[9] So, citing goals like (a)–(e) that seem primarily to require some divine *relational* hiddenness doesn't do much to help explain the level of divine *epistemic* hiddenness we seem to find in the world.[10] And the latter is what the first premise of the Hiddenness Argument focuses on. At a minimum, then, we can conclude that, absent additional argumentation, citing goals like (a)–(e) will leave the Hiddenness Argument more or less intact.

---

[9] Moser, 'Cognitive Idolatry and Divine Hiding,' p. 127.

[10] Readers still wondering whether divine epistemic hiddenness from humans might be an effective partial enabler of human filial knowledge of God will, we think, find it instructive to ask the parallel question about child–parent relationships among humans. Suppose you want a child of yours to grow into a *proper* child–parent relationship with you. Might relieving your child of whatever justification s/he now has to think you exist—or preventing her from gaining such justification in the first place—be an effective partial enabler of a proper child–parent relationship between the two of you? Putting it mildly, an affirmative answer is somewhat implausible. All the argument currently under construction in the main text needs is the analogous claim concerning God and humans (which, again, we think Moser will accept [p. 110])—viz., that it's (at best) somewhat implausible to think divine epistemic hiddenness is an effective partial enabler of human filial knowledge of God (which includes satisfaction of goals like [a]–[e] that Moser cites).

As we've said, though, Moser's Divine Purposes Reply comprises another important element that hasn't yet been put into play. This is what we call the Cognitive Idolatry Argument. In light of the worry just voiced about the portion of the Divine Purposes Reply already on the table, we submit that Moser's reply stands or falls with the Cognitive Idolatry Argument, which the following passages helpfully summarize:

In *cognitive* idolatry, we deny... God's supreme authority in commending ways of knowing God's reality. [...] Such idolatry rests on a cognitive standard, whether empiricist, deductivist, rationalist, or some hybrid, that doesn't let God be authoritative Lord over our knowing God's reality. Cognitive idolatry typically aims to protect one's lifestyle from serious challenge by the God who would authoritatively and lovingly call, judge, and seek to reconcile humans. [...] Cognitive idolatry exploits epistemological standards... to refuse to let God be supremely authoritative in a person's life, initially in the cognitive area of life. A cosmic authority problem regarding a perfectly authoritative and loving God lies behind much cognitive idolatry and, for that matter, idolatry in general. In cognitive idolatry, we seek to control the terms for knowing God's reality in a way that devalues God's preeminent authority. (p. 102)

[Cognitive idolatry] often rests on a principle of this form: Unless God (if God exists) supplies evidence of kind K, God's existence is too obscure to justify reasonable acknowledgement. The problem isn't with a principle of this form but is rather with the specification of kind K. Some philosophers specify K in a way that disregards what would be the distinctive personal character and redemptive intentions of a perfectly authoritative and loving God. They thereby isolate themselves from any divine challenge of volitional attunement, and risk cognitive idolatry too. Such idolatry arises from a cognitive commitment designed... to exclude God as Lord in our lives. It stems from the human desire to be, or at least to appoint, the ultimate authority for our lives, as if we humans were entitled to this. Such idolatry would obscure for us important purposively available evidence of God's reality, by obscuring or distorting what we attend to, and would thus obscure for us the truth about God's reality. [...] Tragically, supposed mere spectators complaining from remote regions may in fact remain out in those regions by their own self-isolating choices. (pp. 121–3)

Let's restate this fascinating line of objection to the Hiddenness Argument's first premise more formally:

The Cognitive Idolatry Argument

1. Even if God existed, some cognitively normal adult humans might culpably endorse overly restrictive requirements on evidence for God's existence—requirements that aren't sensitive to 'the distinctive personal character and redemptive intentions of a perfectly authoritative and loving God.'
2. If you culpably endorse such requirements on evidence for God's existence, then you're thereby culpably keeping yourself from gaining available evidence for God's existence.

C. Even if God existed, it might still be that some cognitively normal adult humans culpably lack adequate evidence that God exists (and so, aren't justified in believing God exists).

We should pause briefly to note the importance of the 'culpably' in 2's (and so, C's) consequent. Presumably, most (if not all) parties to the debate over the Hiddenness Argument will (quite correctly, we think) want to at least leave the following position open:

- There couldn't be a cognitively normal adult human who *nonculpably* lacks adequate evidence for God's existence.

Few (if any) critics of the Hiddenness Argument will try to rebut its first premise by plumping for the possibility that God exists yet some cognitively normal adult humans nevertheless nonculpably lack adequate evidence that he exists. Instead, most (if not all) of those attempting to rebut the first premise will employ the same kind of strategy Moser does in presenting the Cognitive Idolatry Argument—viz., advocate the possibility that God exists yet some cognitively normal adult humans somehow *culpably* lack adequate evidence for his existence.

It's time to draw together this section's main findings. Moser presses four interrelated objections against the Hiddenness Argument. One of these (the Spirit of God Argument) seems a nonstarter, while another (the Transformative Gift Argument) is parasitic on the Purposively Available Evidence Argument—which, together with the Divine Purposes Reply, are Moser's two potentially successful objections to the Hiddenness Argument. Further, the Divine Purposes Reply depends crucially on the Cognitive Idolatry Argument. So, if the Cognitive Idolatry Argument fails, Moser's reply to the Hiddenness Argument reduces to the Purposively Available Evidence Argument.

In the next section, we'll argue that the Cognitive Idolatry Argument does indeed fail. We'll then conclude by reflecting on Moser's reply's prospects for success, given that it arguably stands or falls with the Purposively Available Evidence Argument.

3 The failure of the Cognitive Idolatry Argument

We'll start with a quick-and-dirty preliminary objection to the Cognitive Idolatry Argument's second premise. After considering a likely defense of that premise, we'll develop our preliminary objection into a serious problem for the argument.

According to premise 2 of the Cognitive Idolatry Argument, you can keep yourself from acquiring available foundational evidence for God's existence simply by endorsing overly restrictive requirements on evidence for God's existence. But parallel claims concerning other kinds of foundational evidence are not very compelling. Plausibly, your current visual experience justifies you in believing there are mind-independent physical objects—*even if* you're an 'external world skeptic' who endorses mistaken views on which such experiences don't justify such beliefs for you. Similarly, it seems you could have foundational a priori justification to believe certain propositions, *even if* you're an 'a priori skeptic' who endorses mistaken views on which you don't have such justification for any belief. (Supposing your skepticism about the a priori is justified by philosophical argument[s], won't at least certain of your premises be justified a priori if at all?) More generally, it seems you can't keep yourself from gaining available foundational evidence of a certain kind simply by denying that such evidence exists. You don't have *that* kind of control over *that* part of your cognitive life. Since 2 of the Cognitive Idolatry Argument counterintuitively implies you do, that argument fails.

Now we see a natural way for Moser to reply to this preliminary objection. The quotations in the last section suggest Moser thinks that endorsing overly restrictive criteria for evidence of God's existence can keep you from having such evidence. But other passages suggest a somewhat different, subtler view:

> We rarely criticize or even consider idols in the *cognitive* domain, because they are too close to us and too protective of our closely held preferences. Still, they flourish in the cognitive domain with real harm to their owners. We all set up or otherwise adopt . . . cognitive standards for what is (reasonably) to count as real. There's no problem here in principle, but we thereby may obscure or otherwise damage our perspective on significant features of reality. For instance, if we require that available evidence of reality be *reproducible* in ways we can control, we will potentially obscure for ourselves available evidence for the reality of any being that doesn't leave such reproducible evidence. Alternatively, if we require that all available evidence of reality be *sensory*, we will exclude (*at least from our acknowledgement* [italics added]) available evidence for any being that doesn't leave sensory evidence. Our cognitive standards thus matter significantly, and may obstruct our apprehension of reality. Bad epistemology can cloud what's real. (pp. 12–13)

> Some people have a psychological attitude-set closed or even opposed to a divine redemptive program of all-inclusive reconciliation by a gift of divine-human fellowship in unselfish love. Their attitude-set, in guiding *what they attend to and how they interpret what they attend to* [italics added], obscures or even blocks for them purposively available evidence of the reality of God. The volitionally sensitive evidence of God's reality is, I contend, actually available . . . People need, however, appropriate, God-sensitive 'ears to hear and eyes to see' the available evidence aright, and this requires their willingness to receive the evidence for what it is intended to be: an evident authoritative divine call, via conscience, to repentance and divine-human fellowship. (p. 112)

In contrast with the passages quoted in the last section—which focus on evidence acquisition and possession—these suggest that what your embracing mistaken criteria for evidence that God exists prevents is your *acknowledging* or *correctly interpreting* whatever evidence for God's existence you may have. Your endorsing overly restrictive requirements on evidence that God exists, Moser is suggesting, may keep you from *treating* or *responding to* relevant parts of your total evidence as what it really is: adequate evidence for God's existence. Notably, much recent epistemological work in the philosophy of science discusses (often under the label 'salience') the plausible, widely held view that Moser seems to be invoking here—viz., that 'the bearing of a given piece of evidence on a given hypothesis depends on considerations of background theory.'[11,12]

---

[11] T. Kelly, 'Evidence' in E. Zalta (ed.), *The Stanford Encyclopedia of Philosophy* (2006), <http://plato. stanford.edu/entries/evidence> (accessed July 5, 2010). Seminal discussions of this issue include R. G. Collingwood, *The Idea of History* (Oxford, Oxford University Press, 1956); T. Kuhn, *The Structure of Scientific Revolutions* (Chicago, University of Chicago Press, 1962).

[12] We note in passing that Moser couldn't plausibly claim that the alleged phenomenon of cognitive idolatry is just a particular instance of the more general alleged fact that 'perception is theory-laden'

The above passages recommend a somewhat different understanding of the Cognitive Idolatry Argument from that we offered in the last section:

The Revised Cognitive Idolatry Argument

1. Even if God existed, some cognitively normal adult humans might culpably endorse overly restrictive requirements on evidence for God's existence.
2. If you culpably endorse such 'requirements, then you're culpably keeping yourself from treating certain of your evidence as what it really is—viz., evidence for God's existence.
3. If you're culpably keeping yourself from treating certain of your evidence as what it really is—viz., evidence for God's existence—then you're culpably keeping that evidence from making you justified in believing [God exists].

C. Even if God existed, it might still be that some cognitively normal adult humans culpably lack justification to believe that God exists.

We have two objections to the Revised Cognitive Idolatry Argument,[13] which we'll express in (what we think is) order of ascending strength. Our first objection is that the Hiddenness Argument can be modified so as to circumvent the Revised Cognitive Idolatry Argument without losing much (if any) of its force. Here's the modified version we have in mind:

The Modified Hiddenness Argument

1. If God existed, then *most* cognitively normal adult humans would be justified in believing that God exists.
2. A cognitively normal adult human would be justified in believing that God exists only if she had adequate spectator evidence that God exists.
3. So: If God existed, then *most* cognitively normal adult humans would have adequate spectator evidence that God exists.
4. *Many* cognitively normal adult humans lack adequate spectator evidence that God exists.

C. So: God doesn't exist.

This argument makes two modifications to the original one. In step 1, it replaces 'every cognitively normal adult human' with 'most cognitively normal adult humans,'

(for influential discussion, see N. R. Hanson, *Patterns of Discovery* (Cambridge, Cambridge University Press, 1961); Kuhn, *The Structure of Scientific Revolutions*). For one thing, there's vigorous debate over the claim that perception is theory-laden (cf. Kelly, 'Evidence'). For another thing, there is (to put it mildly) serious tension between the claim that perception is theory-laden and Moser's 'best available explanation' account of how perceptual experience epistemically supports 'external world' beliefs (pp. 85–6). Briefly: If perceptual experience is theory-laden, such experience is 'epistemically posterior' to beliefs about the external world, and so (plausibly) can't justify such beliefs.

[13] Incidentally, readers can verify that these objections apply (*mutatis mutandis*) to the initial version of the argument as well.

yielding a somewhat weaker first premise. And it replaces 'some' with 'many' at step 4, yielding a somewhat stronger—but (we submit) not markedly less plausible—fourth premise.

Now to engage this Modified Hiddenness Argument, the first premise of the Revised Cognitive Idolatry Argument would have to be strengthened to

- Even if God existed, *many* cognitively normal adult humans might culpably endorse overly restrictive requirements on evidence for God's existence.

We don't find that thought very plausible. Even supposing God does exist, we doubt that many people even implicitly endorse *any* requirements on evidence for God's existence, overly restrictive or otherwise. The fact that certain key passages where Moser articulates the Cognitive Idolatry Argument are restricted to *philosophers* (p. 122) suggests that he's at least somewhat sensitive to this worry. We suspect that culpable endorsement of overly restrictive conditions on evidence for God's existence explains only God's hiding from a small number of the more reflective among us, if such endorsement can explain any divine epistemic hiddenness at all.

But we can set aside the above objection to the Revised Cognitive Idolatry Argument; that won't deliver it from failure. The bigger problem is its third premise:

3. If you're culpably keeping yourself from treating certain of your evidence as what it really is—viz., evidence for God's existence—then you're culpably keeping that evidence from making you justified in believing [God exists].

This claim implies that *even if* you have what's in fact adequate evidence E for proposition P, you can culpably keep E from justifying P for you *by* culpably keeping yourself from treating E as evidence for P. We think the following argument casts serious doubt on the indicated implication of 3:

An Argument against Premise 3 of the Revised Cognitive Idolatry Argument

1. If you're culpable for failing to treat E as evidence that P, then you have a choice about whether you treat E as evidence that P.[14]
2. If you have a choice about whether you treat E as evidence that P, then E's justifying P for you doesn't require that you treat E as evidence that P.[15]
3. So: If you're culpable for failing to treat E as evidence that P, then E's justifying P for you doesn't require that you treat E as evidence that P.

---

[14] For recent discussion and defense of such principles (from, e.g., so called 'Frankfurt-type Cases'), see T. Warfield, 'Metaphysical Compatibilism's Appropriation of Frankfurt' (2008), *Oxford Studies in Metaphysics*, 3, pp. 283–95.

[15] This is the argument's shakiest step. See below for a supporting argument.

4. If E's justifying P for you doesn't require that you treat E as evidence that P, then failing to treat E as evidence that P won't all by itself keep E from justifying P for you.

5. So: If you're culpable for failing to treat E as evidence that P, then failing to treat E as evidence that P won't all by itself keep E from justifying P for you.

C. So: Even if you're culpable for failing to treat certain evidence you have as evidence that God exists, that failure isn't all by itself keeping the relevant evidence from rendering you justified in believing [God exists].

So far as we can see, 2 is the above argument's shakiest step. Fortunately, there's a strong supporting argument available for it.

Suppose (for conditional proof) that E's justifying P for you requires that you treat E as evidence that P. Suppose also (for nested reductio) that you have a choice about whether you treat E as evidence that P. It follows that you have a choice about whether your evidence E justifies P for you (at the time in question). But you *don't* have a choice about that. While you may *across time* have significant control over (e.g.) what evidence you have, you don't *at a given time* have much (if any) control over what the evidence you then have supports or justifies for you. So you don't have a choice about whether you treat E as evidence that P. The overall conclusion: If E's justifying P for you requires that you treat E as evidence that P, then you don't have a choice about whether you treat E as evidence that P. Contrapositively: If you *do* have a choice about whether you treat E as evidence that P, then E's justifying P for you *doesn't* require that you treat E as evidence that P. We've now arrived at step 2 of our second, stronger (so we think) objection to the Revised Cognitive Idolatry Argument.

4 Conclusion

In light of the objections to the Cognitive Idolatry Argument pressed in the last section, we conclude that that argument fails. Combining this result with the main findings of the section before last serves to whittle Moser's reply to the Hiddenness Argument down to the (Revised) Purposively Available Evidence Argument. Should this be cause for concern?

Provided there aren't significant obstacles to the Purposively Available Evidence Argument's success, the fact that Moser's reply to the Hiddenness Argument stands or falls with it needn't be cause for much concern. (So what if the Hiddenness Argument's failure isn't *over*determined, as long as it in fact fails?) On the other hand, if significant challenges *can* be raised to the Purposively Available Evidence Argument, they'll thereby constitute significant challenges to Moser's treatment of the Hiddenness Argument. And so our final question arises: *Are there* significant obstacles to the success of the Purposively Available Evidence Argument?

Recall step 2 of (the revised version of) the argument:

2. If one of God's main aims for you were that you freely submit to such a relationship with him, then your having adequate evidence for his existence *might* involve your receiving 'an evident authoritative call to volitional fellowship with God.'

Your receiving such a call, according to Moser, would include your gaining via conscience certain experiential evidence that justifies your believing certain moral propositions about both yourself and God—where those experiences justify the relevant moral propositions in virtue of the latter qualifying as the best available explanation of the former:

Firsthand evidence of God's authoritative call to volitional fellowship wouldn't itself be an *argument* for God's existence. Instead, it would be akin to evidence from conscience regarding, for instance, either the duty ... to undertake an act of self-giving kindness or the duty ... not to perform an act of needless torture. [...] One's firsthand experience of what is evidently God's authoritative call ... wouldn't be an argument of any kind; nor would it be a propositional answer to skeptical questions. Instead, it would be experiential acquaintance ... with what is evidently God's authoritative call on a person's life, via that person's conscience. Consider a situation where the best available undefeated explanation of such an experience is that a perfectly authoritative and loving God has actually intervened in one's life with a call to volitional fellowship with God. Many relatively normal people would suggest that their own experience exemplifies just such a situation, and they aren't in an asylum or otherwise irrational. [...] The foundational evidence in experiential acquaintance with what is evidently a personal God wouldn't reduce to a premise, a conclusion, or an argument of any kind, and this is in keeping with experiential foundational evidence in general. (pp. 62, 65)

Moser's Purposively Available Evidence Argument thus presupposes that at least some cognitively normal adult humans are noninferentially justified in believing certain moral propositions about themselves and God in virtue of those propositions' being their best available explanation of certain 'conscience' experiences they have. Any significant obstacle to the success of this position in moral epistemology would be an obstacle to the success of Moser's reply to the Hiddenness Argument (given the reply's dependence on the Purposively Available Evidence Argument). So: *Are there* significant challenges to the thought that cognitively normal adult humans have 'conscience' experiences, the best available explanation of which is a proposition like [I have been convicted and forgiven by God for all my wrongdoing]? We're afraid so, and will close by briefly explaining why.

We expect many readers will be aware of the growing body of literature at the intersection of moral philosophy and cognitive science strongly suggesting that ex-periences prompting moral beliefs are often influenced (if not generated) by personal bias (against, as well as toward, others and yourself), illusions (e.g., so called 'framing effects'), culture, society, biology, and so on.[16] This work confirms something we

---

[16] See (e.g.) chapter 9 of W. Sinnott-Armstrong, *Moral Skepticisms* (Oxford, Oxford University Press, 2006), as well as W. Sinnott-Armstrong (ed.), *Moral Psychology, Volume 2: The Cognitive Science of Morality: Intuition and Diversity* (Cambridge, MA, MIT Press, 2008).

(cognitively normal adult humans) already had reason to believe via informal study of, and reflection on, our own and others' moral beliefs—viz., that experiences prompting moral beliefs (and so, moral beliefs themselves) are often influenced (if not generated) by a wide range of 'non-truth-conducive' sources and factors. One consequence is that, for any cognitively normal adult, there will be multiple explanations available for the 'conscience' experiences Moser points to, competing with propositions like [I'm being convicted and forgiven by God for all my wrongdoing]. To put it mildly, it's quite unclear whether a moral proposition of the indicated kind will for many cognitively normal adults turn out to be the best explanation available to them for the relevant experiences. And of course, *even if* some moral proposition of the indicated kind turns out to be the best explanation available to some cognitively normal adults for certain of their 'conscience' experiences, it may well turn out that the proposition has too narrow a margin of victory over available competing explanations for the relevant experiences to endow the proposition with positive epistemic status sufficient to meet the justification condition on knowledge (which is Moser's concern throughout his work on this topic).

We wouldn't want to claim that the envisaged worries about the position in moral epistemology required by Moser's Purposively Available Evidence Argument are insurmountable. We do, however, think the case against that moral epistemology arising from such worries is serious enough to merit additional careful attention. Absent such attention, Moser's Purposively Available Evidence Argument won't qualify as anything like a decisive objection to the Hiddenness Argument.

Our overall conclusion, then, is that Moser's reply to the Hiddenness Argument depends crucially on some currently controversial claims in moral epistemology. For our part, we hope—and are even somewhat inclined to suspect—that recent challenges to the moral epistemology Moser requires can be overcome. The fact remains, however, that elaboration and defense of the required moral epistemology remains important unfinished business for Moser's distinctive brand of evidentialism about theistic belief and the novel reply to the Hiddenness Argument it enables *if* tenable.

7

An Evolutionary Objection to the Argument from Evil

Thomas M. Crisp

'The argument from evil,' let us say, is any argument that concludes to the non-existence of God from premises citing facts about the existence, distribution or amount of evils contained in our world, where 'God,' let us say, is shorthand for 'the extremely powerful, extremely wise, wholly good creator of all things.' In this paper, I shall put a very general objection against the argument from evil. I shall conclude with some brief remarks about the bearing of my objection on other atheological arguments (other arguments that conclude to the non-existence of God). My objection is inspired by Plantinga's widely discussed evolutionary argument against naturalism,[1] though as will become clear, the premises I shall require are considerably weaker than those deployed by Plantinga.[2]

The argument from evil, we learned at mother's knee, comes in two main varieties. There are so-called *logical* arguments from evil, purporting to show the existence of God logically or perhaps broadly logically incompatible with the existence of evil. And there are so-called *evidential* arguments from evil, purporting to show that the existence, distribution or amount of evil contained in our world renders it improbable that God exists. I shall focus on the latter sort of argument, though it'll be clear by the end of the paper that my objection applies to the former sort as well.

The evidential arguments from evil one finds in the literature rest on certain key premises, premises like those found in (1):

---

[1] See, e.g., Alvin Plantinga, *Warranted Christian Belief* (Oxford, Oxford University Press, 2000), and James K. Beilby (ed.), *Naturalism Defeated? Essays on Plantinga's Evolutionary Argument Against Naturalism* (Ithaca, N.Y., Cornell University Press, 2002).

[2] My argument has affinities with an unpublished paper by Richard Otte ('Science, Naturalism, and Self-Defeat'), which came into my possession as I was finishing this paper. There Otte argues, as I'll argue here, that the cognitive faculties responsible for belief in abstract scientific and philosophical matters are not likely to be reliable given that they were produced by naturalistic evolutionary processes. The conclusions he draws from this are similar to mine, but our arguments differ in several important respects. Argument in the same basic family may also be found in Victor Reppert, *C. S. Lewis's Dangerous Idea: In Defense of the Argument from Reason* (Downer's Grove, IL, InterVarsity Press, 2003).

(1a) Probably, no reason would justify an extremely powerful, extremely wise, wholly good creator of all things in permitting the existence of evils of the sort contained in our world.[3]

(1b) The probability, given that God exists, that there should be the distribution of evils we observe is much lower than that probability given naturalism.[4,5]

Below I shall put a very general objection against claims of the sort found in (1). It'll be handy to have a name for such claims. I shall group them together under the label 'the Key Premise' (since claims like those in (1) are key premises in the various versions of the evidential argument from evil) and use that label as a loose way of talking about the claims in (1) and close cousins of those claims.

1 Objection to the Key Premise

1.1 Setup

My objection rests on four theses, which I shall now explain and briefly defend.

First Thesis: The question whether the Key Premise is true is a recondite philosophical question.

That is to say, the question whether the Key Premise is true is deep and difficult. Claims like those in (1) have been the subject of perennial philosophical dispute stretching back through the history of philosophy. On one side, you find inter alia the Stoics, Augustine, Thomas Aquinas, and Leibniz rejecting claims like those in (1), holding that God has good reasons for permitting evil and offering suggestions as to what they are; on the other, you find, for example, Epicurus, Hume, Voltaire and Russell endorsing claims like those in (1). Much like the questions *What is causation?*, *What is freedom of the will?*, *What is it for an object to persist through time?*, the question whether the Key Premise is true is a perennially disputed and deeply difficult philosophical question. As we'll put it, it's a recondite philosophical question.

Next, there's this

Evolutionary Thesis: If God doesn't exist—if *atheism* is true—then it is highly likely that we humans and our cognitive faculties are the product of evolutionary processes of the sorts described by contemporary evolutionary theory,

where I'll think of likelihood here à la Keynes,[6] Carnap,[7] and Swinburne:[8] as an objective, quasi-logical relation of probability between propositions which conforms

---

[3] Cf. William L. Rowe, 'The Problem of Evil and Some Varieties of Atheism' (1979), *American Philosophical Quarterly* 16, pp. 335–41.

[4] Naturalism: roughly, the view that there is no God or being like God.

[5] Cf. Paul Draper, 'Pain and Pleasure: An Evidential Problem for Theists' (1989), *Nous* 23, pp. 331–50.

[6] John Maynard Keynes, *A Treatise on Probability* (London, Macmillan and Co., 1921).

[7] Rudolph Carnap, *Logical Foundations of Probability* (Chicago, University of Chicago Press, 1950).

[8] Richard Swinburne, *The Existence of God* (Oxford, Oxford University Press, 1979).

to the probability calculus. (There is much debate, of course, on whether this is the right way to think about probability. Not much turns on it for our purposes. The arguments to follow are easily recast in terms of other theories of probability.) Consider, then, the proposition that we and our cognitive faculties are the product of evolutionary processes of the sort investigated by contemporary evolutionary theory (call it 'E'), our evidence for contemporary evolutionary theory ('K'), and the proposition that God does not exist ('A'). Letting 'P(p/q)' be short for 'the logical probability of p given q,' my claim comes to this: P(E/A&K) is high.

Why think so? Why think P(E/A&K) high? Because, if God doesn't exist, it's extremely difficult to see how we could have got here if not by the processes described by contemporary evolutionary theory. Given that there is no God, evolution is by far the most plausible explanation how we arrived on the scene. (Say many: given that there *is* a God, evolution is by far the most plausible explanation how we arrived on the scene. That's as may be. For present purposes, all that matters is that, given atheism, evolution is plausible.)

Next, there's this

Thesis of Unreliability: The probability that we humans have much by way of reliable insight into recondite philosophical matters, given atheism and that we and our faculties are the product of evolutionary processes of the sort described by contemporary evolutionary theory, is either low or such that we have no way of knowing its value. That is, letting 'R_R' stand for the proposition that our cognitive faculties are reliable with respect to recondite philosophical matters, P(R_R/A&E) is low or inscrutable.

Why think this thesis true? There are two possibilities to consider here. First, there's the possibility that A&E holds and that the evolutionary processes that gave rise to humans and their cognitive faculties were *unguided*: not orchestrated or superintended by any intelligent agent—*blind*, to use Dawkins' term.[9] Second, there's the possibility that A&E holds and that the evolutionary processes that gave rise to us were *guided* by some sort of non-theistic intelligence.

Consider each in turn. What's the probability of R_R on the first option, *unguided A&E*, let us call it? Well, consider this question: Is there some reason, given that atheism holds and that we and our cognitive faculties arose via unguided evolutionary processes of the sort described by contemporary evolutionary theory, to *expect* those processes to have endowed us with much by way of reliable insight into recondite philosophical matters—matters quite beyond the exigencies of normal human life? Surely the answer here is 'no.' Given unguided A&E, the main explanation why our evolutionary ancestors evolved cognitive faculties of the sort they did was that those faculties were adaptive: useful for feeding, flying, fighting, reproducing and so forth. But why would cognitive faculties selected for their success at those tasks have required reliability with respect to abstruse philosophical matters, matters quite unconnected to

---

[9] Richard Dawkins, *The Blind Watchmaker* (New York, W. W. Norton, 1986).

the concerns of everyday life? From a fitness point of view, such cognitive capability seems wholly unnecessary. Given unguided A&E, the probability of R_R, one thinks, is low. (Though there's this possibility to consider: perhaps reliability on recondite philosophical matters far removed from the everyday concerns of life is a 'spandrel'—a non-adaptive byproduct of some adaptively selected trait, in the way that, for example, abstract mathematical abilities could be non-adaptive byproducts of the adaptive ability to do simple arithmetic and geometry. Perhaps; it's hard to say. Since at this point anyway, no one has been able to produce a convincing argument that we should *expect* reliability on recondite philosophical matters as a byproduct of adaptively selected cognitive traits, perhaps the best thing to say about the probability of R_R on A&E is that it is inscrutable—such that we simply don't know what it is.)

What about the second option, *guided A&E*? The idea here is that the evolutionary processes that produced us were somehow guided by a non-theistic intelligence, by a being or beings that were not extremely powerful, extremely wise and wholly good. What's the probability that evolutionary processes superintended by such beings— beings of middling or minimal power, knowledge or goodness—should have produced creatures capable of commanding much by way of reliable insight into recondite philosophical matters? Hard to say. If these beings weren't terribly powerful, perhaps they lacked the means to create creatures capable of recondite philosophical speculation. If they weren't terribly knowledgeable, perhaps they lacked the know-how. If they weren't terribly good, perhaps they wanted to deceive us about deep and important matters. Perhaps. I should think we have no way of knowing, no way of sensibly deciding the probabilities here. The probability of R_R given guided A&E, I should think, is inscrutable.

Supposing all this right, we still have this question: What's the probability of R_R given A&E? Letting 'U' stand for the proposition that evolution was unguided by any intelligent being and 'G' for the proposition that it was guided by some intelligent being, it follows from the probability calculus and the fact that U is true iff G is false that

$$P(R_R/A\&E) = P(R_R/A\&E\&U)\times P(U/A\&E) + P(R_R/A\&E\&G)\times P(G/A\&E).$$

If I'm right to think that the values of '$P(R_R/A\&E\&U)$' and '$P(R_R/A\&E\&G)$' on the right side of the equation are each inscrutable, we may conclude, then, that the value of '$P(R_R/A\&E)$' on the left side of the equation is likewise inscrutable, and thus that our Thesis of Unreliability holds.

So far, then, some considerations in favor of the Thesis of Unreliability. Note well: I am not arguing, Plantinga-style, that, given A&E, the probability that our cognitive faculties are *generally* reliable is low or inscrutable. I am not claiming that, given A&E, we've reason to suspect global cognitive unreliability. I am arguing for something much weaker, and, I think, much more easily defended. Objectors to Plantinga's argument have claimed that, *pace* Plantinga, given A&E, we should *expect* our faculties to be generally reliable, generally truth-conducive, especially with respect to matters that would have been necessary for the evolutionary success of our ancestors.[10] For present purposes, I needn't dispute that. I claim only that, given A&E, the probability that we'd have got faculties reliable with respect to abstruse philosophical matters is low or inscrutable. And that might well be, even if, given A&E, we should expect some sort of general cognitive reliability.

The crucial point, then: my objection relies on a premise considerably weaker than the crucial premise of Plantinga's evolutionary argument against naturalism.[11]

Finally, there's this

Principle of Defeat: If for some cognitive faculty F, you have good reason[12] for belief[13] that F is in state S, and if you have good reason to withhold or deny the proposition that P(F is reliable/F is in S) is high, and if there is no state S* such that you have good reason for belief that (a) F is in both S and S*, and (b) P(F is reliable/F is in both S and S*) is high, then you have a defeater for any proposition p such that you have good reason for belief that F is your only source of information about p,[14]

where, for present purposes, you have a defeater for a proposition p iff you have good reason to withhold or deny p. Why accept this principle? I have no argument from first principles. I argue from cases.[15] Suppose you have good reason to think your pool thermometer unreliable. Then, one thinks, you should not believe what the thermometer says about the water's temperature unless you have some other source of information to go on. Or: Suppose I think it likely that my perceptual faculties are unreliable if I'm plugged into the Matrix and have good reason to think I'm plugged into the Matrix. I'm not aware of any mitigating factors: I'm not aware of anything about me or my faculties that would offset the perceptual impairment caused by being

---

[10] See, e.g., Evan Fales, 'Darwin's Doubt, Calvin's Calvary' in James K. Beilby (ed.), *Naturalism Defeated? Essays on Plantinga's Evolutionary Argument Against Naturalism* (Ithaca, N.Y., Cornell University Press, 2002), pp. 43–60; Brandon Fitelson and Elliot Sober, 'Plantinga's Probability Arguments Against Evolutionary Naturalism' (1998), *Pacific Philosophical Quarterly* 79:2, pp. 115–29; Jerry Fodor, 'Is Science Biologically Possible?' in Beilby, *Naturalism Defeated?*, pp. 30–42; William Ramsey, 'Naturalism Defended,' in Beilby, *Naturalism Defeated?*, pp. 15–29.

[11] My Thesis of Unreliability and supporting argument is closely connected to Michael Rea's claim in *World Without Design: The Ontological Consequences of Naturalism* (Oxford, Oxford University Press, 2002) that the probability that human *intuition* is reliable, given A&E, is not high, where intuition, for Rea, is the faculty whose outputs are 'conscious episodes, not involving memory, sense perception, or inference, in which a proposition seems to be [necessarily] true' (p. 174). Note that my Thesis is stronger than Rea's claim: the faculties subtending recondite philosophical speculation include intuition, but more besides. Also, my argument relies on a different (and, I think, more defensible) principle of defeat than Rea's.

[12] You have good reason to believe (invest considerable confidence in, withhold, deny, etc.) p, for present purposes, iff accepting (investing considerable confidence in, withholding, denying, etc.) p is a rational response to your total evidence.

[13] I shall understand talk of 'belief' here and in the sequel in such a way that S believes that p if either (a) S accepts p, full stop, or (b) S invests a high degree of confidence in p.

[14] For a related but interestingly different principle of defeat, see Rea, *World Without Design*, p. 186.

[15] I am indebted here to Plantinga's discussion of like cases (e.g., Alvin Plantinga, *Warranted Christian Belief* (Oxford, Oxford University Press, 2000), p. 237 ff., and Alvin Plantinga, 'Introduction,' in Beilby, *Naturalism Defeated?*, p. 251.

thus connected to the Matrix. Then, one thinks, I should doubt any proposition p such that I have good reason for believing my perceptual faculties my only source of information about p. Reflection on these and like cases, I suggest, lends strong support to our Principle of Defeat.

There are a couple of responses to Plantinga's Evolutionary Argument Against Naturalism in the large literature that has grown up around that argument that might be thought to make trouble for my Principle. Let us look briefly into those.

A central suggestion of Plantinga's argument is that one who believes one's faculties the product of naturalistic evolutionary processes and comes to believe that P(one's faculties are reliable/they were thus produced) is low or inscrutable thereby acquires a defeater for the belief that one's faculties are reliable and for any belief emanating from those faculties. Trenton Merricks[16] thinks this suggestion unobvious and that Plantinga's arguments for it fail. In the process of arguing the latter, Merricks gives various cases in which one has reason to think, with respect to someone other than oneself, that that person's faculties F are in a state S such that P(F is reliable/F is in S) is low or inscrutable. But, he argues, one has no reason in these cases to doubt the beliefs emanating from F.

For example:[17] suppose you come to believe of a hypothetical population of humans that their cognitive faculties are reliable, owing to the fact that you have lived among them, interacted with them, and thereby acquired powerful observational evidence of their cognitive reliability. You then come to believe (a) that their cognitive faculties are the product of naturalistic evolution and (b) that the probability that their faculties are reliable given that they are thus produced is low or inscrutable. It is not obvious, says Merricks, that you've thereby acquired reason to doubt their reliability. Seems like the rational thing to think here is that their faculties are indeed reliable and that they beat the odds. Here's a case, then, in which you have good reason to think of the members of this hypothetical population that their faculties F are in a state S such that P(F is reliable/F is in S) is low or inscrutable but get no defeater for the deliverances of F.

I agree with all of this. But it's perfectly compatible with my Principle of Defeat. For though it's true in this case that you have good reason to believe the faculties of the imagined population in a state S such that P(their faculties are reliable/they are in S) is low or inscrutable, it's *not* true that there is no state S* such that you have good reason for belief that (a) their faculties are in both S and S*, and (b) P(their faculties are reliable/they are in both S and S*) is high. For in the imagined case, you have good reason to think their faculties are in the state S* of having been observed by you to display a long history of reliability, and you've good reason to think P(their faculties are reliable/they are in both S and S*) is high. Merricks's case is interesting, but does no damage to my Principle of Defeat. Analogously with the other cases he presents. (Note

[16] Trenton Merricks, 'Conditional Probability and Defeat' in Beilby, *Naturalism Defeated?*, pp. 165–75.
[17] Ibid. 170–3.

well: I'm not here objecting to anything Merricks says. He nowhere claims to be objecting to a principle like my Principle of Defeat. I am merely pointing out that his cases make no trouble for my Principle.)

Erik Wielenberg[18] likewise takes a dim view of Plantinga's suggestion that one who believes one's faculties the product of naturalistic evolutionary processes and comes to believe that P(one's faculties are reliable/they were thus produced) is low or inscrutable thereby acquires a defeater for the belief that one's faculties are reliable (and for beliefs emanating from those faculties). Wielenberg presents several cases in which one comes to believe of oneself that one's faculties are in a state S such that P(one's faculties are reliable/they're in S) is low or inscrutable. But in none of these cases, he argues, does one thereby acquire reason to doubt the reliability of one's faculties or the beliefs emanating therefrom.

For example, the 'Unknown Process Scenario':[19] I come to believe that my faculties were created by some process or other and that I have no idea what that process was. Thus I have good reason to think my faculties in the state S one's faculties are in iff one is in the dark about their provenance and good reason to think P(they're reliable/they're in S) is inscrutable. Does this give me a defeater for my belief that my faculties are reliable? Obviously not, thinks Wielenberg. To suppose it does is to suppose that all the evidence I have for the reliability of my faculties is somehow undercut by the realization that I don't know where my faculties came from, and Wielenberg thinks this implausible.[20]

I'm not so sure it's implausible. I should think my evidence for the reliability of my faculties *would* be undercut by my realization that I don't know where my faculties came from. But suppose not. Suppose I've evidence E for the reliability of my faculties and, as per Wielenberg's suggestion, my realization that I don't know where my faculties came from leaves E intact. Then I'm in this situation: I have good reason to think my faculties in a state S such that P(they're reliable/they're in S) is inscrutable, where S is the state one's faculties are in iff one is in the dark about their provenance, and I have good reason to think they're also in a state S$\star$ such that P(they're reliable/they're in S and S$\star$) is high, where S$\star$ is the state one's faculties are in iff E is true of them. The upshot: If the case works the way Wielenberg says it does, it gives no counterexample to the Principle of Defeat.

Likewise with the other cases he considers. In his 'Less Mysterious Machine Scenario,'

I believe I was created by a certain machine. I believe that the machine operates according to certain principles, and I understand the most fundamental of these principles. Still, I believe that there are many unknown factors that affect what sort of output the machine will provide in a given case.[21]

---

[18] Erik J. Wielenberg, 'How to be an Alethically Rational Naturalist' (2002), *Synthese* 131, pp. 81–98.
[19] Ibid. 87–8.   [20] Ibid. 88.   [21] Ibid. 90.

Here, says Wielenberg, P(my faculties are reliable/I was created by the machine in question) is low or inscrutable.[22] But realization of this fact gives no defeater for my belief that my faculties are reliable, since

I have all sorts of evidence for the reliability of my faculties. For example, most of my perceptual beliefs about medium-sized physical objects turn out to be true; such beliefs are deliverances of perception, so perception seems to be reliable. I know all sorts of things, and I wouldn't know these things if I weren't reliable.[23]

The suggestion here again then: I have all sorts of evidence E for the reliability of my faculties, and the realization that P(my faculties are reliable/I was created by the machine in question) is low or inscrutable does not undercut E. But if so, I've good reason to think my faculties in a state S such that P(they're reliable/they're in S) is low or inscrutable, where S is the state one's faculties are in iff they were created by the machine in question, and I have good reason to think they're also in a state S* such that P(they're reliable/they're in S and S*) is high, where S* is the state one's faculties are in iff E is true of them. The upshot here again: If the case works the way Wielenberg says it does, it gives no counterexample to the Principle of Defeat.

As best I can tell, then, Merricks's and Wielenberg's objections to Plantinga, interesting as they are, give no reason to doubt our Principle of Defeat.

1.2 The upshot

I take the upshot of our three theses and Principle of Defeat to be this: if you are a reasonably well-informed, intellectually sophisticated atheist,[24] you have a defeater for the Key Premise. This because (a) you have good reason to accept the First and Evolutionary Theses and the Thesis of Unreliability, and (b), if so, then given the Principle of Defeat, you have a defeater for the Key Premise.

With respect to (a): I take the arguments of the above section to have shown that the First and Evolutionary Theses and the Thesis of Unreliability are plausible on some widely known facts about perennially difficult philosophical questions, evolutionary theory, and probability. These facts, I take it, are known by the reasonably well-informed, intellectually sophisticated among us, suggesting that, if you're a reasonably well-informed, intellectually sophisticated atheist (for short, a *sophisticated* atheist), you have good reason to accept the First and Evolutionary Theses and the Thesis of Unreliability.

With respect to (b): Call those of your cognitive faculties responsible for forming and maintaining belief in recondite philosophical matters your *philosophical* faculties and suppose you are a sophisticated atheist. Then since you are among the sophisticated and

---

[22] Ibid.   [23] Ibid.
[24] Cf. Philip L. Quinn, 'In Search of the Foundations of Theism' (1985), *Faith and Philosophy* 2, pp. 468–86. An 'atheist,' for present purposes, is someone who fully believes the proposition that there is no God or invests a high degree of confidence in that proposition.

have good reason for accepting the Evolutionary Thesis and Thesis of Unreliability, you have good reason for belief that your philosophical faculties are in the state S of having been produced by atheistic evolutionary processes, and good reason to withhold or deny that P(your philosophical faculties are reliable/they're in state S) is high.

More, so far as I can see, there is no state S★ such that you have good reason for belief that your philosophical faculties are in both S and S★ and P(your philosophical faculties are reliable/they're in both S and S★) is high. For what would such a state be?

1.2.1 A track-record argument? Maybe you'll reply, 'Well, my faculties are in the state one's faculties are in if one has enjoyed a considerable track-record of success at answering recondite philosophical questions. I have observed in myself a long history of successful philosophical inquiry and thus have good reason to think my faculties in a state S★ such that P(my philosophical are reliable/they're in both S and S★) is high.'

But if you're a sophisticated atheist, there's this problem with your suggestion. Consider the first bit B_1 of philosophizing on some recondite philosophical question you performed which is such that, by your lights, it was a success—by your lights, it delivered up recondite philosophical truth. Since you have good reason for thinking your philosophical faculties in the state S of having been produced by atheistic evolutionary processes, and thus good reason to withhold or deny that P(your philosophical faculties are reliable/they're in state S) is high, by the Principle of Defeat you have good reason to doubt the deliverances of B_1 unless there is some state S★ such that you have good reason for belief that your philosophical faculties are in both S and S★ and P(your philosophical faculties are reliable/they're in both S and S★) is high. We're presently exploring the suggestion that your reason for thinking your faculties in the relevant state S★ is a track-record argument; wherefore, you have good reason to doubt the deliverances of B_1—your first bit of putatively successful philosophical theorizing—unless you have evidence that, subsequent to B_1, you produced a track-record of philosophical successes. Well, consider your second bit B_2 of putatively successful philosophical theorizing. You have good reason to doubt *its* deliverances unless you've evidence of a track-record of success either prior to B_2 or subsequent to B_2. Since B_1 is in doubt unless you have evidence of philosophical success later than it, all depends here on whether you've evidence of successful philosophical theorizing after B_2. Likewise with your third bit B_3 of putatively successful philosophical theorizing: you have good reason to doubt *its* deliverances unless you can point to a considerable number of successes after B_3. Likewise with your fourth bit, and your fifth, and so on, until you get to your most recent philosophical theorizing, which you have reason to doubt and no later successes to point to.

The upshot, I propose, is this: if you have good reason for thinking your philosophical faculties in the state S of having been produced by atheistic evolutionary processes and thus good reason to withhold or deny that P(your philosophical faculties are reliable/they're in state S) is high, and your *only* reason for thinking your philosophical faculties in a state S★ such that P(they're reliable/they're in both S and S★) is high is that you have noticed in yourself a track-record of philosophical aptitude, then, pretty clearly, you *don't* have good reason to think yourself in the relevant S*.

Is there some other S* such that you have good reason for belief that (a) your philosophical faculties are in both S (the state of having been produced by atheistic evolutionary processes) and S*, and (b) P(your philosophical faculties are reliable/ they're in both S and S*) is high? Perhaps.

1.2.2 Reid to the rescue? Michael Bergmann has offered an objection to Plantinga's Evolutionary Argument Against Naturalism inspired by Thomas Reid.[25] To borrow an example of Plantinga's,[26] suppose there is powerful circumstantial evidence that you stole a certain letter yesterday from the office of one of your colleagues, but that you clearly remember being alone for a walk in the woods at the time the letter was stolen. Your colleagues doubt your claim to have been alone in the woods at the relevant time (call that claim 'W') on grounds that P(W/k) is low, where k, say, is the conjunction of the propositional evidence against you. We can suppose that you have basically the same propositional evidence k as do your colleagues and that you agree that P(W/k) is low. But you have a source of *non-propositional* evidence not available to your collea-gues: your memorial experience of its seeming clearly to you that you were out for a walk at the time the letter was stolen. And this experience, if sufficiently vivid, can make it rational for you to continue believing W, even if fully aware that the probability of W on your total propositional evidence k is low. The lesson, Plantinga concludes, is that it can be perfectly rational to believe something improbable on your total propositional evidence if you have sufficiently strong non-propositional evidence for the belief in question.

Bergmann agrees but thinks this makes trouble for Plantinga's Evolutionary Argu-ment.[27] For as Reid pointed out,[28] our belief in the reliability of our cognitive faculties is not plausibly thought of as inferential, as based on other beliefs we hold. On Reid's view,[29] belief in the reliability of our faculties is grounded, rather, in a certain sort of *non*-propositional evidence, viz. an experience of the emotion of *ridicule*. He thought of belief in the axioms of logic and mathematics, the reliability of our faculties, and other truths of 'common sense' as grounded in this emotion, as follows: when one considers the contrary of one of these truths—when one entertains the possibility that, for example, modus ponens is *not* a valid rule of inference, that 2 + 2 is *not* equal to 4, or that I am massively deceived about the world around me—an emotion of ridicule

[25] Michael Bergmann, 'Commonsense Naturalism' in Beilby, *Naturalism Defeated?*, pp. 61–90.

[26] Alvin Plantinga, 'Epistemic Probability and Evil' in Daniel Howard-Snyder (ed.), *The Evidential Problem of Evil* (Bloomington, Indiana University Press, 1996), pp. 69–96.

[27] Bergmann, 'Commonsense Naturalism,' pp. 66–8.

[28] See, for example, Thomas Reid, *Essays on the Intellectual Powers of Man* (Cambridge, MIT Press, 1969), pp. 593 and 630.

[29] I'm following Bergmann's exposition of Reid (Bergmann, 'Commonsense Naturalism,' pp. 66–8) pretty closely here.

naturally arises in one, prompting in one a thought like 'that's crazy, ridiculous!' Such experience, then, grounds belief in the common sense truth whose contrary presents itself to one as thus ridiculous.

Reid's point, says Bergmann, suggests this reply to Plantinga:[30] Even if the naturalist came to believe that P(her faculties are reliable/they were produced by naturalistic evolutionary processes) is low or inscrutable, she needn't thereby acquire a defeater for her belief that her faculties are reliable. For her belief might be backed by sufficiently strong non-propositional evidence of the sort Reid described, evidence strong enough to make it perfectly rational to continue holding that belief, even if her total relevant propositional evidence k was such that P(her faculties are reliable/k) was low or inscrutable.

It also suggests an answer to my question whether the sophisticated atheist has good reason for belief that her faculties are in a state $S^\star$ such that P(her philosophical faculties are reliable/they're in both S and $S^\star$) is high (where S, recall, is the state one's faculties are in iff they were produced by atheistic evolutionary processes). For suppose her belief that her philosophical faculties are reliable is grounded in powerful non-propositional evidence of the sort Reid described. Then, it would seem, she has good reason to think her philosophical faculties in a state $S^\star$ such that P(her philosophical faculties are reliable/they're in both S and $S^\star$) is high, where the $S^\star$ in question is the state one's faculties are in iff they are *reliable*.

Accordingly: if you are a sophisticated atheist and have strong non-propositional evidence of the sort Reid described for your belief that your philosophical faculties are reliable, then the answer to my above question whether there is some $S^\star$ such that you've good reason for belief that (a) your philosophical faculties are in both S (the state of having been produced by atheistic evolutionary processes) and $S^\star$, and (b) P(your philosophical faculties are reliable/they're in both S and $S^\star$) is high, is *yes*.

By way of reply, I wonder this. Why don't *I* have such non-propositional evidence for my belief that *my* philosophical faculties are reliable. I don't experience any emotion of ridicule when I entertain the possibility that my cognitive faculties are unreliable with respect to abstruse philosophical matters far removed from the everyday concerns of life. That possibility doesn't strike me as crazy or ridiculous. I don't notice any powerful seeming or seeing to be true when I consider the proposition that my philosophical faculties are reliable; it doesn't strike me as just *obvious* that they are. In fact, when I consider the multitude of crazy views philosophers have defended over the centuries and the rampant disagreement among philosophers over almost of everything of substance, I find it wholly *unobvious* that we humans, myself included, have reliable philosophical faculties. More, my attitude seems *appropriate* to the foregoing evidence. Given that evidence, it *shouldn't* strike us as just obvious that our philosophical faculties are reliable—the possibility that those faculties are unreliable

---

[30] Bergmann, 'Commonsense Naturalism,' p. 68.

shouldn't strike us crazy or ridiculous. My worry then: If you are a sophisticated atheist and have Reidian non-propositional evidence for the reliability of your philosophical faculties—you find it just *obvious* that your philosophical faculties are reliable—then I suspect you are not being appropriately responsive to the evidence. I suspect that your total evidence undercuts your Reidian non-propositional evidence—that given your awareness of widespread philosophical disagreement on almost all matters of substance and the variety of crazy views defended by philosophers over the centuries, a Reidian emotion of ridicule at the thought that perhaps your philosophical faculties aren't reliable is an unreasonable response to your evidence. But if so, then if your only evidence for belief in the reliability of your philosophical faculties is Reidian non-propositional evidence, you *don't* have good reason for thinking your philosophical faculties in a state S* such that P(your philosophical faculties are reliable/they're in both S and S*) is high.

Let us rehearse the logic of the situation. I argued above that, if you are a sophisticated atheist, you have good reason for belief that your philosophical faculties are in the state S of having been produced by atheistic evolutionary processes, and good reason to withhold or deny that P(your philosophical faculties are reliable/they're in state S) is high. More, I said, as best I can tell, there's no state S* such that you have good reason for belief that (a) your philosophical faculties are in both S and S* and (b) P(your philosophical faculties are reliable/they're in both S and S*) is high. We considered and rejected the possibility that you have a good track-record argument for thinking your philosophical faculties in a state S* such that P(your philosophical faculties are reliable/they're in both S and S*) is high. We then considered and rejected the possibility that you have good non-propositional reason, of the sort Reid described, for thinking your philosophical faculties in a state S* such that P(your philosophical faculties are reliable/they're in both S and S*) is high.

That leaves us, then, with the question whether there is some *other* S* such that you have good reason for belief that (a) your philosophical faculties are in both S (the state of having been produced by atheistic evolutionary processes) and S*, and (b) P(your philosophical faculties are reliable/they're in both S and S*) is high. It's hard indeed to see what state S* could do the job. I think there is no such state. If I'm right, then it follows from our Principle of Defeat that you have a defeater for any proposition p such that you have good reason for belief that your philosophical faculties are your only source of information on p. But, you *have* good reason for belief that your philosophical faculties are your only source of information on the Key Premise. This because you have good reason for accepting the First Thesis, the claim that the Key Premise is a recondite philosophical matter, and your philosophical faculties are, by definition, the faculties whereby you form and maintain belief about recondite philosophical matters. Wherefore, you have a defeater for the Key Premise; belief in the Key Premise is unjustified for you.

Our reasoning has led us to this conclusion: If you are a sophisticated atheist, belief in the Key Premise is unjustified for you. For the sophisticated anyway, the evidential argument from evil is *not* a good argument for atheism: it's not an argument one could rationally hold atheistic belief on the basis of. For as we've seen, if you are among the sophisticated and you accept the conclusion of the evidential argument (that there is no God), belief in the argument's key premise is unjustified for you.

Such is my objection to the evidential argument from evil; in short: if you're a reasonably well-informed, intellectually sophisticated denizen of the contemporary scene, you can't rationally accept the conclusion of the evidential argument on the basis of its premises. The argument gives you no good grounds for being an atheist.

2 Three objections

First objection:[31]

Consider

(*) No reason would justify an extremely powerful, extremely wise, wholly good creator of all things in permitting the existence of evils of the sort contained in our world.

If (*) is true, then, plausibly, it's a *conceptual truth*: a sentence S a priori knowable by anyone with an adequate understanding of the concepts expressed by the constituent terms of S. So take 'no married male is a bachelor.' It is a conceptual truth in our sense: anyone with an adequate grasp on the concepts *bachelor*, *married*, and *male* can see a priori that it's true. Likewise, plausibly, with (*): mastery of the concepts 'good,' 'justification,' and so forth, should enable one to see a priori that it's true (if it's true).

Suppose so. Then even if it's right that the probability given atheistic evolution that we should command reliable insight into fundamental metaphysical truths—truths about the fundamental structure of the world—isn't high, there's good reason to think that the probability given atheistic evolution that we'd be reliable on *conceptual* matters—that we'd be good at discerning conceptual truths—is high. Reliability of the latter sort, one thinks, is a matter of having reliable a priori access to the conditions of satisfaction of our concepts and to the logical relations holding among them. Plausibly, reliability of this sort would have been fitness enhancing for our ancestors. A creature with the concepts of, say, *danger* or *food*, who lacks a reliable grip on the conditions under which such concepts are satisfied or on the logical relations holding among related concepts will fare poorly in the evolutionary game. Faculties capable of reliable belief about the satisfaction conditions of our concepts and the logical relationships holding among them are not at all surprising on the evolutionary story. Wherefore, reliability in the domain of conceptual truths is not at all surprising on the evolutionary story. But if so, the probability given atheistic evolution that we'd be reliable on the Key Premise and like claims isn't low, since these are quite plausibly thought of as conceptual truths. But if so, your above argument fails.

---

[31] Thanks to Mike Rea for helpful correspondence on this and the next objection.

Such is our first objection. A couple points in reply. First, is it right that reliability with respect to conceptual truths is not at all surprising on the evolutionary story? Here the distinction between, on the one hand, having beliefs about a rule, and on the other, having *internalized* the rule—having a set of behavioral dispositions keyed to the content of the rule—is relevant.[32] Think about rules you might learn from your golf teacher about how to swing a club. You start by forming beliefs to the effect that the rule for thus-and-such situation is thus-and-so. You then consciously apply rules learned thus to your swing. Eventually, if things are going well, you *internalize* the rules: encode them in a set of dispositions and bodily habits sensitive to the content of the rule so that your bodily behavior conforms to the rule without your having to consciously attend to it. Given enough time, you may even forget the rules in the sense that you no longer possess propositional representations of them.

The distinction between having beliefs about a rule and having internalized a rule in hand, return to the concept of *danger*. Our objector suggests that a creature who possesses the concept of danger but lacks a reliable grip on its conditions of satisfaction will fare poorly in the evolutionary game. Much depends, though, on what's meant by talk of having a 'reliable grip' on the conditions of satisfaction of the concept of danger. One way of understanding such talk: to have a reliable grip on the conditions of satisfaction of the concept of danger is to have internalized the concept: to have encoded a set of dispositions and bodily habits sensitive to the satisfaction conditions of the concept in such a way that one can reliably avoid those conditions in which the concept is satisfied. Another way of understanding such talk: to have a reliable grip on the conditions of satisfaction of the concept of danger is to be able to form true beliefs of the form 'the concept danger is satisfied under thus-and-such conditions.'

Now, this much seems right: It's not at all surprising that evolution should have crafted creatures with a reliable grip on the conditions of satisfaction of the concept of danger, in the first sense of that notion. So it's not at all surprising that evolution should have crafted creatures who had internalized the concept of danger: who had encoded a set of dispositions and bodily habits sensitive to the satisfaction conditions of the concept in such a way that they could reliably avoid dangerous situations. But is it likewise unsurprising that evolution should have crafted creatures with the ability to form true *beliefs* about that concept, its application conditions, its logical relations to other concepts, and so forth? That part isn't as obvious. So long as the concept is internalized, whether or not one has faculties capable of reliability on the relevant metalevel beliefs about the concept would seem to be irrelevant from the perspective of evolution. But if so, contrary to our objector, faculties capable of reliable belief about the satisfaction conditions of our concepts and the logical relationships holding among them *is* surprising given the evolutionary story.

---

[32] For insightful discussion of the difference between propositional knowledge of rules and internalized rules, see John R. Searle, *Intentionality* (Cambridge, Cambridge University Press, 1983), pp. 150ff, and John R. Searle, *The Construction of Social Reality* (New York, Simon and Schuster, 1995), pp. 140ff.

Second, it's not very plausible, I think, that (*) is the sort of claim a priori knowable by anyone with an adequate understanding of the concept of *goodness, justifying reason* and the like. There is considerable disagreement in the history of philosophy about (*). Leibniz thought it false; Russell thought it true. Was this because one or the other didn't understand the concept *goodness* or *justifying reason* well enough? That strikes me as dubious. I should think Russell and Leibniz understood the concepts in play in (*) perfectly well, but that understanding of those concepts isn't sufficient for ascertaining the truth of (*). Ascertaining the truth of (*) requires a grip on those concepts, to be sure, but more besides: for example, a grip on the space of evil-justifying reasons available to a being like God. While we've a perfectly good grip on the concepts *goodness, justifying reasons*, and so forth, we have a lousy grasp on the space of evil-justifying reasons available to a being like God. That strikes me as a much more plausible explanation of our perennial disagreement about (*) than does the suggestion that (*) is a conceptual truth whose component concepts are unclear to us. My central suggestion here, then: (*) isn't plausibly thought of as a conceptual truth in the sense relevant to the objection.

Thus far our first objection and some reply. Here's a second objection:

Even if you're right that an atheist couldn't sensibly base atheistic belief on the evidential argument, it's consistent with what you say that for many (maybe even most), the evidential argument constitutes good reason for *agnosticism* with respect to theistic belief. Consider the Key Premise. As was suggested earlier, the question whether the Key Premise is true is perennially difficult—philosophers have disputed about it for centuries. The fact of the matter is, it's not obvious what to think about it.

Imagine someone, then, with no other evidence for or against theism who considers the Key Premise and the various arguments for and against it, finds herself unsure what to think and adopts an attitude of agnosticism toward the Key Premise—in Chisholm's terminology, she withholds the Key Premise. Seeing the implications of the Key Premise for theism (if the Key Premise is true, likely theism isn't), she likewise withholds the proposition that God exists. Arriving at agnosticism thus on the basis of the evidential argument would seem to be perfectly rational. The evidence for the Key Premise is ambiguous; it's hard to know *what* to think about it. Withholding the Key Premise seems a reasonable response to the evidence. For one with no other evidence for or against theism who withholds the Key Premise and sees the connection between it and theism, withholding theism seems reasonable as well.

So we get this: even if your above arguments are on target and the evidential argument isn't a good basis for atheistic *belief*, it's perfectly consistent with what you've said that, for many people, the evidential argument constitutes excellent grounds for agnosticism with respect to the theism/atheism debate.

Such is our second objection. Note by way of reply that even if this objection is right— even if all my above arguments shows is that the evidential argument does not constitute good grounds for atheistic belief—we still have an interesting result. In my experience, quite a few atheists report holding atheistic belief on just these grounds.

What to say about the objection, then? Is it right? Yes, I think it is. It's consistent with what I've said that, for many people, the evidential argument constitutes excellent grounds for agnosticism with respect to the theism/atheism debate. I would point out, though, that for the sophisticated among us, there is a steep epistemic cost associated with agnosticism toward the Key Premise. For as was pointed out by our objector, the reasonable response to agnosticism about the Key Premise is agnosticism about theism. But if you are agnostic on theism, you are, we may suppose, agnostic on the question whether your cognitive faculties are the product of atheistic evolutionary processes. And if you are agnostic about *that*, then by a principle similar to our above Principle of Defeat, you have a defeater for any proposition p such that you've good reason for thinking your philosophical faculties your only source of information on p.

Here I have in mind this

Revised Principle of Defeat: If for some cognitive faculty F, you are agnostic on whether F is in state S, and if you have good reason to withhold or deny the proposition that P(F is reliable/F is in S) is high, and if there is no state S$\star$ such that you have good reason for belief that (a) F is in both S and S$\star$, and (b) P(F is reliable/F is in both S and S$\star$) is high, then you have a defeater for any proposition p such that you have good reason for believing F your only source of information about p.

Why accept this revised principle? Here again, I have no argument from first principles. Cases like those mentioned above make the principle plausible. Suppose you are agnostic about whether your pool thermometer is reliable. Then, one thinks, you should not believe what the thermometer says about the water's temperature unless you have some other source of information to go on. Or: Suppose I think it likely that my perceptual faculties are unreliable if I'm plugged into the Matrix and am agnostic about whether I've been plugged into the Matrix. I'm not aware of any mitigating factors: I'm not aware of anything about me or my faculties that would offset the perceptual impairment caused by being thus connected to the Matrix. Then, one thinks, I should withhold any proposition p such that I have good reason for believing my perceptual faculties my only source of information on p. Reflection on these and like cases, I suggest, lends strong support to our Revised Principle of Defeat.

My claim, then: if you are agnostic on the question whether your cognitive faculties are the product of atheistic evolutionary processes, then by the Revised Principle of Defeat, you have a defeater for any proposition p such that you have good reason for thinking your philosophical faculties your only source of information on p. This is because, if you are agnostic on the question whether your cognitive faculties are the product of atheistic evolutionary processes, then you are agnostic on the question whether your philosophical faculties are in the state S of having been produced by atheistic evolutionary processes. Since, by hypothesis, you are among the sophisticated and thus have good reason for accepting the Thesis of Unreliability (or, at any rate, no good reason for rejecting it—more on this below), it follows that you have good reason to withhold or deny that P(your philosophical faculties are reliable/they're in S) is high. Since, as best I can tell, there is no state S$\star$ such that you have good reason to think (a) your philosophical faculties are in both S and S$\star$, and (b) P(your philosophical faculties are reliable/they're in S and S*) is high, we get, by the Revised Principle of Defeat, that you have a defeater for any proposition p such that you have good reason for thinking your philosophical faculties your only source of information on p. For most any recondite philosophical claim you accept, then, you aren't justified in accepting it.[33]

In summary: if you are agnostic on the Key Premise and among the sophisticated, you should be agnostic on pretty much any recondite philosophical claim. This is the steep epistemic cost I referred to earlier when I suggested that, for the sophisticated among us, there is a steep epistemic cost associated with agnosticism toward the Key Premise.

Perhaps you'll reject my claim that the cost here is steep. Perhaps you think this sort of philosophical skepticism (philosophical skepticism: skepticism about recondite philosophical matters) attractive. If so, I would point out that consistency on this point would seem to require a disciplined program of agnosticism on more than just matters in the far reaches of abstruse metaphysics, philosophy of mathematics and the like, but also on most of the deliverances of the theoretical parts of the natural sciences (the parts working on quantum theory, relativity and the like).

Perhaps you're okay with this; you think agnosticism the appropriate attitude toward all such theoretical endeavor. If so, you are rare—among the sophisticated anyway. Most of the reasonably well-informed, intellectually sophisticated folks I meet hold firm views, and lots of them, on abstruse issues in philosophy and the sciences and take themselves to be reasonable in doing so.

If you are in the latter camp—you are reasonably well-informed and intellectually sophisticated, hold various beliefs on abstruse matters in philosophy and the sciences, and think you're reasonable in doing so—then, I want to suggest, you have a powerful reason for denying the Key Premise.[34] For if my earlier arguments are on target and you are among the sophisticated, you can't rationally *accept* the Key Premise. And if my more recent arguments are on target and you are among the sophisticated who reject philosophical skepticism, you can't rationally withhold the Key Premise either. The thing for you to do, I suggest, is to deny it.

I conclude, then, that, for the sophisticated who reject philosophical skepticism anyway, the evidential argument does not constitute good grounds for agnosticism with respect to the theism/atheism debate.

And finally, here's a third objection.[35]

Your Thesis of Unreliability looks an awful lot like a recondite philosophical claim. If it is, then by your own reasoning, the sophisticated atheist/agnostic can't rationally accept it—she has no good reason for accepting it. But if she has no good reason for accepting it, then she has no good reason for withholding or denying that P(her philosophical faculties are reliable/A&E) is high, and your argument collapses.

---

[33] For related argument on the epistemic costs of agnosticism about the origins of our cognitive faculties, see Plantinga, *Warranted Christian Belief*, pp. 218–27.

[34] Cf. Alvin Plantinga, *Warrant and Proper Function* (Oxford, Oxford University Press, 1993), pp. 214–15.

[35] Thanks to Nathan Ballantyne for helpful correspondence here.

By way of reply, it's unclear whether the Thesis of Unreliability counts as a recondite philosophical claim, owing to the looseness with which I characterized that notion at the start of the paper. Suppose it is, though. Nothing very interesting follows. If it is a recondite philosophical claim, my argument gets us that if you are a sophisticated atheist, you can't rationally believe it. But of course it doesn't follow that, therefore, if you are a sophisticated atheist, you can rationally *deny* it—that you can rationally accept its negation. I think it's clear that, given our evidence, there's no good reason to accept its negation—its negation is not a priori obvious, nor, so far as I can tell, are there any good arguments for it. If my Thesis of Unreliability *is* a recondite philosophical claim, then, it looks like the rational attitude for the sophisticated atheist toward it is *agnosticism*.

But if you are a sophisticated atheist and are agnostic on the Thesis of Unreliability, then by our Principle of Defeat, you still get a defeater for any proposition p such that you have good reason for thinking your philosophical faculties your only source of information on p. You have, let us suppose, good reason for belief that your philosophical faculties are in the state S of having been produced by atheistic evolutionary processes. As we've just seen, you likewise have good reason for agnosticism on the question whether P(your philosophical faculties are reliable/they're in state S) is high. Since, presumably, there is no state S⋆ such that you have good reason to think (a) your philosophical faculties are in both S and S⋆, and (b) P(your philosophical faculties are reliable/they're in S and S⋆) is high, we get that, by the Principle of Defeat, you have a defeater for any proposition p such that you have good reason for thinking your philosophical faculties your only source of information on p, and the argument goes on just as before.

The upshot: even if the Thesis of Unreliability counts as a recondite philosophical thesis, the argument goes through as before: you still get a defeater for most any abstruse philosophical claim, including the Key Premise.

3 Conclusion

I have argued that the evidential argument gives you no good grounds for atheistic belief if you are a reasonably well-informed, intellectually sophisticated denizen of the contemporary scene. Nor does it give you good grounds for agnosticism about theism (if you're thus sophisticated and reject philosophical skepticism).

My reasoning, of course, has application to arguments beyond just the evidential argument from evil. Any atheological argument (argument to the non-existence of God) resting on recondite philosophical premises will be subject to the same objection, suggesting that if you are a sophisticated atheist or agnostic and your only grounds for this are philosophical—your only grounds are arguments resting on recondite philosophical premises—then your atheism (agnosticism) is poorly grounded.[36]

[36] For helpful comments and conversation on earlier drafts of this paper, kind thanks to Nathan Ballantyne, Richard Otte, Michael Rea, Donald Smith, Gregg Ten Elshof, and Erik Wielenberg.

PART III

Evidence and Religious Belief

8

Consensus Gentium: Reflections on the 'Common Consent' Argument for the Existence of God

Thomas Kelly

As the human intellect, though weak, is not essentially perverted, there is a certain presumption of the truth of any opinion held by many human minds, requiring to be rebutted by assigning some other real or possible cause for its prevalence. And this consideration has a special relevance to the inquiry concerning the foundations of theism, inasmuch as no argument for the truth of theism is more commonly invoked or more confidently relied on, than the general assent of mankind.

John Stuart Mill, *Theism*

1 Introduction

I want to take up an argument that might seem a better candidate for contempt than for serious scrutiny. In its crudest and least sophisticated form, the Common Consent Argument for the Existence of God runs as follows:

(Premise) Everyone believes that God exists.
(Conclusion) God exists.

So stated, the argument is not exactly an overwhelming one, suffering as it does from the twin defects of transparent invalidity and the having of an obviously false claim as its sole premise. In a slightly less crude form, the premise of the argument is that almost everyone, or the great majority of humankind, believes that God exists. More generally, proponents of the argument contend that the *prevalence* of the belief that God exists is itself evidence for the truth of that belief.

The common consent argument has a venerable history. An explicit statement appears as early as Plato's *Laws*.[1] A list of prominent thinkers who endorsed some

---

[1] See Book X, 886, where the character Clinias appeals to the fact that 'all mankind, barbarians as well as Greeks, believe in them' as one way of proving the existence of the gods.

recognizable variant of the argument would include Cicero, Seneca, Calvin, the Cambridge Platonists, Gassendi, and Grotius.[2] In addition, it was discussed critically by (among many others) Locke, Hume, and Mill.[3]

More recently, the argument has fallen on hard times as an object of philosophical attention. It is seldom taken seriously, even in circles in which arguments for the existence of God are still taken seriously. It is, for example, rarely if ever included among the usual rogues' gallery of arguments for the existence of God in anthologies or course syllabi devoted to the philosophy of religion. Among the more sophisticated, book-length critical surveys of such arguments, it is not so much as mentioned in Mackie's *The Miracle of Theism*, Sobel's *Logic and Theism*, or Swinburne's *The Existence of God*. Nor does any reference to it appear in the *Oxford Handbook of Philosophy of Religion* or Blackwell's *A Companion to Philosophy of Religion*, each of which runs to well over five hundred pages. In short, although the argument still occasionally appears in popular apologetics,[4] it seems to have virtually disappeared as an object of discussion among professional philosophers.

Perhaps there are good reasons for the more or less complete neglect of the argument among contemporary philosophers of religion, in contrast to the attention that it received from previous generations of thinkers. Nevertheless, despite the apparently anachronistic character of the enterprise, I want to inquire into what might be said for and against a relatively modest version of the argument. In particular, I will be concerned with what I take to be the core thought behind the appeal to common opinion: viz. that the fact that theistic belief is widespread among the human population is itself a significant piece of evidence that God exists, and thus a fact that can boost the rational credibility of theism for those who are aware of it. By my lights, this thought is neither absurd nor obviously correct. Moreover, I believe that some of the issues that arise in connection with it are of interest not only for the epistemology of religious belief but also for philosophy more generally.

To forewarn the reader: what I have to say on this topic will be quite inconclusive, even relative to the typically inconclusive standards of philosophy. For reasons that I indicate below, I do not believe that we are currently in a good position to say anything definitive about the evidentiary value of appeals to common opinion about the existence of God. (In any case, I am certain that I am not in a position to do so.) What I hope to provide instead is something like a prolegomena to future reflection on

---

[2] For an overview of this tradition, see the useful survey in Paul Edwards, 'Common Consent Arguments for the Existence of God' in Edwards (ed.), *The Encyclopedia of Philosophy*, vol. 2 (New York, Macmillan, 1967), pp. 147–55.

[3] Locke, *An Essay Concerning Human Understanding* (many editions), Book I, section IV; Hume, *The Natural History of Religion* (many editions), section XII; Mill, 'Theism,' reprinted in *Three Essays on Religion* (Amherst, NY, Prometheus Books, 1998), pp. 155–60.

[4] See, e.g., Peter Kreeft and Ronald Tacelli, *Handbook of Christian Apologetics* (Downers Grove, IL, Intervarsity Press, 1994), pp. 83–5. Even here, however, the argument hardly enjoys pride of place: of the twenty arguments for the existence of God presented by Kreeft and Tacelli, the common consent argument appears nineteenth.

this kind of argument, and, perhaps, a small step towards its rehabilitation as a topic of interest among philosophers.

I will begin with some remarks about common consent arguments in general and then turn my attention to the specific application to the case of theistic belief.

2 Common consent arguments

The idea that the sheer *popularity* of an opinion might provide a respectable reason for thinking that that opinion is true has not found many takers in the Western philosophical tradition. Indeed, one might very well date the beginning of the Western philosophical tradition from Socrates' adamant insistence that the mere fact that certain views and practices are dominant among his fellow Athenians is not itself a good reason for accepting those views and practices. The Socratic injunction to 'follow the argument where it leads' is, among other things, an injunction against the uncritical acceptance of prevailing orthodoxies, and a call to consider radical alternatives with an open mind.[5]

Following Socrates' lead, a good part of the subsequent history of philosophy has been devoted to the consideration of radically revisionary views in metaphysics, epistemology, and ethics. In general, it has not been considered a good objection to such views to simply note that they conflict with what is generally believed about what there is, what we know, or what we should do. Significantly, the idea that inconsistency with prevailing opinion is not itself an objection to radical views in philosophy has generally been accepted not only by proponents of such views, but also by their critics, who have sought to discredit the revisionary views on other, ostensibly more intellectually respectable grounds. When philosophers argue for and against claims by offering reasons, they do not cite surveys of public opinion. Indeed, for the most part it seems to have been assumed (at least implicitly) that the actual distribution of opinion with respect to a philosophical view has no normative significance whatsoever.[6]

Moreover, it is not simply that standard philosophical practice seems to treat the distribution of opinion among the philosophically unsophisticated masses as normatively irrelevant; the distribution of opinion among the (presumably) more sophisticated philosophers is similarly ignored. For example, perhaps few if any contemporary philosophers are full-fledged skeptics about our knowledge of other minds, in the sense of believing that there is some sound argument that has as its conclusion the claim that

---

[5] For a discussion of the relevant intellectual ideal, see my 'Following the Argument Where It Leads' (forthcoming in *Philosophical Studies*).

[6] A notable exception to this general tendency is the so-called 'common sense' tradition, as embodied by figures such as Thomas Reid and G. E. Moore. Both Reid and Moore regularly return to the fact that the propositions denied by radical skeptics and revisionary metaphysicians are the objects of universal or near universal belief. Moreover, both men clearly take this fact to have considerable normative significance and to tell against the views in question. For discussion of this aspect of the common sense tradition, see Part I of my *Believing with Reason* (manuscript).

'for all I know, my mind is the only thing of its kind in existence.'[7] Nevertheless, it would not be considered a good objection to arguments for skepticism about other minds to simply note that such arguments have failed to inspire conviction among the vast majority of philosophers who are acquainted with them. In short, if one were to judge by standard philosophical practice, one might easily be led to the conclusion that contingent, empirical facts about the distribution of opinion among any given group of people are one thing, and considerations relevant to normative questions about what one should believe are an entirely different matter. One might thus be tempted to conclude that *any* common consent argument is fallacious, on the grounds that it is simply a mistake to treat the fact that people believe as they do as evidence for the truth of what they believe. After all, when one says: 'Everyone believes that, but there is simply no evidence that it's true'—surely one does not *contradict* oneself.

However, it is clear that, at least outside of the philosophy seminar room, we regularly treat the beliefs of others as evidence for the truth of what they believe, revising our own views in the light of what they think, and that (often enough) it is reasonable for us to do so. For example, if I initially believe that this week's recycling is scheduled to be picked up tomorrow, but I subsequently learn that everyone else on our block thinks that the pick-up is scheduled for today (perhaps I observe that others have already placed their recycling bins on the curb this morning), then I will change my view. Moreover, barring very unusual circumstances, surely this is the reasonable thing for me to do. Similarly, if I perform some non-trivial mathematical calculation but subsequently learn that others who performed the same calculation arrived at a different answer, then I should treat this as evidence of my having made a mistake. Our tendency to treat the views of others as evidence is perhaps most salient in cases of disagreement (when one becomes less confident or even abandons one's original view upon learning that others think something else) or in cases in which one initially holds no view at all about the question at issue (consider cases in which one is otherwise ignorant but defers to the view of an expert upon learning what she thinks). But we also appropriately treat the views of others as evidence that warrants a change of mind in cases in which they agree with views that we already hold. Thus, if I learn that others who performed the calculation arrived at the same answer that I did, then it is reasonable for me to increase my confidence in my original answer in response.

Of course, there are some cases in which it is appropriate to give no weight at all to the fact that others believe as they do, even if the view from which one dissents is a consensus opinion. Indeed, in some cases the appropriate course is to give no weight at all to the consensus opinion, even if one knows that *all* of the members of the consensus

---

[7] Of course, many philosophers have defended skeptical arguments by attempting to show that particular objections to their soundness are misguided, or even that all extant objections are misguided. Some philosophers no doubt believe that we have yet to produce good objections to skeptical arguments, or even that we can reasonably hope to find good objections to skeptical arguments in the future. But all of these broadly sympathetic stances vis-à-vis skepticism are much weaker than genuine skepticism, in the sense specified in the text.

are *perfectly reasonable* in believing as they do. For example, suppose that my loathing of the butler leads me to frame him for some crime that he did not commit. Suppose further that I execute my plan impeccably: due to my efforts, the authorities and members of the general public come to possess large quantities of misleading evidence, all of which suggests that the butler is guilty. When I subsequently note with satisfaction the (near) universality of the belief that the butler is guilty, I might very well judge that all of those who hold the belief hold it reasonably. Nevertheless, in these circumstances, I will not treat the fact that everyone else reasonably believes that the butler is guilty as any reason at all to think that this proposition is true.

Notwithstanding such exceptions, the range of cases in which we are prepared to treat the beliefs of others as at least some evidence for the truth of what they believe is impressive. As the examples above make clear, we do so in ostensibly a priori domains such as mathematics as well as when it comes to questions that are straightforwardly empirical, such as those concerning recycling schedules. We often treat the views of others as evidence in cases in which those views are arrived at non-inferentially. (Consider, for example, perceptual judgments: if it looked to me like Horse A crossed the finish line slightly ahead of Horse B, but everyone around me thought that Horse B won the race, then it will typically be reasonable for me to revise my opinion in the direction of the consensus.) But we do the same with respect to inferential judgments that are the deliverances of some piece of reasoning (as in a case mathematical calculation) or based on a body of evidence.

Consider cases in which it is clear that the truth cannot be discerned directly; if it is available at all, one must rely on evidence, broadly construed. In such cases, there are at least two distinct motivations for why one might treat the views of others as evidence. First, others might very well possess relevant evidence that one lacks, or have had relevant experiences that one has not had. To the extent that one regards the others as generally competent interpreters of their evidence and experience, one would expect the probative force of their evidence and experience to be reflected in their beliefs. By giving at least some weight to their beliefs, one gains a kind of indirect access to their evidence and experience. In treating their beliefs as evidence, one is in effect treating their beliefs as a *proxy* for the first order evidence and experience on which those beliefs are based. In this way, one improves the pool of evidence and experience that plays a role in influencing one's own beliefs.

The beliefs of other people often provide our best or only access to relevant evidence: this fact guarantees that the practice of giving weight to the beliefs of others will play a pervasive role in any epistemically well-conducted life. However, if one took the view that this proxy function *exhausts* the evidential value of the beliefs of others, then one might naturally embrace the following picture: in any case in which one *does* have direct access to the grounds on which the other person bases her view, one should in effect 'look through' the fact that she believes as she does. One should not give any additional or independent weight to the fact that she believes as she does, once one has taken into account the grounds that prompt her to believe in this way.

In fact, something like this picture seems to be assumed by many participants in the classical debate over the status of common consent arguments. Here, for example, is Mill:

It may doubtless be good advice to persons who in point of knowledge and cultivation are not entitled to think themselves competent judges of difficult questions, to bid them content themselves with holding that true which mankind generally believe . . . or that which has been believed by those who pass for the most eminent among the minds of the past. But to a thinker the argument from other people's opinions has little weight. It is but second-hand evidence; and merely admonishes us to look out for and weigh the reasons on which this conviction of mankind or of wise men was founded.[8]

In this passage, Mill significantly underestimates the evidential value of the opinions of other people. For even in the unusual case in which one gains direct access to all of the 'first-hand' evidence on which others base their belief, it will still often make sense to give additional weight to the fact others have responded to that evidence by adopting a certain opinion. For inasmuch as one acknowledges that one is a fallible evaluator of the relevant kind of evidence (as 'thinkers' surely should), the fact that others have responded to the evidence in a certain way is itself a potentially valuable piece of evidence or information: it is evidence that bears on the accuracy of one's own assessment of the (original, first hand) evidence in this particular case, and thus should affect how confident one ought to be of the view at which one has arrived.[9]

The set of beliefs that a person holds at any given time constitutes a unique perspective on the world. In effect, it says: 'This is how things look from here.' Of course, that perspective is not simply a reflection of how things appear from some point in physical space (as is perhaps suggested by the locational demonstrative 'here'). Rather, it also reflects the individual's past history and experience, the particular ways in which she interpreted or responded to those experiences, her background assumptions and starting points, and much else besides. A proposition that was the object of genuinely *universal* belief (as opposed to, say, a proposition that was believed by all of the homeowners on my block, or by everyone who had been exposed to the evidence that a certain individual committed some crime) would be a part of any actual perspective on the world.

Even with respect to a universally held belief, one can imagine acquiring evidence that would undermine the potential epistemic significance of the fact that it is universally held. (For example, imagine a possible world in which literally everyone believes

---

[8] Mill, 'Theism,' p. 156. Among those who took the common consent argument to have at least some value, a dispute arose as to whether widespread belief in God was itself a reason to believe that God exists or rather merely an 'indication' that such reasons existed. For examples of the latter view, which is similar to Mill's in the epistemic role that it assigns to the opinions of others, see Robert Flint, *Theism* (New York, Charles Scribner and Sons, 1903), p. 349 and Cardinal Joseph Mercier, *A Manual of Modern Scholastic Philosophy* (London, Kessinger, 1926), p. 55.

[9] For more on this point, see David Christensen, 'Epistemology of Disagreement: the Good News' in *Philosophical Review* 116 (2), pp. 187–217, and Thomas Kelly, 'Peer Disagreement and Higher Order Evidence,' in Richard Feldman and Ted Warfield (eds.), *Disagreement* (Oxford, Oxford University Press, 2010).

that God exists, but in which scientists discover the following fact: because of the character of that world, belief in God has proven evolutionarily advantageous for non-truth-related reasons, and because of this all members of the species are now born with such belief hard-wired into their brains.) However, absent some compelling under-mining explanation, we can see why genuinely universal belief that p would seem to provide impressive evidence that p is true. For the fact that p is part of every actual perspective shows that the belief that p is not the result of *idiosyncrasy*. That is, it is not due to idiosyncratic judgment, past history, course of experience, interpretation, background assumptions or starting point. Rather, it is among the things that are left over when one abstracts away from such idiosyncrasies.

Notwithstanding the intuitive plausibility of such a picture (at least, when it is described in sufficiently broad outline), one might still harbor suspicions about the idea that the mere belief that p (no matter how widespread) could by itself ever amount to full-fledged, independent evidence that p is true. For suppose that there is originally no evidence whatsoever that p is true, but that large numbers of people nevertheless unreasonably come to believe it for bad reasons, or for no reasons at all. If widespread belief in p constitutes genuine evidence that p is true (at least, in the absence of the availability of some undermining explanation), then those who baselessly believe p would seem to have magically brought evidence for p into existence merely by believing it in the absence of any evidence. Here we seem to have gotten something from nothing, and the way seems clear for all sorts of dubious bootstrapping maneu-vers, by which ill-supported views come to be reasonably believed merely by once having been believed unreasonably.

However, although this phenomenon can look strange when viewed in certain lights, it is a genuine one. For example, suppose that the following improbable event were to occur: every person in our group happens to make exactly the same mistake while performing some non-trivial mathematical calculation, and thus independently arrives at the same mistaken answer. At the moment we learn what the others think, each of us should increase his or credence that the mistaken answer is correct. In this case, the beliefs of others constitute genuine (albeit misleading) evidence for the mistaken conclusion. Nevertheless, there is a clear sense in which, prior to becoming aware of what the others think, none of us had a legitimate basis for believing as we did. After all, given that the case involves a mathematical mistake, not only do the truths from which we reason fail to support the answer at which we arrive, but they literally entail the falsity of that answer. The moral: the fact that a proposition is widely believed can constitute strong evidence that that proposition is true, even if there would be no evidence that it is true in the absence of its being believed.

In various ways then, our practice of treating the beliefs of others as evidence serves as a crucial epistemic resource and check on our own thinking. More specifically, in many cases—although certainly not all—when one finds oneself out of step with some consensus, it is reasonable to adjust one's own view in the direction of the prevailing view. Thus, at least one natural criticism that someone might make of common consent arguments in general—that to cite the fact that a large number of people believe that p as evidence for p is a kind of category mistake—misses the mark. Moreover, notice that with respect to the specific case of religious belief, many atheists and agnostics will also insist that the actual distribution of opinion is normatively significant. So, for example, many atheists and agnostics will think that the diversity of theological beliefs among theists (i.e., the fact that the theists are divided among Muslims, Jews, Christians, and others) provides evidence against the theists' more specific theological commitments.

Consider some cases in which, intuitively, I am justified in believing some proposition because I know that that proposition is believed by all or almost all of the members of some salient group. For example, if a non-trivial math problem is given to ten individuals, then, even if I myself am ignorant of the parameters of the problem, I will typically be justified in believing that the correct answer is '138' upon learning that that is the answer that each of the ten came up with. And the same will be true, presumably, if only eight or nine of the ten came up with that number.

Suppose next that I am one of the ten individuals who is given the problem. In a case in which I learn that the other nine arrived at the same answer that I did, I should increase my confidence in that answer. On the other hand, if I learn that the other nine arrived at some different number, it will typically be reasonable for me to give up my original belief and conclude that their answer is correct. Moreover, notice that this will typically be the rational course even if I am the most reliable of the ten individuals when it comes to the relevant kind of math problem, and I know that I am. For even if I have compelling evidence (perhaps on the basis of our past track records) that I make fewer mistakes than the second most reliable person in the group, it will typically be much more likely that I've made a mistake in this case, than the others have managed to mistakenly arrive at the same wrong answer.[10]

How should we understand the inference from 'The dominant opinion in the group is p' to 'p is true' or 'p is probably true'? I suggest that we construe the inference as an inference to the best explanation.[11] In general, I am justified in concluding that p is the case on the basis of the fact that p is the dominant opinion in the group only if the truth of p is part of the best explanation of the fact that p is the dominant opinion in the group. That p is the case and most of the group has managed to pick up on this is one among many *potential* explanations of the fact that p is the dominant opinion: roughly, it is the kind of thing that would *actually* explain why p is the dominant opinion *if it were*

---

[10] Notice that the relevant comparison is not the probability that I've made a mistake versus the probability that each of the nine others made some mistake, but rather the probability that each of the nine made a mistake given that they arrived at the same answer. In a case in which I know that we each arrived at our answers independently, the last probability might very well be astronomically low, even if each of the nine individuals frequently makes mistakes.

[11] On inference to the best explanation, see especially Peter Lipton's *Inference to the Best Explanation* (London, Routledge, 1991) and Roger White, 'Explanation as a Guide to Induction,' in the *Philosophers Imprint* 5 (2005), pp. 1–29. A seminal paper is Gilbert Harman, 'The Inference to the Best Explanation,' in *The Philosophical Review* 74 (1965), pp. 88–95.

true.[12] To say that it is the *best* potential explanation is to say that it scores higher than any other, rival potential explanation when evaluated by the usual criteria of plausibility, fit with background knowledge, explanatory power, simplicity, and so forth. Of course, even if it is in fact the best potential explanation with respect to these criteria, that does not guarantee that it is the true or actual explanation: inference to the best explanation, like inductive inference more generally, is fallible even when impeccably performed. This is as it should be, for to claim that the truth of p is (part of) the best explanation for why p is the dominant opinion is not to deny the obvious fact that the convergence of opinion regarding p is consistent with the falsity of p. (For example, perhaps all of those who arrived at the number '138' just happened to make exactly the same mistake in their calculations.) Rather, it is to say that no potential explanation of the convergence that fails to mention the truth of p is as good as some potential explanation that does invoke the truth of p.

The attractiveness of construing the relevant reasoning as an inference to the best explanation is perhaps most clear in cases in which the relevant inference is *not* warranted. For example, suppose that I know that although all of the other members of the group arrived at some specific answer other than the one at which I arrived, only one person performed the calculation on his own: the rest either copied their answer from him, or copied from someone who copied from him. In that case, the 'truth explanation' is trumped; there is no need to invoke the truth of the claim that '138' is the correct answer in accounting for why that belief is dominant in the group, for we can account for its dominance in a way that does not appeal to its truth. Given that I am aware of how this convergence came about, the numbers drop out: I should give no more credence to '138' than I would upon learning that that was the answer arrived at by the individual who worked on the problem on his own. And if I know that I am more reliable than any other individual in the group, I should give less credence to that answer than to the one at which I arrived. Here, being greatly outnumbered counts for nothing.

More generally, the epistemic significance of the existence of consensus with respect to a given issue depends on how the existence of that consensus is best explained. (When in *The Structure of Scientific Revolutions* Thomas Kuhn attributed the ability of the natural sciences to achieve consensus to the fact that its practitioners are commonly educated into the reigning paradigm, many took this thesis as potentially undermining the epistemic significance of widespread agreement within the natural sciences.) Some explanations of a prevailing consensus might reinforce its status as an indication of truth, other explanations might undermine its status as such.

---

[12] On potential versus actual explanations, see Lipton, *Inference to the Best Explanation*, pp. 56–66. As Lipton notes, the equation between 'true potential explanation' and 'actual explanation' is not quite right: being a true potential explanation seems to be a necessary, but not quite sufficient condition for being an actual explanation. Sufficiency fails in cases of (e.g.) causal preemption. The existence of such cases will not make a difference in what follows.

3 Common consent arguments for theism: some comments on the traditional debate

As a historical matter, the traditional arguments for the existence of God have often been offered as 'proofs,' where it is a necessary condition for an argument's being a genuine proof that its premises entail its conclusion. Judged by this standard, any version of the common consent argument is a clear failure, for even if there is universal agreement that p is the case, that does not entail that p is the case. This obvious point is generally conceded by proponents of the argument, who typically make weaker claims on its behalf. For example, Kreeft and Tacelli acknowledge that widespread belief in God is consistent with the truth of atheism, but claim that, in the absence of a compelling debunking explanation of such belief (which they do not believe is in the offing), believing in God is more reasonable than not believing.[13]

I think that the friend of the common consent argument should aim for a significantly more modest conclusion. The friend of the argument should argue, not that widespread belief in God renders such belief reasonable all things considered, but rather that widespread belief in God is a significant piece of evidence in favor of the truth of that belief. This latter claim, while ambitious and controversial, is nevertheless much weaker than the former. For even if widespread belief in God is a significant piece of evidence for theism—indeed, even if it is sufficiently strong to justify theistic belief in the absence of any other evidence—it does not follow that it is sufficient to do so once all of the evidence is taken into account. After all, insofar as what it is reasonable to believe about some question is determined by one's evidence, what is relevant is one's total evidence, as opposed to some particular piece of evidence that one possesses, or some proper subset of one's total evidence. And of course, one might very well have other evidence that bears on the question of whether God exists, quite apart from one's knowledge of what others believe about this question. For example, many have thought that the existence of evil provides powerful (perhaps even conclusive) evidence against the existence of God; if so, anyone who is aware that the world contains evil has a powerful piece of evidence against the existence of God. Some have thought that certain large-scale structural features of the world constitute significant evidence in favor of the existence of God; if so, then anyone who is aware of those features possesses evidence for the existence of God in addition to whatever evidence (if any) is provided by the fact that others believe as they do. Even if it is true that facts about the distribution of opinion constitute genuine evidence that bears on the question of God's existence, it would be a mistake, I think, to suppose that this is the *only* evidence that is relevant, or that it swamps any other evidence into insignificance.[14]

---

[13] 'Handbook of Christian Apologetics,' p. 84.

[14] In fact, on some views about how we should take the views of others into account, facts about the distribution of opinion do frequently swamp other kinds of evidence, in the sense that they suffice to fix the facts about what one is rationally required to believe. I believe, and have argued at some length, that such views are too strong to be defensible. See Kelly, 'The Epistemic Significance of Disagreement' in Gendler and

Once this point is taken on board, space is cleared for the following possibility: an atheist or agnostic might agree with a proponent of the common consent argument that widespread belief in God is evidence for theistic belief but insist that, nevertheless, belief in God is unreasonable given the kind of evidence that is typically available to would-be believers. Such an atheist or agnostic might agree that a careful statement of the common consent argument results in an *inductively strong* argument (to employ terminology that lacks the currency it once had), but nevertheless deny that belief in God is reasonable on the grounds that the premises of any such argument will fail to encapsulate the total evidence that is available to would-be believers. (And, the atheist or agnostic will add, once premises encoding the missing information are added, the resulting argument will *not* be inductively strong.) Conversely, a theist might hold, alongside many atheists and agnostics, that the actual distribution of opinion with respect to God's existence is significant evidence *against* the existence of God, but maintain that such belief is nevertheless justified on balance, once all of the relevant evidence is taken into account.

To state the obvious: many people do not believe that God exists. Indeed, the rise of secularism in Western Europe was surely a primary cause for the decline in popularity of the common consent argument among religious apologists. Where formerly religious conflict had been almost entirely between adherents of rival theistic traditions who at least shared an underlying belief in God, theism itself came to seem controversial.[15] In such a context, appeals to the 'consensus' that God exists seemed increasingly lame.

Does the evident existence of significant numbers of non-believers fatally under-mine the argument? It is true that many classic presentations of the argument place great emphasis on the putative fact that belief in God is in some sense universal. In response to the apparent existence of non-believers, various strategies were adopted. The most extreme of these was to insist that the apparent existence of non-believers is *merely* apparent. According to this line of thought, even those who sincerely professed not to believe in God at some level really did so; such belief would manifest itself in (e.g.) sufficiently extreme circumstances.[16] (Compare the old saying that 'There are no atheists in foxholes.') Another extreme response was to concede the existence of genuine atheists but to discount their significance on the grounds that they were too anomalous to matter, where 'anomalous' was given a normative spin. Thus, in the course of putting forth his own version of the argument, Pierre Gassendi minimized

Hawthorne (eds.), *Oxford Studies in Epistemology*, vol. 1 (Oxford, Oxford University Press, 2005), pp. 167–96; 'Peer Disagreement and Higher Order Evidence'; and 'Disagreement and the Burdens of Judgment' (forth-coming). Suffice it to say that, if I am wrong and such views are correct, common consent arguments for philosophically interesting conclusions might have even more potential than I credit them with here.

[15] Of course, there had always been atheists and agnostics. But at various times and places, their relative invisibility had been such as to make non-belief seem like a rather marginal (and therefore, practically insignificant) phenomenon. In Western Europe, this had certainly ceased to be true by the middle of the nineteenth century. For a good overview of the relevant history, see Owen Chadwick, *The Secularization of the European Mind in the Nineteenth Century* (Cambridge, Cambridge University Press, 1990).

[16] For a view of this kind, see Charles Hodge, *Systematic Theology* (New York, Scribner, Armstrong, and Company, 1871).

the significance of atheists on the grounds that such people were either 'intellectual monstrosities' or 'freaks of nature.'[17]

No response along these lines is respectable. If the common consent argument depended on a claim to the effect that everyone is 'really' a theist in some sense, or that atheists and agnostics are defective human beings, then it would be unworthy of discussion. In fact, however, neither the interest nor the plausibility of what I have identified as the core thought behind the traditional argument—viz., that widespread belief in God provides evidence for the truth of that belief—presupposes any such claim. After all, in many cases, the fact that a substantial majority of some group shares an opinion is strong evidence that it is true, even if a significant part of the group does not share (and even explicitly rejects) that opinion. Consider then:

The datum: A strong supermajority of the world's population believes that God exists.

In the United States Senate, sixty out of one hundred votes constitutes a supermajority; I use the phrase 'strong supermajority' to capture the fact that, by conventional estimates, the percentage of the world's population that believes in God greatly exceeds sixty percent of the total.[18] While I will raise a question about the datum towards the end of this paper, I will for the most part simply assume that it is true in order to inquire what might follow from it. We can thus restate the core idea behind the common consent argument as follows:

The datum constitutes significant evidence in favor of the proposition that God exists.

In addition to the rise of secularism, there is a second reason for the argument's decline in popularity that we should pause to consider: to a large extent, discussion of the argument was simply swallowed up by the great controversy between empiricists and rationalists.[19] Historically, the argument was closely associated, in the minds of both its proponents and its critics, with the doctrine of innate ideas. Typically, proponents of the argument claimed that the (near) universality of religious belief was due to the fact that the concept of God, and belief in His existence, were part of the innate furniture of the human mind.[20]

---

[17] Quoted in Edwards, 'Common Consent Arguments for the Existence of God,' p. 252. A different kind of universality claim that was sometimes put forward was the following: although there are some non-believers, belief in God is found in every civilization, and moreover, in each civilization, the believers significantly outnumber the non-believers. We might think of this as the Electoral College version of the common consent argument.

[18] See, e.g., the data recently compiled in Phil Zuckerman, 'Atheism: Contemporary Rates and Patterns' in Michael Martin (ed.), *The Cambridge Companion to Atheism* (Cambridge, Cambridge University Press, 2006), pp. 47–68. Zuckerman (a sociologist of religion and an atheist, one of whose avowed purposes is to show that non-belief is more common than is typically claimed) estimates that approximately 88 percent of the world's population believes in God.

[19] On this point, see Walter O'Briant, 'Is There an Argument *Consensus Gentium?*' in *International Journal for Philosophy of Religion* 18 (1985), pp. 73–9.

[20] Notice how this picture fits well with the popular theme that atheists are defective human beings: such people were either born lacking a crucial part of our natural endowment, and thus suffered from a kind of birth defect, or else had become so corrupt that they had lost their grip on what is essentially given to any normal human mind.

Traditional versions of the argument thus frequently came under fire in the context of more general empiricist critiques of innateness claims. For example, in the *Essay Concerning Human Understanding*, Locke explicitly argued that the idea of God (and therefore, belief in God) is not innate. For his part, Mill (1885[1998], pp. 155–60) argued that even if it were conceded that belief in God is innate, this would not provide any respectable reason for thinking that that belief is true. As strong innateness claims increasingly fell out of favor among philosophers, so too did *consensus gentium* arguments.

However, the core thought behind the common consent argument does not presuppose that belief in God is innate, any more than it presupposes the universality of that belief. Indeed, I believe that in some respects the argument is *better off* if belief in God is not innate, but rather acquired after experience of the world. To see this, consider two possible worlds; in each, belief in God is universal among all adult human beings. The difference between the two worlds is the following. In the first world, all human beings are born with the belief that God exists; such belief is simply part of the innate endowment of the human mind. In the second, no one is born with the belief, but everyone acquires it by the time they reach adulthood in response to their experiences of the world. Suppose further that, in each world, the inhabitants know that all adults in their world believe that God exists, and also the manner in which this convergence came about. We can then ask: in which of the two worlds should the inhabitants be more impressed by the convergence of opinion? Although it presumably will matter a great deal how the details are filled in, I believe that a strong case can be made that, all else being equal, inhabitants of the second world have stronger evidence that God exists than inhabitants of the first world. For notice that, in a world in which everyone is simply born believing in God, there will be certain relatively attractive, debunking explanations of the fact that everyone believes in God that are simply not available in the other world. Consider, for example, the kind of evolutionary explanation gestured at in Section 2 above. Explanations of this general form are genuine competitors to truth-invoking explanations in the first world, but are non-starters in the second. More generally, and despite what many participants on both sides of the traditional debate seemed to think, the core thought behind the common consent argument does not presuppose that religious belief is innate as opposed to acquired.[21]

In response to the claim that the datum provides confirming evidence for the proposition that God exists, the critic of the argument might offer a naturalistic, debunking explanation of the datum in the style of Marx, Freud, Durkheim, Weber, or their contemporary successors. Critics of such naturalistic explanations sometimes complain about their speculative character, and the fact that they are typically not accompanied by much in the way of independent evidence.[22] I believe that there is considerable truth to such charges, but also that in the present dialectical context they are not wholly to the point. Again, the proponent of the common consent argument claims that the datum

---

[21] Cf. O'Briant, 'Is There an Argument *Consensus Gentium*?,' pp. 74–5.

[22] See, e.g., Kreeft and Tacelli, *Handbook of Christian Apologetics*, p. 84.

confirms the hypothesis that God exists because the latter is (part of) the best explanation of the former. However, the extent to which a piece of evidence confirms a given hypothesis can be significantly affected by the mere presence of alternative hypotheses in the field, *even in the absence of any reason for preferring those alternative hypotheses*. In general, how strongly a given piece of evidence confirms a hypothesis is not solely a matter of the intrinsic characters of the evidence and the hypothesis. (Nor is it solely a matter of their intrinsic characters together with one's background theory of how the world works.) Rather, it also depends on the presence or absence of plausible competitors in the field. It is because of this that the mere articulation of a plausible alternative hypothesis can dramatically reduce how likely the original hypothesis is on the evidence in question.[23] Thus, the provision of a plausible debunking explanation of the datum can drain the support that it would otherwise lend to the hypothesis that God exists even in the absence of independent empirical evidence to think that the debunking explanation is correct.

Of course, the proponent of the common consent argument might question just how plausible the debunking explanation on offer really is. (After all, just how plausible is Freud's claim that belief in God is rooted in universal dissatisfaction with our own actual fathers qua protectors? Not very plausible, I think.) In response, one who offers the naturalistic explanation might point out that what is at issue is the *comparative* plausibility of hypotheses, and it is not at all obvious why we should think that 'the truth hypothesis' sets a high standard in that regard.[24]

---

[23] Consider a historical example that is often thought to illustrate this normative phenomenon. Many organisms manifest special characteristics that enable them to flourish in their typical environments. According to the *Design Hypothesis*, this is due to the fact that such organisms were so designed by an Intelligent Creator (i.e., God). The Design Hypothesis is a potential explanation of the relevant facts: if true, it would account for the facts in question. How well-supported is the Design Hypothesis by the relevant evidence? Plausibly, the introduction of the Darwinian Hypothesis as a competitor in the nineteenth century significantly diminished the support enjoyed by the Design Hypothesis. That is, even if there had been no reason to prefer the Darwinian Hypothesis to the Design Hypothesis, the mere fact that the Design Hypothesis was no longer the only potential explanation in the field tends to erode (to some extent at least) how much credence the Design Hypothesis merits on the basis of the relevant considerations.

The general epistemological point was forcefully pressed by Hilary Putnam in the 1960s as a reason for doubting that Carnap's vision for inductive logic was a well-conceived research program. The relevant papers are collected in his *Mathematics, Matter and Method* (Cambridge, Cambridge University Press, 1975). A good discussion of the issue is John Earman, *Bayes or Bust* (Cambridge, MA, The MIT Press, 1992), chapter 7.

[24] Indeed, it might be argued that until the defender of the common consent argument offers some story about the *mechanism* by which the putative truth that God exists is grasped, she has not yet offered a genuine potential explanation of widespread belief in God. (According to this line of thought, to simply appeal to the putative fact that p, along with an unspecified ability of many individuals to somehow hit upon that truth is not yet to have offered a genuine potential explanation of why p is widely believed.) As a general matter, I believe that this demand for the specification of a mechanism is misplaced. After all, as is clear from the philosophy of mathematics, we do not currently possess a good story about the mechanism by which individuals recognize the fact that 2+2=4. Nevertheless, it seems that we can be reasonably confident that the correct explanation of why 2+2=4 is (almost) universally believed invokes or entails the fact that that proposition is true. That having been said, there is no question that the specification of a plausible mechanism for theistic belief would greatly strengthen the hand of a proponent of the argument. For a recent attempt, see Alvin Plantinga's *Warranted Christian Belief* (Oxford, Oxford University Press, 2000), which develops ideas he finds in Aquinas and Calvin.

Still, I believe that once things have reached the point of comparing competing hypotheses in this way, considerable ground has been conceded to a proponent of the common consent argument—perhaps more ground than a critic of the argument should feel comfortable conceding. At this point, the proponent of the argument is in a position to go on offense: he can raise doubts about the plausibility of the debunking explanation on offer, and attempt to provide independent reasons for thinking that it is false. If it is conceded that the *only* reason why the datum does not provide evidence for theistic belief is because there is some formidable competing explanation in the field, then to the extent that doubt is cast on that explanation on independent grounds, one's credence in the 'truth hypothesis'—and therefore, in the proposition that God exists—should increase accordingly.

Suppose that one does not have much confidence in any particular naturalistic explanation of theistic belief that has actually been proposed, or even in the disjunction of all such explanations that have been proposed thus far. (For what it is worth, this is the position in which I find myself.) How might one nevertheless resist the suggestion that the datum confirms the proposition that God exists? In the final section of the paper, I want to explore some strategies for minimizing the significance of the datum that do not depend on the availability of formidable naturalistic explanations of religious belief. The strategies that I consider here certainly do not exhaust the possible strategies that one might pursue, nor do I have anything particularly definitive to say about them. I focus on these strategies as opposed to others largely because I believe that each one raises deep and interesting philosophical issues.

4 Some strategies for minimizing the significance of the datum

(i) The datum is relatively insignificant, because the poorly informed/unenlightened/unsophisticated (etc.) are overrepresented among the theists.

The first line of response that I would like to consider proceeds from the correct observation that properly taking into account the opinions of others is not simply a matter of counting heads. Consider a possible norm of belief revision according to which what one should believe about a given question is determined by a kind of hypothetical vote among everyone in the world who has an opinion about that question. Such a radically egalitarian norm is clearly sub-optimal. Among its weaknesses is that it in effect enjoins us to throw out valuable information: with respect to a given question, we might know that some are in a better position to judge than others in virtue of being better informed, or for some other reason. To the extent that one has information that bears on comparative reliability, one should adjust the weight that one gives to the opinions of others accordingly.[25]

---

[25] And of course, this includes the possibility of giving zero or even negative weight to the views of some. (The last option will be appropriate in cases in which one has evidence that suggests that someone is an

Thus, someone attempting to minimize the significance of the datum might claim the following: even if believers greatly outnumber non-believers in absolute terms, the non-believers, considered as a group, are better informed, or more sophisticated, or enjoy some other cognitive advantage. (Presumably, many non-believers think exactly this.) Indeed, someone might very well think that the relevant disparities are sufficiently pronounced that, once opinions are properly weighted, taking into account the distribution of opinion bolsters the case for atheism as opposed to theism, and it is thus the non-believers who should take comfort in the numbers.

Of course, many theists would take issue with any such assumptions. Perhaps unsurprisingly, I will not attempt to say anything here about the respective intellectual merits of believers and non-believers as classes of people, or even whether such very general comparisons are sensible at all. Instead, I will emphasize an important but frequently neglected truth of epistemology that we should bear in mind when assessing strategies of this general kind.

The point is the following: in many cases, even if one knows with certainty that one is in a superior position to judge than another person—say, because one knows that one is better informed, and that one has responded to one's superior evidence impeccably—it is still rationally incumbent upon one to give significant weight to the other person's differing opinion and revise one's own view in response. Here is a toy example that makes the point cleanly:

THE URN: An urn contains a large number of marbles, some of which are black, the rest of which are white. You and I are charged with estimating the ratio of black to white balls in the urn; we base our estimates on observing draws with replacement. Before you enter the room, I observe ten draws and arrive at an estimate. I then leave the room; you enter, and observe the next six draws. Later, I discover that your estimate of the proportion of black marbles in the urn is significantly lower than mine.

In this case, it is uncontroversial that my estimate is significantly better informed than yours. Nevertheless, once I learn what you think, I should revise my estimate of the proportion of black balls downwards. (Certainly, it would be a mistake for me to stick to my guns on the grounds that you are in a worse position to make a judgment than I am, even though that much is clearly true.) Of course, inasmuch as my original estimate was better informed than yours, this should be reflected in my revised estimate, which should be closer to my original estimate than to yours. Notice, however, that as more people who have made at least partially non-overlapping observations weigh in, my own original estimate counts for less and less in determining what it is reasonable for me to believe. At some point, it will be swamped into insignificance, even if all of the other estimates are based on significantly worse evidence than mine.

<hr />

anti-expert with respect to a given domain. On the interesting phenomenon of anti-expertise, see Roy Sorensen, Blindspots (Oxford, Oxford University Press, 1988), pp. 386–97, and Andy Egan and Adam Elga, 'I Can't Believe I'm Stupid,' in John Hawthorne (ed.), Philosophical Perspectives, vol.19: Epistemology (Oxford, Blackwell Publishers, 2005), pp. 77–93.)

Significantly, the lesson that even the opinions of those who are in an objectively worse position to judge often make a difference, indeed a decisive difference, to what it is reasonable for one to believe generalizes far beyond such toy cases. In general, individuals are much more likely to defer to the opinions of perceived experts than to the cumulative judgments of large numbers of non-experts, even though the latter is frequently the better strategy (even in cases in which the perceived experts really are experts, in the sense that they are in a better position to judge than any individual member of the group of non-experts).[26]

At one time, the most popular program in the history of American television was the game show *Who Wants to be a Millionaire?* Contestants attempted to win a million dollars by answering a series of multiple choice questions in ascending order of difficulty. As an added wrinkle, contestants were also given a limited number of 'lifelines' or opportunities to consult other sources when their own judgment about a given question left them uncertain. One such lifeline consisted of the opportunity to poll the studio audience, a relatively large group of ordinary people. An alternative lifeline allowed the stumped contestant to 'phone a friend,' and ask an individual whom she had selected before the show as the person of her acquaintance most likely to correctly answer the kind of question that she would encounter. An interesting fact that soon became apparent to regular viewers of the show was this: in general, the strategy of polling the studio audience was vastly superior to the strategy of consulting the expert-friend.[27] For the typical contestant, deferring to the cumulative judgment of the random group was a better bet than deferring to the person she considered most trustworthy from among her circle of acquaintances.

The cumulative opinion of a large number of people often provides significant evidence even when it conflicts with the opinion held by a comparatively smaller group of people who are in a better position to judge. Thus, even on the supposition that non-believers outnumber believers among those who are best positioned to judge whether God exists, there is no straightforward inference from that supposition to the insignificance of the datum. Of course, there are obvious disanalogies between the case of religious belief and examples like URN and *Who Wants to Be a Millionaire?* Among the most important is this: in the latter cases, but not in the former, individuals arrive at their opinions *independently* of one another. Thus, in the case of the game show, members of the studio audience do not consult with one another (or anyone else) before registering their opinions; the opinion that emerges as dominant is thus the result of an independent convergence. Similarly, in cases like URN, it is assumed that everyone arrives at his original estimate on the basis of his own observations. However, that feature seems to be conspicuously absent in the case of religious belief. This suggests a second strategy for minimizing the significance of the datum.

---

[26] This is a main theme of James Surowiecki's *The Wisdom of Crowds* (New York, Doubleday, 2004), which provides much impressive evidence of the phenomenon.

[27] More exactly, the expert-friend had a roughly 65 percent accuracy ratio, while the studio audience chose the right answer 91 percent of the time. See Surowiecki, *The Wisdom of Crowds*, p. 4.

(ii) The datum is relatively insignificant, because the strong supermajority was not produced by independent convergence.

Recall our example from above: the fact that most of the group thinks that the correct answer is '138' is impressive evidence if each person arrived at that answer independently, but not if they did so by copying from a single member of the group. Indeed, in the latter case, the numbers count for nothing: the evidence supplied by the fact that many think that the answer is '138' is no stronger than the evidence provided by the fact that that was the answer arrived at by the individual from whom the others copied. More generally, impressive evidence that a given view is correct is afforded when a significant number of people independently converge on that view; on the other hand, the less their convergence is an independent matter, the less impressive it is as evidence.[28]

A critic might argue that this fact undermines the evidential value of the datum. Such a critic might very well concede that if billions of religious believers had arrived at their shared belief independently, this would be impressive evidence that it is true, but then point out that we know that nothing remotely like this actually occurred. In the case of the actual history of religious belief, what we find is not independent convergence but rather a convergence that is largely due to mutual influence and influence by common sources. In this respect, the case of religious belief is akin to a case in which students arrive at the same answer by copying from someone they trust. After all, no one thinks that the intellectual case for Islam would be any stronger if birthrates in Muslim countries had been twice as high in past decades as they actually were; nor would the case be any weaker if such birthrates had been significantly lower.

In my judgment, this is the best objection to the claim that the datum provides significant evidence for religious belief. I think that the proponent of the common consent argument should concede straightaway that the datum has significantly less evidential value than it would have had, had the same supermajority come about as a result of independent convergence. Indeed, classical proponents of the argument seemed to recognize the importance of independence, at least implicitly. For they often made much of the fact that something recognizable as religious belief was common not just among 'civilized peoples' but had also been discovered among relatively isolated populations.[29]

---

[28] On the importance and nature of independence, see especially the illuminating discussion in Alvin Goldman, 'Experts: Which Ones Should You Trust?' in *Philosophy and Phenomenological Research*, vol. 63 (2001), pp. 85–110.

As Hartry Field pointed out to me, the need to discount the numbers is not limited to cases in which there is causal dependence present, as in the examples considered above. If I know that two individuals will respond to given evidence in the same manner, then I should treat their having arrived at some particular answer as one piece of evidence, and not two pieces of evidence, in favor of that answer (even if their both having arrived at that answer is in no way underwritten by some causal link).

[29] This led to various heated controversies, among anthropologists and others, as to whether the populations in question really did believe in God, or whether this was a projection of those who had first 'discovered' them. For a flavor of this, see George Hayward Joyce, SJ, *Principles of Natural Theology* (New York, Longmans, Green, and Co.,1923), pp. 179–98.

I believe that this is generally the right approach for a defender of the argument to take: while conceding the importance of independence, and acknowledging the large role that dependence plays in the case of religious belief, she should resist the assimilation of the religious case to cases like that involving the copied answer. Here, in addition to emphasizing the significant measure of independence in the case of religious belief (a significant number of groups that were relatively isolated from one another nevertheless arrived at the same belief), the defender of the argument should also appeal to the impressive *persistence* of religious belief, without which the strong supermajority would not obtain. Even in cases in which individuals initially acquire some belief from a common source, there is for each person the possibility of later abandoning it in the light of subsequent experience or reflection. In the case of religious belief, however, sufficiently many individuals do *not* do this that the strong supermajority persists over time.[30]

Here we note one of the many places where, unsurprisingly, one's views about the significance of the datum will be influenced by one's views about the way in which religious convictions tend to be held. If one thinks, as some do, that religious believers are generally unreflective and uncritical (at least so far as their religious convictions are concerned), then one will be unimpressed with the fact that so many religious believers retain their religious beliefs once having acquired them. On this view, cases in which theistic belief is acquired early on in life and is thereafter retained are no more surprising than cases in which a schoolboy who copies an answer early on during an exam ultimately submits that same answer with the rest of his exam at the end of the period. On the other hand, if one takes a more charitable view of the way in which many religious believers hold their convictions, then the persistence of such belief does call out for explanation.

In this context, the defender of the argument should also point out that the traditional anti-theistic project of providing a fully naturalistic, debunking explanation of religious belief similarly seems to presuppose that there is something left over that calls out for explanation, even after all of the facts about belief dependence have been taken into account. In this respect, Marx, Freud, and the proponent of the common consent argument are bedfellows, albeit exceedingly strange ones. After all, if the

---

[30] Compare: it is extremely plausible that the best explanation of the fact that 2+2=4 is universally believed invokes the fact that this proposition is *obviously true*; here seems like a clear case in which an explanation that includes the truth of the proposition believed (however exactly that explanation is filled out) dominates those potential explanations that do not mention the truth of the proposition. However, notice that people do not typically learn even the most elementary truths of arithmetic autonomously; rather, they are taught such truths by parents, teachers, or others who already believe the truths in question. So in that sense, there is a significant lack of independence in this case as well. Nevertheless, the fact that people are originally taught elementary mathematical truths by authority figures does not account for why these truths continue to strike them as true. And here, it seems that no explanation that does not entail the fact that these claims *are* true could possibly be adequate to account their *seeming* true to so many people over time. My suggestion is that the proponent of the common consent argument should also appeal to the (admittedly much less impressive) persistence of religious belief as something that stands in need of explanation, and that is not accounted for by the fact that believers often acquire their beliefs from others who already hold them.

correct account of why 80 percent of the class came up with the same answer is simply that they copied that answer from a particular student, then there is obviously no need to provide an additional interesting story about why so many students found that answer so tempting or appealing. The same point holds in the case of religious belief: if lack of independence is enough to account for the distribution of opinion that we actually find, then there is no need to provide any additional interesting explanation in terms of wish fulfillment (Freud), consolation for the material hardships of this world (Marx), or truth (the proponent of the common consent argument).

(iii) The datum is actually false.

The most radical strategy for minimizing the significance of the datum is to simply deny that it is true: that is, one might simply deny that a strong supermajority of the world's population genuinely believes that God exists. More modestly, the critic of the argument might argue that we do not know whether the datum is true, or that we lack strong evidence to think that it is.

This might seem like an unpromising line of resistance. After all, that believers greatly outnumber non-believers is generally conceded by both camps, as well as by both those who find this putative fact depressing and those who find it cheering. Nevertheless, legitimate questions can certainly be raised about the quality of our grounds for supposing that this is the actual distribution of opinion. Here I have in mind not only the daunting practical difficulties inherent in any attempt to arrive at a reasonably accurate estimate of 'what the world thinks' about any question, or even the special difficulties that attach to this particular case (e.g. the fact that in many parts of the world, there will be extremely strong incentives for people to misrepresent their true views on this particular issue). Rather, I also have in mind certain more philosophically interesting reasons for doubt, reasons that would remain even if we knew with certainty that a strong supermajority of the world's population would sincerely profess religious belief if given the chance. Consider two such reasons for doubt.

First, I have taken for granted throughout this paper that (e.g.) devout Muslims and Christians, despite their deep theological differences, nevertheless share a particular belief that distinguishes them from atheists and agnostics. This assumption seems safe so long as we assume that 'God' (and its translations into other languages) functions semantically like an ordinary proper name. For on the best account of proper names that we possess, the reference of a name can be preserved even across radical differences in what is believed about the bearer of the name.[31] Thus, a Muslim might convert to Christianity (or vice versa) and in doing so change her theological beliefs radically, while nevertheless continuing to believe, of one and the same divine being, that it exists.[32]

---

[31] See Saul Kripke, *Naming and Necessity* (Cambridge, MA, Harvard University Press, 1980).

[32] Compare the way in which, on the Kripke–Putnam account of natural kind terms, a scientist can change her theory of the electron radically, while nonetheless continuing to refer to one and the same microphysical particle by using the word 'electron' throughout this process. After the scientist has come to accept the new theory, she will think that her past self held a radically false theory about the entity of which

However, Mark Johnston has recently argued, with a great deal of both philosophical and theological sophistication, that 'God' (as well as its standard translations into other languages) does not function semantically as a proper name.[33] Rather, 'God' functions as a descriptive proper name or abbreviated title, neither of which tolerates nearly as much in the way of mistaken belief when it comes to the determination of reference. The upshot of this picture is to render problematic the idea that devout members of very different religious traditions really do 'ultimately worship the same God,' or genuinely share some common belief in the deity. But to call this into question is to call into question the idea that atheists and agnostics lack some particular belief that the rest of the world shares.[34]

But let us set this possibility aside and simply assume the standard view according to which believing Christians, Muslims and Jews (etc.) share a common belief that they do not share with atheists and agnostics. Still, one might question just how common full-fledged theistic belief really is, even among those who would sincerely profess such belief. It is sometimes noted that, given what would seem to be the truly vast differences in world view between theists and atheists, many self-professed atheists and theists behave remarkably similarly in most contexts, including many contexts in which one would expect their putative differences to be manifest. Moreover, it is sometimes argued, with some plausibility, that in many such contexts (e.g., funerals) the behavior exhibited by members of both camps more closely resembles the behavior that one would have expected (at least a priori) from an atheist as opposed to a theist. One might try to leverage these facts in an argument that, for all we know, genuine belief in God is much less common than is ordinarily supposed, even among those who would sincerely avow such belief. One who presses this line of thought can correctly point out that, even though the fact that an individual sincerely avows p is excellent evidence that she believes p, it is nonetheless defeasible evidence, and certainly does not exhaust the considerations that are relevant to whether we are justified in attributing that belief to her. He will then claim that, in the case of theistic belief, we often enough *do* have grounds for not attributing full-fledged belief in God, even to those who would sincerely profess such belief.[35]

At first glance, this line of thought might seem no more plausible than that advanced by those mad-dog defenders of the common consent argument who insisted that belief

she now has a true (or at least, better) theory; she will *not* think that her past self held a theory about something else, or nothing at all. Similarly, the religious convert, viewing things from the perspective of her new theological commitments, will think that her past theological commitments amounted to a radically false theory of the same person or entity of which she now has a better theory.

[33] See his *Saving God: Religion After Idolatry* (Princeton, NJ, Princeton University Press, 2009).

[34] As Johnston puts it: 'Believing in God is not a mere psychological state. It is more akin to an achievement... That is why belief in God may be a much rarer thing than has been almost universally supposed' (*Saving God*, pp. 29–30).

[35] For a recent, particularly lively presentation of the kind of doubt at issue here, see Georges Rey, 'Does Anyone Really Believe in God?' in D. Kolak and R. Martin (eds.), *Experience of Philosophy*, 6th edn (Oxford, Oxford University Press, 2006), pp. 335–53.

in God really is universal, and that individuals who sincerely profess not to believe in God are self-deceived. However, the current line of thought is significantly more plausible than the latter. For the mad-dog defender of universal belief in God insists that *anyone* who sincerely professes atheism or agnosticism has a false belief about whether she believes in God. On the other hand, the proponent of the current line of thought insists, not that everyone who takes himself to be theist has a false belief about whether he believes in God, but only that the phenomenon is common enough to render the datum false. It is, of course, compatible with this hypothesis that there are some—indeed, many millions—of full-fledged believers.

For my part, I am inclined to believe that the datum is true, and that neither of the considerations raised in this section should lead us to abandon it. Nevertheless, I also believe that an adequate treatment of these issues would inevitably require the resolution of quite subtle questions in the theories of reference and belief attribution. If that is correct, then fully getting to the bottom of the common consent argument might very well require further inquiry, not only in epistemology, but also in the philosophies of language and mind.[36]

[36] An earlier version of this paper was presented at a joint Princeton–Rutgers philosophy of religion workshop in the Spring of 2008. I am grateful to the audience present on that occasion for feedback, to Dan Garber and Dean Zimmerman for organizing the workshop and inviting me to speak at it, and to the Departments of Philosophy and Religion at Princeton, the Rutgers Philosophy Department, and the Princeton Theological Seminary for their sponsorship of the event. Finally, I would like to thank Kelly Clark and Ray VanArragon for the invitation to write up those thoughts for the present volume.

9

Morality and Happiness

Kelly James Clark and Andrew Samuel

1 Introduction

In Dostoevski's *The Brothers Karamazov*, Smerdyakov claims 'If God does not exist, everything is permitted.' This quotation has often been taken to imply Dostoevski's belief that morality is essentially dependent upon God; hence, if there is no God, then there is no right or wrong and everyone may do whatever they please. But Dostoevski may have had something different in mind. He may have meant that if God does not exist, human beings will lose their motivation to be moral. Remove the divine judge and human beings will simply do as they please. There is an objective moral standard, on this construal, but there is no motivating reason to abide by it.

On this construal of Dostoevski's famous phrase, the perennial problem of morality comes into focus: Why Be Moral? If one can be immoral and get away with it (i.e., avoid punishment), is one more likely to be happy? Is morality an obstacle to human happiness and contrary to the satisfaction of human desire? Is it in our best interest to be moral?

Current social contract theorists offer well-developed answers to the question 'Why Be Moral?'[1] According to social contract theories of morality, right and wrong are constituted by the agreement among rationally self-interested individuals to give up the unhindered pursuit of their own desires and interests for the security of living in peace with one another. In order to secure this peace, one willingly forgoes the liberty of total self-determination and takes on the constraints of conventional morality. It is in my best interest, so the argument goes, to have my desires constrained by entering into a society where the desires of everyone are constrained by an agreed upon power.

We shall argue that the social contract theory is motivationally deficient and that theism provides a better motivation for rationally self-interested persons to be moral. We shall defend rational belief in a post-mortem life within a community similar to

---

[1] Recent defenders of social contract theories of morality include Kurt Baier, *The Moral Point of View: A Rational Basis of Ethics* (Ithaca, NY, Cornell University Press, 1958) and David Gauthier, *Morals By Agreement* (New York, Oxford University Press, 1986).

Kant's kingdom of ends. The temporary squelching of desire required by morality makes sense, we shall argue, only if the moral project continues into the next life.

In this essay we shall make (at least) one undefended assumption: That we are rational, self-interested persons. The assumption that humans are self-interested is one of the better attested theories of human nature. The commitment to rationality, on the other hand, is simply an ideal, for we often behave in a less than rational manner; but our arguments are directed toward what is in our *rational* self-interest; that is, what would be in our best interest if we were fully rational. We define rationality in the sense that Gauthier defines it as doing one's best to fulfill one's preferences. A rational being, on this construal, is a self-interest maximizer.

Let us first consider the problem 'Why Be Moral?'

2 The moral problem

In Plato's *Republic*, Thrasymachus claims: 'Justice is really the good of another.... They [i.e., the just] make the one they serve happy, but themselves not at all' (Grube/Reeve 343c). Justice is really another's good and for the inferior who obeys it is a personal injury; it makes the other happy, but not oneself. Morality, Thrasymachus argues, is an obstacle to human happiness as it runs contrary to the satisfaction of our desires and interests. Consider the demands of justice to see whose interests are protected. Suppose I see Gordon's wallet on the table with $1,000 inside. I need $1,000 and consider stealing it. Assume that I can easily steal it and get away with it. Whose interests are protected by morality in this instance? Gordon's, not mine. In this instance, morality is *his* good, not mine. Suppose I get angry at Mary and wish to strike her on the nose. Assume I can punch her with impunity. Again, whose interests are protected by morality in this instance? Hers, not mine. Examples abound: we ought to keep promises, tell the truth, be faithful to our spouses, avoid murdering others, etc. According to Thrasymachus, morality only protects the interests of the other and is not in my own interest. Of course, if one is unjust, gets caught and is adequately punished, it is not to one's advantage. So the most powerful person is the one clever enough to conceal her injustice, perhaps under the guise of justice, and get away with it. Justice is, of course, in *my* interest when Gordon wishes to steal my wallet and Mary wishes to punch my nose. Thrasymachus's point seems to be that when I am under obligation to behave morally, that is from the perspective of the person performing the action, it is the interests of the other that are protected and not my own.

Since our intention is to compare the motivational force of theistic and non-theistic moral theories, we need to understand the kinds of goods that are attainable on either theory. The goods attainable by a non-theistic moral theory, that is, the goods attainable on the assumption of metaphysical naturalism, are, so far as we can tell, restricted to what we shall call, rather cumbersomely and archaically, 'this-worldly goods':

(1) A good is this-worldly if and only if it is a good that can be attained *ante-mortem* such as pleasure and avoidance of pain, and whatever human desire-satisfaction and happiness are attainable in life.

The goods that are attainable if theism is true include both this-worldly goods and what we shall call, admittedly quaintly, 'other-worldly goods':

(2) A good is other-worldly if and only if it is a good that can be attained *post-mortem* such as complete pleasure and avoidance of pain, total satisfaction of desire, full human happiness, and moral perfection.

Corresponding definitions could be offered of this- and other-worldly evils. If, as naturalism presupposes, post-mortem existence is untenable, we are restricted in our attainment of goods—only this-worldly goods are available to us. According to theism, however, both this- and other-worldly goods are available to us.

The problem 'Why Be Moral?' looms large: morality appears, at first glance, to be designed to favor the protection of the this-worldly goods of the other and not of me. It is sometimes not in my this-worldly interest for me to be moral. In terms of this-worldly desire satisfaction, essential to the attainment of this-worldly human happiness, morality seems to favor the satisfaction of the desires of others and to constrain my own personal satisfaction. How might the social contract theory motivate us, given these temptations to immorality, to be moral?

3 Social contract theories of morality

The social contract theorist argues that it is in my best interest to agree to live in a society which enforces morality. Society protects the rights and interests of its members with both the threat and manifestation of force. Outside of society, that is, in the state of nature, where sufficient power is lacking to force people to respect the interests of others, life is chaotic, life expectancy is radically uncertain, and the prospects for the enjoyment of one's own projects are dim. So it is in my best interest to leave this state of nature, to give up my claim, primarily to total self-determination, and to abide by the conventional standards of morality which constrain my desires.

This much seems obvious—it is better to leave the state of nature, under specified conditions, than to remain in it given that in the state of nature the prospect of being able to satisfy my desires is precarious. The executive power in a civil society creates a situation where my life and what is left of my liberty are sufficiently protected from the wiles of other selfish creatures to permit at least the modest pursuit of happiness. It is vastly preferable for rationally self-interested persons to leave the state of nature where their pursuit of happiness is unhindered but also unprotected and to give up certain rights to secure at least a modicum of happiness.

But has the naturalist social contract theorist adequately answered the question 'Why Be Moral?' It is clearly in my best interest to live in a society which embraces conventional morality and also protects its members from offenders who violate the moral standards and harm its citizens. But Thrasymachus's challenge remains: Why not be immoral in such a society, if one can get away with it?

Those who enter into the social contract are faced with decisions to abide by morality or defect from morality. Presumably, defectors will selectively abide and occasionally defect. Will complete moral compliance or selective defection conduce to the this-worldly satisfaction of human desires?[2] Abiding by morality will satisfy one's desires only on the assumption that most people with whom one deals also abide by morality. If others do not abide by morality and one does, then the likelihood of being taken advantage of, and having one's own desires regularly thwarted, is maximized. As Thomas Hobbes writes:

He that would be modeste and tractable and perform all the promises in such time and place where no man els should do so, should but make himself prey to others, and procure his own ruin, contrary to all Laws of Nature, which tend to Nature's preservation.[3]

But even if everyone else were moral, would abiding by morality be the most likely way of attaining this-worldly human happiness? If Thrasymachus is right, morality constrains the satisfaction of my desires and correspondingly protects the interests of others. The best situation of all, if we are restricted to this-worldly goods, would be to defect from morality where we can get away with it. One might add the additional proviso that the maximally best situation, if restricted to this-worldly goods, is to be selectively immoral and get away with it where I can in a society of people who are moral, that is, within a society of people who abide by the social contract. For they will abide by a standard of morality which ensures the protection of my interests and I will be acting immorally where I can, that is, in ways that conduce to my this-worldly interests as well. My immorality and their corresponding morality ensure the maximal satisfaction of my this-worldly desires.[4]

4 Gauthier's defense

David Gauthier, a contractarian in morality, attempts to rebut this argument with appeal to only this-worldly goods; he does so by resolving the following paradox: 'Duty overrides advantage, but the acceptance of duty is truly advantageous.'[5] He frames the social contract paradox in a prisoner's dilemma situation where acting

---

[2]   This is more properly conceived of in terms of strategies and outcomes. The strategies will be to abide by or violate conventional morality and the outcomes may not be simply up to the individual. Which outcome obtains will depend in part on the way the world is.

[3]   *Leviathan*, chapter 15.

[4]   Here our argument extends George Mavrodes' argument in 'Religion and the Queerness of Morality,' in Robert Audi and William Wainwright (eds.), *Rationality, Religious Belief and Moral Commitment* (Ithaca and London, Cornell University Press, 1986), pp. 213–26.

[5]   David Gauthier, *Morals By Agreement* (Oxford, Clarendon Press, 1986), p. 2.

Player 1

		Cooperate	Defect
Player 2	Cooperate	6, 6	0, 10
	Defect	10, 0	4, 4

Figure 9.1

ethically (or abiding by the social contract) consists of 'cooperating' with other players even when it is not in one's self-interest to do so. In Figure 9.1 each player can choose to cooperate or defect. If both choose to cooperate, society's total payoff can be maximized (at 12 units). Thus, societies that abide by the social contract increase their total payoffs. The paradox exists because the commitment to cooperate is not individually rational. Either player can *unilaterally defect* and increase their own personal payoff at the expense of society. Thus, both players will defect and will achieve the worst possible outcome for themselves and for society (4 units each). Gauthier argues that individuals will prefer to live in a society where everyone cooperates and conforms to the social contract because it increases both their and society's payoff. Therefore, he argues that any rational person will choose a society in which all individuals conform to the social contract. His framework implicitly assumes the standard model of rational choice, where fully-informed individuals rank choices according to the ante-mortem benefit (or happiness) associated with each alternative. In the absence of morality rational, self-interested individuals will always defect because it produces a higher payoff *irrespective of the other players' choices*. However, according to Gauthier, rational individuals will choose to conform to society's moral norms because they know (or believe) that doing so will provide them with higher ante-mortem benefit.

Before considering Gauthier's argument more closely, it is important to clarify a common misunderstanding regarding prisoner's dilemma games. It is often pointed out that when PD games are repeated, the cooperative outcome (*cooperate, cooperate*) can be sustained because players can use future rounds of the game to punish each other.[6] For example, the two players may meet beforehand and make the following arrangement: 'We will each cooperate as long as the other player also cooperates. However, if one of us cheats by defecting, the other will "punish" the defector by defecting in every period thereafter.' Under this agreement, the threat of future defection serves as a credible punishment mechanism. Therefore, for each player the payoffs from defection (and the resulting cost of punishment) are lower than the payoffs from cooperation. Consequently, the cooperative outcome (*cooperate, cooperate*) can be sustained in equilibrium.

---

[6] Robert Axelrod, *The Evolution of Cooperation* (New York, Basic Books, 1984).

Since real societies frequently involve repeated interactions, it has been argued that repeated interactions solve the prisoner's dilemma.[7] However, there are two important caveats to this 'solution' to the prisoner's dilemma. First, for repeated interaction to sustain cooperation, the game must be played infinitely. To see why this must be so, consider the very last round of a finitely repeated prisoner's dilemma. In the ultimate round of the game, defection is no longer punishable because there is no future round in which to punish the defector. Therefore, both players know that (*defect, defect*) is the only rational outcome in the ultimate round. However, this implies that the ultimate round no longer serves as an effective means of punishment for the penultimate round. Consequently, in the penultimate round players will not have any incentive to cooperate. By applying recursive logic, it follows that players will never have any reason to cooperate—even in the first round! Thus, for repeated prisoner's dilemma to solve this dilemma, it must be repeated infinitely.

More importantly, however, the claim that '(infinitely) repeated PD solves the prisoner's dilemma is based on the following logical fallacy: an infinitely repeated PD is not isomorphic to a one-shot PD game; therefore, the insights (or results) from an infinitely repeated PD cannot be applied to a one-shot PD. In fact, in contrast to a one-shot PD, in a repeated PD, when players agree to punish each other's defection by defecting in every future round of the game, the payoffs from cooperating are higher than the payoffs for defecting (for both players).[8] Therefore, once 'prisoner's dilemma' is repeated infinitely, *there is no longer any dilemma to be solved!* Repeated prisoner's dilemma, therefore, does not solve the original dilemma, it simply removes the dilemma. In order to provide a solution, one needs to understand why people may choose to cooperate *in one-shot games*, even when there is no threat of future punishment. Therefore, if Gauthier's approach attempts to solve a genuine dilemma, he must be understood to be referring to the one-shot PD game.[9]

The problem is not one of initially accepting the social contract—it is surely better for one to live within a society in which the pursuit of individual interest is constrained by standards of justice and morality (enforced by a sufficient power). So it is more rational for self-interested persons to join a society than to remain in the state of nature. Furthermore, one's insufficiency at satisfying one's needs entirely on one's own will make it doubly rational to seek society for the mutual and maximal satisfaction of human needs. Rationality is, according to Gauthier, self-interest maximizing: 'the rational person seeks the greatest satisfaction of her own interests.'[10] Hence, the joining of a civil society is rational. The question is whether or not it is rational to violate, or in Gauthier's terms to 'defect from,' that contract when one can get away with it without

---

[7] Another way of saying this is that people's desire to build a good reputation enforces cooperation.

[8] Technically, cooperation is a dominant strategy as long as players care sufficiently about the future.

[9] For a complete discussion of Gauthier's game-theoretic problems, see Ken Binmore, *Game Theory and the Social Contract*, Vol 1 (Cambridge, MIT Press, 1992).

[10] Gauthier, p. 7.

causing the breakdown of society. In order to prevent defections, Gauthier argues that we must cultivate the disposition not to ask ourselves on each occasion 'Does this maximize my interest?' The Straight Maximizer is the person who asks such questions and seeks to maximize personal utility in every decision. If one were so to do, one would surely see that, on certain and perhaps many occasions, it is not in one's best interest to be moral. Gauthier believes that adopting such a disposition is rational because people can tell if one is sincere in one's commitment to the social contract. If people adjudge that one is not sincere, one will not gain the cooperative benefits that drove one to rationally affirm the social contract in the first place. Rationality requires, therefore, the development of the disposition of 'Constrained Maximality.'

5 Gauthier critiqued

The development of such a disposition, 'Constrained Maximality,' in the face of the evidence that morality is sometimes not in our own best interest would require systematic and massive self-deception. A procedure that crucially relies on self-deception is surely not epistemically rational, but is it Gauthier-rational? Is it rational in the sense of maximizing self-interest? Let us pursue this question in the succeeding paragraphs.

Because of the difficulty to tell when someone is insincere in one's commitment to the social contract, one can occasionally violate it without loss of cooperative benefits. Gauthier concedes that 'the ability to detect the dispositions of others must be well developed in a rational CM [constrained maximizer]. Failure to develop this ability, or neglect of its exercise, will preclude one from benefiting from constrained maximization.'[11] While Gauthier does recognize the problems that arise from the inability to detect the dispositions of others, he does not realize the extent to which it undermines his project. To illustrate this issue, consider a population with two types of individuals, CMs and Straight Maximizers (SMs). If CMs and SMs were easily identifiable, then there would be no problem with Gauthier's argument. CMs would only interact with each other, would always cooperate, and would receive a higher ante-mortem payoff from their commitment to the social contract (as in Figure 9.1). However, within this framework there are incentives for SMs to become crafty maximizers; straight maximizers who develop a disposition to appear sincere while violating the social contract. These crafty SMs will be able to enjoy the benefits of participating in a society that, for the most part, abides by the social contract without having to pay the costs associated with being a CM. Therefore, crafty SMs will outwit CMs and CMs will receive fewer ante-mortem goods from conforming to the social contract.

This issue is exacerbated by the fact that, in reality, these sincere dispositions are typically observed by noticing emotional cues or signals that are not very precise. This issue is worth examining more formally. Consider a population with two types of

---

[11] Gauthier, p. 181.

individuals: SMs (who may be crafty SMs) and CMs who are sincerely committed to the social contract. In this population an individual may be genuinely sincere (a CM), denoted by $I = 1$, or insincere (an SM), denoted by $I = 0$. By extension, the probability $P(I = 1)$ denotes the fraction of the total population that is sincere. It is also the likelihood that a randomly drawn individual from the population is a sincere CM. Similarly, the probability $P(I = 0)$ represents the likelihood that a randomly drawn individual from the population is an SM. Individuals signal their true motives (or types) using emotional dispositions. We let $S = 1$ denote a sincere signal and $S = 0$ denote an insincere signal. These signals are not precise but are correlated with a person's true motives and can be represented as conditional probabilities:

$$P(S = 1|I = 1) = \alpha$$
$$P(S = 1|I = 0) = \beta$$

The first conditional probability, α, represents the ability of sincere individuals ($I = 1$ types) to send a signal $S = 1$. The second probability, β, captures the presence of crafty maximizers; it is the probability of receiving a sincere signal ($S = 1$) from an insincere individual ($I = 0$ type). It can be interpreted, more generally, as a measure of the cost of mimicking a sincere CM. When the value of β is small or close to zero, the cost of mimicking sincerity is prohibitively expensive; insincere individuals find it difficult to send a sincere signal and be crafty SMs. Whereas, when β is large, sincerity is 'cheap'; insincere individuals can easily fake sincerity.

When both sincere CMs and SMs can send out sincere signals ($S = 1$), the signal becomes an imprecise indicator of a person's true type. The precision of a sincerity signal is the likelihood (or the probability) that a person is a sincere CM given that one has just observed them send out a signal $S = 1$. Formally, this precision is the conditional probability: Using Bayes' rule this probability is:

$$P(I = 1|S = 1)$$

$$P(I = 1|S = 1) = \frac{\alpha P(I = 1)}{\alpha P(I = 1) + \beta P(I = 0)}$$

It represents the likelihood that a person is a sincere CM type ($I = 1$), given that that person has sent out a sincere signal ($S = 1$). When this conditional probability is close to 1, the sincerity signal is precise, whereas when it is close to 0 the signal is imprecise. Two issues are worth noting in this context. First, the precision of this signal does not depend on the value of α alone. Even if sincere individuals were perfectly capable of sending a sincere signal all the time (i.e. when $\alpha = 1$), the precision of the signal $P(I = 1|S = 1)$ may still be quite small. For example, when β is large and the proportion of SMs, $P(I = 0)$, is large the precision may be quite low even with $\alpha = 1$. Second, when β is 0 the cost of mimicking sincerity is prohibitively expensive and SM's ($I = 0$ types) will not be able to send out a signal $S = 1$. In this case the precision of the sincerity signal may be close to 1 *even when α is small.* In this case one can be reasonably certain that the person sending a signal $S = 1$ is sincere. Thus, the precision of the sincerity signal does not depend only on the value of α but also on the value of β and on the proportion of insincere types ($I = 0$ types). As β increases (i.e. the costs of mimicking sincerity fall), the above probability decreases and the signal $S = 1$ becomes a less precise indicator of a person's sincerity. Similarly, as the proportion of insincere types increases, the probability of encountering such a person, $P(I = 0)$, also increases and the precision of the sincerity signal is lowered. Thus, this sincerity signal can become quite imprecise when the proportion of insincere types is large ($P(I = 0)$ increases), or because they become increasingly adept at mimicking the signal (β falls).

Herein lies Gauthier's problem: when insincere maximizers can mimic the signal $S = 1$, they automatically lower the precision of even those signals originating from *genuinely* sincere CMs. Thus, a crafty SM places an additional burden on a sincere CM's ability to prove his or her own sincerity. If CMs find it hard to detect genuine sincerity, their ante-mortem benefits from entering into the social contract will diminish significantly.[12] Furthermore, even if these conditions are satisfied initially, CMs are likely to enter the social contract only if they can be sure that crafty SMs will not mimic their signals *at some point in the future.* Therefore, for Gauthier's argument to hold, he must be able to show that β will always remain small and that there will always be a very small proportion of crafty SMs ($P(S = 0)$ is small).[13] However, there is nothing within Gauthier's framework that can ensure that both of the above conditions will always be satisfied.[14]

Societies like America, where people usually obey but occasionally violate the social contract, are relatively stable and provide the best state of affairs for the satisfaction of the crafty and powerful straight maximizer. If one were in the initial position—ignorant of one's potentialities—then one would rationally will to develop the disposition not to ask the question 'Is this in my interest?' But we are not in the original position when making characterological choices and if we reasonably assess that our interests will be maximized by occasional defections from the social contract then we would reasonably develop the disposition to appear sincere when we are not (we can fool people and violate the social contract with impunity). So Gauthier hasn't resolved the paradox because he must concede that it is often not

---

[12] Since the CM's decision to enter the social contract is conditional upon his or her ability to detect sincerity.

[13] These dispositions can also be manipulated quite easily. Recent research in Neuroeconomics has shown that the neuroactive hormone oxytocin can facilitate trust between strangers. For example, when this hormone is introduced to subjects they naively cooperate in prisoner's dilemma games.

[14] In fact, it is conceivable that within an evolutionary game-theoretic framework, β will increase over time. For example, consider a population starts out with a small β and a small proportion of SMs Gauthier's framework may work initially. However, there will be evolutionary advantage for this small proportion of SMs to develop better mechanisms to fake sincerity. Since, they will frequently encounter sincere CMs, they will gain at their expense and may reproduce faster.

really in one's own interest to be moral (one has simply dispositionally repressed the question).[15]

A second problem, and one that is particularly relevant to the thesis of this paper, is that moral motivations in Gauthier's framework are driven entirely by the ante-mortem gains associated with conforming to the social contract. The problem with this approach is that, since Gauthier appeals only to ante-mortem gains (or losses), the value of any decision is always measured in terms of its ante-mortem benefits. When the value of all choices have a common measure, however, all decisions (and the value of their consequences) are fundamentally commensurate. Hence, any choice and its consequence, whether ethically relevant or irrelevant, will be commensurate with the value of any other choice. Consequently, even a constrained maximizer will violate the social contract whenever the benefits received from that violation are sufficiently large. For example, consider the decision of a constrained maximizer who is faced with the choice of deciding whether to return a lost wallet (with a large amount of money inside). Within Gauthier's framework, since all gains are ante-mortem, even the sincere constrained maximizer may violate the social contract if the money inside the wallet is sufficiently large, because she will simply trade (or exchange) one ante-mortem benefit (the money) for the ante-mortem benefits associated with conforming to the social contract. Therefore, if all choices, regardless of their ethical implications, are valued according to ante-mortem gains, then there is, in principle, a dollar value or price for every moral act. Hence, in Gauthier's framework, even a constrained maximizer who is paid a sufficiently large sum of money will violate the social contract.[16]

If we are restricted to this-worldly goods, then we are most likely to attain them if we endorse and live in a society of individuals that abide by the social contract yet do all that we can to violate it with impunity. Social contract theories, therefore, have a serious motivational problem: The social contract is insufficient to motivate rationally self-interested people to be moral.

The principal motivational defect of social contract theories is clear: If we are restricted to goods attainable in this earthly life, it is not always in my best interest to be moral. It may be in my best interest to lie, cheat or steal (if I can get away with it), if there is no next life with which to contend. If only this-worldly goods are available to us, then morality will surely be perceived as an obstacle. This is not hard to see with moral demands which are so severe that no this-worldly good could accrue to oneself from their performance—the giving up of one's life for one's child, say, or a

---

[15] The literature on Gauthier's views is vast. For other critiques of his defense of constrained maximization see Peter Danielson, 'Closing the compliance dilemma: How it's rational to be moral in a Lamarckian world' in Peter Vallentyne (ed.), *Contractarianism and Rational Choice* (New York, Cambridge University Press, 1991), pp. 291–322; Maarten Franssen, 'Constrained Maximization Reconsidered . . . ,' *Synthese* 101, 2, Nov. 1994, pp. 249–72; and J. Howard Sobel, 'Straight Versus Constrained Maximizers,' *Canadian Journal of Philosophy* 23, 1, Mar. 1993, pp. 25–54.

[16] A further question that one might ask Gauthier here is whether he would be willing to accept a moral system that places a price on moral action.

lifetime of sacrifice for one's severely mentally retarded child, or remaining in a deeply troubled marriage for the sake of one's children, or speaking up when someone else is falsely blamed even when assuming responsibility may prove costly to oneself. Even less demanding duties—to declare all of one's income on one's tax returns, not to overbill to cover one's deductible when making a claim for damages to one's insurance company, or not to exceed the speed limit or run a red light in one's car while running late for an important meeting, or to return the extra money that the salesperson mistakenly gave you for change—are often contrary to one's own good (assuming one can violate these duties with impunity).

6 Defective theistic solutions

How might the theist answer the question 'Why Be Moral?' One reply is that morality is properly motivated by fear of eternal punishment and desire for eternal bliss. God sees all that we do, judges justly, and will punish us in the eternal fires if we are wicked or reward us with eternal bliss if we are righteous. While this may be true and should motivate rationally self-interested persons to be moral, such motivation is selfish and morally inadequate. It is not difficult to see the moral defectiveness of such a motivation. One might behave in a manner that is perceived as kind, self-sacrificial, patient or generous; but one's motive is invidiously selfish if one's desire is only for the good of one's self. Just as we would properly judge as base the person who is generous simply to gain a good reputation or a public office, so too we would properly judge as base the person who is moral simply to gain God's favor or eternal bliss. The other, who has indeed benefited from such actions, has been used as a mere tool, simply the means to an end. Selfishness debases apparently other-regarding actions and diminishes the moral value of such actions. The demands of the moral life include not only other-regarding behavior but also the proper concern, desire, or feelings for the other.[17]

So we will assume the obvious: that bringing post-mortem punishments and rewards into play would rationally motivate morality. But moral motivation cannot lie simply or even chiefly in the offer of the greatest reward or avoidance of the worst punishment. To do so reduces moral motivation to selfishness. We will, therefore look at motivating morality from a more thoroughly Christian perspective. This moves us away from the thin conception of human motivation (and hence of the moral life)

---

[17] Kant's more nuanced view is that while our primary motive for action is duty to others we nonetheless have duties for our own happiness. Kant's intention in the preceding quotation is simply to isolate the primary and most important motivation to act morally for everyone in every situation—to heed the call of duty, regardless of one's desire for happiness. Here is another way to clarify Kant's apparently severe point about duty vs. inclination. Human beings are a curious admixture of inclination and duty. We have a sense of obligation but we are also creatures of need. In the good person, which is subordinate to which? It is clear in Kant: in the person of good will, inclinations and desires are subordinate to their sense of duty (and vice versa for the wicked person). Kant is not opposed to inclination or desire, but he is interested in understanding the proper order of motivations in the good person. Kant so fears the intrusion of the 'dear self' into our moral deliberations that appeals to self-interest are entirely inappropriate to the motivation of the moral life.

assumed by social contract theorists and its assumption of commensurate goods. We shall treat some goods as more morally salient or valuable than others.[18]

7 Preference hierarchies and post-mortem goods

There may yet be ways to consider how morality is good for us without degenerating into selfishness. Rational agents will conform to the moral law, even when the ante-mortem costs from doing so are large, if they ascertain that the gains from acting ethically are somehow incommensurate with any ante-mortem benefits (or costs) associated with ethical action. This condition is necessary because, as we have seen earlier, ethical decisions that are evaluated according to their ante-mortem gain may be exchanged for alternatives that provide greater ante-mortem gains. However, if the measure of value of acting ethically is incommensurate with any other ante-mortem gains, then individuals will remain committed to the social contract even when there are no obvious ante-mortem gains.

An obvious source of a measure of value that is incommensurate with ante-mortem motivations is a measure that is based on the post-mortem gains associated with a choice. Post-mortem gains, particularly within a Judeo-Christian theistic framework, will presumably be incommensurable with the ante-mortem gains of an action. A theist will regard her duty towards the post-mortem goals above her desire to satisfy her ante-mortem desires. Therefore, individuals who evaluate moral choices according to their post-mortem gains will act ethically even when the ante-mortem costs from doing so are large. Thus, theism can motivate the moral life by providing individuals with the motivation to live a virtuous life, even at the expense of losing ante-mortem satisfaction.

A formal way to capture this incommensurability is to introduce a hierarchy of preferences to represent an individual's decision process. Moral individuals within this framework use two sets of preference rankings to evaluate choices and make decisions. They first evaluate alternative choices according to an 'ethical preference ranking' that represents the post-mortem benefits associated with each choice, and only afterwards evaluate the alternatives according to their ante-mortem benefits. In this approach, ethical preferences take hierarchical precedence over ante-mortem preferences and, therefore, take priority over ante-mortem preferences in the decision making process. The ante-mortem consequences of an act are considered only after the decision has been evaluated according to its post-mortem or ethical preference ranking.

There are two implications that are worth noting in this context. First, the post-mortem ranking acts as a constraint on the ante-mortem ranking only when there is a

---

[18] Here we are making a Pascalian move. While Pascal's wager, if successful, would show that it is in one's best interest to believe (wager) that God exists, Pascal does not believe that such a selfish calculation is a fit basis for true faith. So he entices the unbeliever into seeing that faith in God is to his advantage with the hope of moving the unbeliever into true faith which involves love of God for its own sake and for his benefit. So, too, we shall argue that game theoretical decisions can demonstrate that it is in one's best interest to be moral, but true virtue involves love of the other for their own sake and also for one's own sake.

conflict between the two rankings. Consider a moral individual who finds a wallet full of money on a deserted street. According to the ante-mortem ranking the person must keep the money, but according to the ethical preference ranking the person must return the wallet. A moral individual in this instance will first consider the rightness or wrongness of his act by evaluating it according to his ethical preference ranking *and afterwards* evaluate his decision according to the ante-mortem ranking.[19] Thus, the higher-level ethical ranking acts as 'meta-ranking' that can constrain lower-level choices. Second, in situations where the post-mortem ranking is not inconsistent with the ante-mortem ranking, the post-mortem ranking becomes irrelevant. Thus, for example, if the person recognizes that the wallet belongs to a close friend (from whom he, presumably, would not steal), then his ante-mortem ranking would not be in conflict with his ethical preference ranking and, therefore, it places no constraint on his choices. This will also be true if the wallet happened to be empty, since there would be, effectively, no ante-mortem reason to steal the wallet. Hence, in one sense a person's duty or 'pursuit of virtue' constrains the choices that are driven by the ante-mortem inclinations of an individual, when those inclinations conflict with duty.

The above model provides a rational, consistent framework to understand moral choices when dutiful and selfish inclinations conflict. Within this framework an individual who believes in the reality of a post-mortem world will find it perfectly rational to conform to the moral law even when: (1) the ante-mortem benefits of defection are large and (2) there are large numbers of straight maximizers in society.

This model of hierarchical preferences is consistent with Kant's view of morality in which 'the good maxim is where one puts duty first and happiness second.' Kant writes that:

The distinction between a good man and one who is evil cannot lie in the differences between the incentives which they adopt into their maxim (not in the content of their maxim) but rather must depend upon subordination (the form of the maxim), i.e., which of the two incentives he makes the condition of the other. Consequently man (even the best) is evil only in that he reverses the moral order of the incentives when he adopts them into his maxim. He adopts, indeed, the moral law along with the law of self-love; yet when he becomes aware that they cannot remain on a par with each other but that one must be subordinated to the other as its supreme condition, he makes the incentive of self-love and its inclinations the condition of obedience to the moral law; whereas, on the contrary, the latter, as the supreme condition of the satisfaction of the former, ought to have been adopted into the universal maxim of the will as the sole incentive. (Kant, *Religion Within the Bounds of Reason Alone*, translated by Theodore M. Greene and Hoyt H. Hudson (New York, Harper and Brothers, 1960), pp. 31–2)

Kant appears to be concerned with the order of incentives; that is, whether it is proper to pursue one's happiness, if one primarily pursues one's duty. Our framework of hierarchical preferences shows that rational individuals (who are also virtuous) can be

---

[19] The decision making process in this model is thus sequential; individuals first evaluate choices according to their post-mortem values and only afterwards allow their ante-mortem values to influence their decision.

motivated by both duty and personal happiness and are capable of resolving any conflicts that may arise between duty and their own happiness.[20]

8 Virtue and happiness

Without the hope that the pursuit of virtue will lead to happiness, rationally self-interested persons will be demoralized. How can theism properly motivate the moral life without degenerating into selfishness?

Let us proceed by way of example. Suppose one is considering whether or not to have children. Consider the selfish parent-to-be. She will have children if she supposes they will bring her happiness, perhaps to satisfy her desires for holding small, cuddly things or to give her something to boast to her friends about or to financially provide for her in her old age or because she is lonely and can't make any adult friends. She may be good to her children but she does so simply as a means to her own happiness. But the morally virtuous parent will have children both for her own sake and for the sake of the child. She will surely want the child and the benefits of child-rearing but will also desire the good of the child itself. She may have talents, finances, opportunities or love which are better shared than kept to herself. Her behavior toward her child will not be motivated primarily by the benefits that might accrue to herself. Her devotion to her child will be motivated primarily by her desire for the good of the child itself.

The morally virtuous parent also hopes that her sacrifices will create an environment of security, freedom, honesty, peace, joy, fun and reciprocal love which will redound to her own benefit as well. The burdens of child-rearing are lessened to the extent that the parent creates an atmosphere of mutual self-satisfaction. The parent gives and gets, thus creating a healthy environment both for the child and for herself. Morality demands self-sacrifice without neglecting the satisfaction of one's own interests. Deprive a parent of the hope that doing her duties towards her child will result in a greater good both for the child and for herself and that parent will be demoralized. Deprive parents in general of such hope and the project of parenting will be quickly abandoned. The self-sacrifice demanded of the parent requires that the parent believe that her actions will redound to the greater good both of her child and of herself.

What we've said about parenting can be extended to other members of one's moral community as well. Becoming virtuous or doing one's duty must be properly

---

[20] A further feature of this hierarchical model is that it is not consequentialist. John Broome, in 'Deontology and Economics' (1992), *Economics and Philosophy* 8, pp. 269–82, p. 270, points out that consequentialist/utilitarian models of choice are typically concerned with the *goodness* that results as a consequence of an act, whereas deontological models are typically concerned with the *rightness (or wrongness)* of performing that act itself. In the above model the post-mortem (ethical) ranking can be used to represent the post-mortem value of the 'act of choosing' some alternative. Since this ethical preference ranking takes precedence over the ante-mortem ranking, the post-mortem ranking becomes decisive in determining choice, and the ante-mortem consequences of actions become less relevant (or irrelevant).

motivated by genuine concern for the other. This does not, however, require one to abandon all self-interest. One ought to desire one's efforts to contribute to a community of mutual satisfaction in which every person both desires and seeks to attain the good of the other. This is not unlike the creation of what Kant calls 'the kingdom of ends.' Kant maintains that the third version of the categorical imperative, 'treat people as ends and never merely as means,' requires me to endeavor to further the ends of others, 'for the ends of a subject who is an end in himself must, if this conception is to have its *full* effect in me, be also, as far as possible, *my* ends.'[21] I am required, that is, to share as far as possible the ends of others and to make their ends my ends. In striving towards the kingdom of ends we are striving towards a community devoted to the welfare of each of its members.

While we should strive for the kingdom of ends, we need not eliminate all regard for the self.[22] Fortunately, self-interest is not inconsistent with our moral aspirations (although selfishness is). It is possible, as it is for the good parent, to primarily desire the good of the other and yet to desire one's own good. In attempting to realize the kingdom of ends, one is attempting to bring about a situation of maximum desire satisfaction both for others and for oneself. In Kantian terms, the order of inclination must be duty first and happiness second. The desire for one's own happiness can be subordinated (but not sublimated) to desire for the good of the other.

The moral life demands an intrinsic connection between virtue and happiness. Kant, however, contends that virtue is not instrumentally connected to happiness: 'Morals is not really the doctrine of how to make ourselves happy but of how we are to be *worthy* of happiness [his emphasis].'[23] And, so, social contract theories of morality are doubly defective: they are instrumental and concerned primarily with one's self-interest. The kingdom of ends, as we have described it, seeks through the life of virtue both the happiness of the other and the happiness of oneself. The virtue of every member of the moral community is essential to the happiness of every other member.

In order for morality to be good for me and not an obstacle to my own happiness, the kingdom of ends must be attainable. Moral motivation of rationally self-interested people requires the hope that I and everyone else can become virtuous and that everyone's desires, including mine, can be mutually satisfied. What, precisely, should be our hope? What should we hope for if we wish to properly motivate the moral life? We agree with Aristotle that human flourishing takes place when two conditions

---

[21] Kant, *Groundwork of the Metaphysics of Morals*, trans. H. J. Paton (New York, Harper & Row, 1964), p. 98.

[22] It is not clear that Kant does either. He simply argues that morality requires making self-interest subordinate to duty.

[23] Kant, *Critique of Practical Reason*, p. 130. There is a connection between virtue and happiness, according to Kant. God grants happiness insofar as an individual merits it according to her virtue. He continues: 'Only if religion is added to it can the hope arise of someday participating in happiness in proportion as we endeavored not to be unworthy of it.'

are met: (1) One attains a life of virtue and (2) External conditions of life are arranged such that human desires are satisfied. The pursuit of happiness requires both (1) and (2).

But here's the problem—our ante-mortem existence, in some cases, favors wickedness in pursuit of (2). There is no necessary connection ante-mortem between devotion to virtue and human desire-satisfaction. If restricted to this-worldly goods, wickedness may be the best policy to secure human happiness. But becoming virtuous cannot be seen as an obstacle to attaining happiness. We cannot reasonably adjudge that our interests are better served by immorality.

What rationally self-interested beings require, therefore, is hope that there is a next life in which the kingdom of ends is fully realized and in which virtue results in happiness. There must be a next life, with other-worldly goods, if justice is to prevail. It should motivate us because we will believe that our best but invariably puny efforts to flourish will not be in vain. Deprive us of that hope, and we will believe that since the moral struggle cannot be won it is not worth fighting; better to gain all of the this-worldly goods—pleasures and avoidance of pains—that one can for oneself.

But should we hope for a better world simply to gain our own happiness? Aren't we led back to selfishness once again? Here the demands of virtue are clear, and as is emphasized by most theists, our own interests cannot be completely satisfied unless and until they include the interests of others. But if one desires the interests of others, isn't one being selfish? Here the reply seems obvious—wanting to help others is the opposite of selfishness, indeed it is altruism at its finest. The altruistic person need not ignore her own interests, of course, and her interests include the interests of others as well. The life of virtue is acquired by ridding ourselves of unwarranted and exclusive devotion to our self and taking on the interests of others (while not denying a healthy self-interest). In so doing, one finds one's deepest desires satisfied—to know and to be known, to care for and be loved by others, to take delight in the joys and grieve at the sorrows of others (who likewise grieve and rejoice with oneself); the intrinsic reward of altruism is deep desire satisfaction. The virtue is the reward, so to speak, in the kingdom of ends. When virtue and justice embrace, an ideal community of people is formed who genuinely delight in one another's good. Mutual satisfaction of our deepest human desires ensues.

The moral life that we have been describing suggests a double source of desire satisfaction. First, the virtuous person secures the satisfaction of her desires to be kind, just, loving, generous and patient toward others. Second, the virtuous person, when fully a member of the kingdom of ends, is part of a community devoted to her happiness as well. Neither of these states of affairs is attainable ante-mortem and is thus not available to motivate the naturalist, social contract theorist. But if we are to respond to the moral demand, to sacrifice ante-mortem happiness and even life itself for the good of another, then rationally self-interested persons must believe that it is possible to attain virtue and happiness in the next life.

So far our argument supports the belief that insofar as the demand to be moral is rational, it is rational to believe in the next life. There is no necessity, so far, for one to believe in God. But if one supposes, as does Kant, that we are in bondage to sin, that is, to the evil maxim whereby duty is subordinate to self-interest, then virtue is not attainable in this life. If virtue is not attainable, then neither is deep, human fulfillment (according to our argument). So, if we are in bondage to sin, neither virtue nor happiness is attainable. If virtue and happiness are not believed to be attainable, it is not rational to have them as ends. If it is rational to have virtue and happiness as ends, they must be believed to be attainable. So rationality requires, if there is a legitimate moral demand to pursue virtue and happiness, both the belief that they are attainable in the next life and that God exists to assist in the transformation of will from the evil maxim to the good maxim or, in our terms, from being selfish to being morally virtuous.[24]

Theistic belief unites the altruistic imperative of the life of virtue with the attainment of human happiness. Neither virtue nor human happiness is guaranteed in this life; if they are attainable there must be post-mortem existence where virtue is consonant with happiness. If either virtue or happiness through virtue is not attainable, then the motivation to strive for them is diminished. Restricting ourselves to this-worldly goods, therefore, is demoralizing: the moral life is not sufficiently motivated and one might more reasonably choose the life of wickedness. Motivating the moral life, therefore, rationally demands hoping for a next life in which virtue is attainable within a community of likeminded people and intrinsically issues forth in happiness. This requires the belief that God can and does offer assistance in the transformation of the will. And finally, if there is a God in whom we find our deepest desires satisfied, as Boethius, Aquinas and Pascal contend, then the life of virtue will include devotion to him and the kingdom of ends will become the kingdom of God.

9 Conclusion

We have argued that Christian belief has moral advantages in that it can adequately motivate rationally self-interested people to be moral. A prominent alternative motivation is the social contract theory which, we have argued, is desperately inadequate.[25] Only if there is a next life in which virtue is attainable and issues forth in happiness may one be properly motivated to be moral. This is crucial when morality is demanding. If this moral argument were the sole reason offered in defense of theism, belief in God would be held on poor grounds indeed. We might recognize the truth of our argument and simply be demoralized; the sober truth might just be that it is often in our best interest to be wicked.

---

[24] This argument has been developed in detail in John Hare, *The Moral Gap* (Oxford, Oxford University Press, 1996). Hare points out the defects in Kant's understanding of divine assistance and offers a more adequate solution.

[25] There are, of course, other non-theistic answers such as those offered by eudaimonistic theories. It is beyond the scope of this essay, but we contend that the best eudaimonistic theories are likewise theistic. If we agree with Aristotle that the conditions necessary for happiness must obtain to secure eudaimonia and that virtue is not always its own ante-mortem reward, then eudaimonistic theories are best located within a context of post-mortem rewards.

But suppose we were to locate this debate within the context of a larger theistic argument in which we were able to demonstrate that theism is roughly equal in explanatory power to naturalism.[26] In such a case, the moral advantages of theism might tip the scales in favor of belief in God. No doubt there are pragmatic advantages to theism as well, concerning, say, the meaning of life or the grief suffered when loved ones die. These pragmatic advantages may provide additional reasons to believe in God. All things being equal, it is surely more reasonable to accept an explanatory theory which has more moral and pragmatic advantages than its competitors. As for motivating the moral life, theism has the advantage.

---

[26] That it can and perhaps has been so argued, see William L. Craig and Quentin Smith, *Theism, Atheism and Big Bang Cosmology* (Oxford, Oxford University Press, 1993).

10

Divine Perfection and Freedom

William Rowe

> Though God is a most perfectly free agent, he cannot but do always what is best
> and wisest in the whole.
>
> Samuel Clarke

Many thinkers in the theistic tradition have held that in addition to omnipotence and
omniscience God's attributes must include perfect goodness and freedom. For the
theistic God deserves unconditional gratitude and praise. But if a being were to fall
short of perfect goodness, it would not be worthy of unreserved praise. So, too, for
divine freedom. If God were not free in some of his significant actions, if he always
lacked the freedom not to do what he in fact does, we could hardly make sense of
thanking him or praising him for anything that he does. He would not be deserving of
our gratitude and praise for the simple reason that he would act of necessity and not
freely. So, along with omnipotence and omniscience, perfect goodness and significant
freedom are fundamental attributes of the theistic God.

Some attributes are essential to a being. That being could not exist were it not to
possess those attributes. Other attributes are such that the being could still exist were it to
lack them. If the theistic God does exist, to which class do his attributes of omnipotence,
omniscience, perfect goodness, and freedom belong? Are they essential to that being?
Does that being possess those attributes in every possible world in which he exists? Or are
they not essential? Most thinkers in the theistic tradition have held the view that these
attributes are constitutive of God's nature; they are essential attributes of the being that
has them. With this view in mind, my aim in this essay is to consider the question of
whether God's perfect goodness, specifically his moral perfection, is consistent with his
being free in many significant actions. Throughout, we will suppose that if God exists he
is *essentially* omnipotent, omniscient, perfectly good, and free in many of his actions.
What I want to determine is whether there is a serious problem of reconciling God's
essential goodness and moral perfection with any significant degree of divine freedom.[1]

---

[1] I take God's moral perfection to be logically implied by his perfect goodness.

My principal aim is to show that there is a serious problem here. I'll also briefly consider how the problem might be solved or at least diminished.

Consider the question of whether God is ever free to do an evil (morally wrong) act. Of course, being morally perfect, omnipotent, and omniscient, God will never in fact do an evil act. No being who knowingly and willingly performs an evil act is morally perfect. Since being free to do an evil act is consistent with never in fact doing an evil act, it may seem initially plausible to think that God could be free to perform such an act. But if God is free to perform an evil act, then he has it in his power to perform that act. And, if God has it in his power to perform an evil act, then he has it in his power to deprive himself of one of his essential attributes (moral perfection). But no being has the power to deprive itself of one of its essential attributes.[2] Therefore, God does not have it in his power to perform an evil act.

The reasoning in this argument proceeds as follows.

1. God has it in his power to bring it about that he performs an evil act. (Assumption to be refuted)
2. From God's performing an evil act it follows that God is not morally perfect.
3. If a being has it in its power to bring about p, q follows from p, and q does not obtain, then that being has it in its power to bring about q.[3]
4. God has it in his power to bring it about that he is not morally perfect. (from 1–3)
5. Being morally perfect is an essential attribute of God.
   Therefore,
6. God has it in his power to bring it about that he lacks one of his essential attributes.

Because (6) is clearly false, we must deny the initial assumption that God has power to bring it about that he performs an evil act. But if God does not have it in his power to perform an evil act, then performing an evil act is not something God is free to do.

It may seem that my argument to show that God is not free to do an evil act has already produced a serious difficulty in the theistic concept of God. For if God cannot do evil, what becomes of his omnipotence? After all, even we humans, with our quite limited power, are able to perform evil deeds. If God does not have the power to do what even we can do, how can we reasonably hold that he is essentially omnipotent?

So long as we hold that omnipotence does not imply power to do what is not possible to be done, we need not conclude that God's lacking power to do something

---

[2] It is understood here that a being has the power to deprive itself of a property only if there is some possible world in which that being exists but does not have that property.

[3] (3) is expressed without reference to time in order that its central idea can be more quickly grasped. A more extended formulation of (3) is as follows: If a being has it in its power to bring it about that p obtains at t, p's obtaining at t entails q's obtaining at t, and q does not obtain at t, then that being has it in its power to bring it about that q obtains at t.

morally wrong renders him less than omnipotent.[4] For, as we've seen, it is strictly impossible for a being who logically cannot be other than morally perfect to do something evil.

If God is not free to do a morally wrong action, might he be free to do a morally right act? 'Morally right act' may mean either what is morally obligatory or what is morally permissible. If we are willing to countenance refraining from performing a certain action as itself an 'action' then it is clear that God is not free in performing any action that is morally obligatory for him to perform. For in order for God to be free in performing an action, it must be both in his power to perform it and in his power to refrain from performing it. But since refraining from a morally obligatory action would be morally wrong, and, as we've seen, God is not free to do anything that is morally wrong for him to do, he does not have the power to refrain from doing what is morally obligatory. In short, God does what is morally obligatory of necessity, not freely.

The way I've just put the point about God doing what is morally obligatory for him to do is not quite right. For it suggests that even though God does not freely do what he is morally obligated to do, he nevertheless does (of necessity) what he has a moral obligation to do. But the truth is that no action is such that God can have a moral obligation to perform it. For an agent can have a moral obligation to do a certain thing only if the agent is free to carry out the obligation. Now if a person freely does some act, then it was in the person's power not to do it.[5] But since it would be morally wrong for God not to do what he is morally obligated to do, and, as we've seen, God cannot do what is morally wrong, it follows from our previous argument that God does not freely do what he is morally obligated to do. So, since one cannot be morally obligated to do what one is not free to do, there are no actions God has a moral obligation to perform. At best we can say that God does of necessity those acts he would be morally obligated to do were he free to do them.

We've seen that because he is essentially a morally perfect being, God is neither free to do a morally wrong action nor free in doing a morally obligatory action. We've also seen that no action can be such that God has a moral obligation to do it (or not to do it). It looks, then, as though our initial efforts have yielded the result that God's absolute moral perfection places significant restraints on the scope of divine freedom.[6] However, the fact that God is neither free to do what is wrong nor free in doing what is morally obligatory (what would be morally obligatory were God free with respect to doing or not doing it) may still leave considerable scope for God's freedom to be

---

[4] For a discussion of this point see Joshua Hoffman, 'Can God Do Evil?' (1979), *Southern Journal of Philosophy* 17, pp. 213–20.

[5] To avoid Frankfurt type counter-examples, we should say that when an agent freely performs some action she caused her action and had the power not to cause that action. The power not to cause one's action is *not* the same as the power to prevent one's action. I ignore this complication in the text.

[6] If we take significant freedom, as Alvin Plantinga does, to be the freedom to do or refrain from doing what is morally obligatory, it can be shown that God cannot be significantly free. See Wes Morriston, 'Is God Significantly Free?' (1985), *Faith and Philosophy* 2, pp. 257–64.

exercised. For, so long as some of his important actions are morally permissible but not morally obligatory, we thus far have no reason to deny that God is free with respect to all such actions, that he has it in his power to do them and in his power not to do them. For example, it has long been held that God's action in creating the world was a free action, that God was free to create a world and free not to create a world.[7] Creating the world is certainly a very significant act, involving, as it does, a vast number of divine acts in actualizing the contingent states of affairs that constitute our world. If God enjoys freedom with respect to the world he creates, then, although his freedom is constrained in ways that ours is not, there would not appear to be any insurmountable problem of perfection and freedom.[8] To pursue our investigation of a possible conflict between God's moral perfection and his freedom, therefore, it will be helpful to turn our attention to God's action in creating the world. Specifically, we need to consider whether God's moral perfection leaves God free with respect to his creation of the world.

It is important to distinguish two questions concerning God's freedom in creating a world. There is the question of whether God is free to select among creatable worlds the one he will create.[9] There is also the question of whether God is free not to create a world at all. In what follows, I will focus primarily on our first question (whether God is free to select among creatable worlds the one he will create).

In an important article, Robert Adams argues that it need not be wrong for God to create a world that is *not as good as* some other world he could create.[10] Adams supposes that the world God creates contains creatures each of whom is as happy as it is in any possible world in which it exists. Moreover, no creature in this world is so miserable that it would be better had it not existed. Let's suppose there is some other possible world with different creatures that exceeds this world in its degree of happiness, a world that God could have created. So, God has created a world with a lesser degree of happiness than he could have. Has God wronged anyone in creating this world? Adams argues that God cannot have wronged the creatures in the other possible world, for merely possible beings don't have rights. Nor can he have wronged the creatures in the world he has created, for their lives could not be made more happy. Adams notes that God would have done something wrong in creating this world were the following principle true.

---

[7] For an excellent discussion and critical evaluation of the classical Judeo-Christian views on God's freedom with respect to creation see Norman Kretzmann, 'A General Problem of Creation' and 'A Particular Problem of Creation' in Scott MacDonald (ed.), *Being and Goodness* (Ithaca and London, Cornell University Press, 1990).

[8] There is a problem of understanding what God's moral perfection comes to, given that he can have no moral obligations. But this problem may not be unresolvable. See Thomas Morris, *Anselmian Explorations* (Notre Dame, University of Notre Dame Press, 1987), pp. 31–41.

[9] Since there may be possible worlds that an omnipotent being cannot create, we need to restrict our discussion to the class of worlds creatable by God.

[10] Robert Adams, 'Must God Create The Best?' (1972), *Philosophical Review* 81, pp. 317–32.

It is wrong to bring into existence, knowingly, a being less excellent than one could have brought into existence.[11]

But this principle, Adams argues, is subject to counter examples. Parents do no wrong, for example, when they refrain from taking drugs that would result in an abnormal gene structure in their children, even though taking the drugs would result in children who are superhuman both in intelligence and in prospects for happiness.

Suppose we agree with Adams on these points. Suppose, that is, that we agree that God is not morally obligated to create the best world that he can, that it would be morally permissible for God to create the best world he can, but also morally permissible for God to create any of a number of other good worlds of the sort Adams describes. If so, can't we conclude that there is no unresolvable conflict between God's being essentially morally perfect and his enjoying a significant degree of genuine freedom? For it now appears that God's moral perfection does not require him to create the best world. In short, he is free to create (or not create) any of a number of good worlds.

As forceful and persuasive as Adams's arguments are, I don't think they yield the conclusion that God's perfect goodness imposes no requirement on God to create the best world that he can create. What Adams's arguments show, at best, is that God's moral perfection imposes no *moral obligation* on God to create the best world he can. His arguments establish, at best, that God need not be doing anything *morally wrong* in creating some world other than the best world. But this isn't quite the same thing as showing that God's perfect goodness does not render it necessary that he create the best world he can. For, even conceding the points Adams makes, there still may be an inconsistency in a morally perfect being creating some world other than the best world he can create. My point here is this. One being may be morally better than another even though it is not better by virtue of the performance of some obligation that the other failed to perform. It may be morally better by virtue of performing some supererogatory act that the other being could have but chose not to perform. Analogously, a being who creates a better world than another being may be morally better, even though the being who creates the morally inferior world does not thereby do anything wrong. Following Philip Quinn, I'm inclined to think that if an omnipotent being creates some world other than the best world it can create, then it is possible there should exist a being morally better than it is.[12] For it would be possible for there to be an omnipotent being who creates the best world that the first being could create but did not. I conclude then that if an essentially omnipotent, perfectly good being

---

[11] 'Must God Create the Best?', p. 329.

[12] Philip L. Quinn, 'God, Moral Perfection, and Possible Worlds,' in Frederick Sontag and M Darrol Bryant (eds), *God: The Contemporary Discussion* (New York, The Rose of Sharon Press, Inc, 1982), pp. 197–213. Quinn remarks: 'An omnipotent, moral agent can actualize any actualizable world. If he actualizes one than which there is a morally better, he does not do the best that he can, morally speaking, and so it is possible that there is an agent morally better than he is, namely an omnipotent moral agent who actualizes one of those morally better worlds' (p. 213).

creates any world at all, it must create the best world it can. For although a being may do no wrong in creating less than the best it can create, a being whose nature is to be *perfectly good* is not such that it is possible for there to be a being morally better than it. If, however, a being were to create a world when there is a morally better world it could create, then it would be possible for there to be a being morally better than it.

What we have seen is that a being who is morally perfect and creates a world must create the very best world it can create. But what if there is no best world among those it can create? This would be so in either of two cases. First, it might be that for any world it creates there is a morally better world it can create. Second, it might be that there is no *unique* best world. Perhaps, instead, there are many morally unsurpassable worlds among the worlds God can create. Let's consider these two cases in turn.

On the assumption that for any world God creates there is a morally better world he can create, it is clear that it is impossible for God to do the best that he can. Whatever he does, it will be the case that he could have done better. This being so, it would seem only reasonable that God's perfect goodness is fully satisfied should he create a very good world. And we may safely assume that there are a large number of such worlds that he can create. So long as he creates one of these worlds he will have satisfied the demands of his morally perfect nature. For the idea that he should create the best world he can is an idea that logically cannot be implemented. Hence, on the assumption of there being no morally unsurpassable world among the worlds God can create, it would seem that God's absolute moral perfection is fully compatible with his freely creating any one of a number of good worlds that lie in his power to create. To complain that God cannot then be perfect because he could have created a better world is to raise a complaint that no creative action God took would have enabled him to avoid. As William Wainwright notes:

The critic complains that God could have created a better order. But even if God had created a better order, He would be exposed to the possibility of a similar complaint. Indeed, no created order better than our own is such that God would not be exposed to the possibility of a complaint of this sort. The complaint is thus inappropriate. Even though there are an infinite number of created orders better than our own, God can't be faulted simply because He created an order inferior to other orders that He might have created in their place.[13]

There is something forceful and right about this reasoning. If, no matter what world an omnipotent being creates, there is a morally better world that being can create, then, provided that the omnipotent being creates a significantly good world, it cannot be morally at fault for not having created a morally better world. But our question is whether a being in such a situation can be a *morally perfect being*. And for reasons we have already uncovered, I think the answer is no. A being is necessarily morally perfect only if it is not possible for there to be a being morally better than it. If a being creates a

---

[13] William Wainwright, *Philosophy of Religion* (Belmont, California, Wadsworth Publishing Company, 1988), p. 90.

world when there is some morally better world that it could have created, then it is possible that there be a being morally better than it. Since our assumption implies that for any world an omnipotent being creates there is a morally better world it can create, it follows that any such being who creates even a very good world cannot be an absolutely perfect moral being. Although the omnipotent being in question could be a very good moral agent and enjoy a significant degree of freedom in creating among a number of very good worlds, it could not be an absolutely perfect moral being. The existence of the theistic God who creates a world is inconsistent with the supposition that among the worlds he can create there is no morally unsurpassable world.[14]

Let's now consider the second way in which it could be true that no creatable world is better than all others. Suppose that among the worlds God can create there are a number of worlds that are morally unsurpassable. For reasons we've already considered, if God creates a world, he cannot create some world that is morally inferior to some other that he can create. Therefore, if there are a number of morally unsurpassable worlds among the worlds he can create, then if he creates at all he must create one of these worlds. But unlike the case when there is exactly one morally unsurpassable world among the worlds he can create, here we do seem to have found a wedge to open up space for some degree of divine freedom to exist in harmony with God's absolute moral perfection. For God would seem to be free to create any one of the morally unsurpassable worlds. In any case, God's absolute moral perfection imposes no requirement on his creation among the set of morally unsurpassable worlds.

Earlier, I distinguished two questions concerning God's freedom in creating a world. We have been discussing the question of God's freedom to select among creatable worlds the one he will create. It is now time to consider the other question of whether God is free not to create a world at all. Here we may limit our inquiry to the possibility that there is exactly one morally unsurpassable world among the worlds creatable by an omnipotent being. As we've seen, in this case God is not free to select any other world to create. If God creates, he must create the one world that is morally best. Our present question is whether in this situation God is free not to create at all.

Some possible world must be actual. What possible world would be actual if God exists but does not create at all? Presumably, it would be a world in which no positive, contingent state of affairs obtains. By 'a positive, contingent state of affairs' I mean any state of affairs such that from the fact that it obtains it follows that some contingent being (other than God, if he should be contingent) exists. Apart from God and whatever necessarily existing entities there are, in a world God inhabits but does not create, no other being would exist. To answer our question of whether God is free not to create a world at all, we must compare the best world God can create with a world whose inhabitants are simply God and whatever necessarily existing entities there are. Assuming such a world would not be morally incommensurate with the morally

---

[14] In the essay by Quinn quoted earlier, it is worth noting that he does not seem to draw the very strong conclusion I've just endorsed.

unsurpassable world among worlds God can create, it is plausible to think that God is not free with respect to whether he will not create at all. For either the world he inhabits but does not create is better than the best world he can create or it is not. If it is better, then he is not free not to create a world at all, he necessarily refrains from creating. If it is worse, then he is not free not to create a world at all, he necessarily creates a world.[15] Might the world he inhabits but does not create be on a moral par with the best world among those an omnipotent being can create? If so, then, as in the case where there are a number of morally unsurpassable worlds omnipotence can create, we again have a wedge to make space for some degree of divine freedom. But, in this scarcely possible situation, God's freedom would be restricted to creating the morally unsurpassable world or not creating at all.

We now can draw together the results of our study of the problem of divine perfection and freedom. The conclusions we have reached may be presented as follows.

1. God is not free to perform any evil act; nor is he free in doing what is morally obligatory.
2. If there is a world creatable by God that is morally better than any world he inhabits but does not create, God is *not* free not to create a world at all. If he exists, he is a creator of necessity.
3. If for any world creatable by an omnipotent being there is another creatable world that is morally better, the theistic God cannot exist and be a creator of anything.
4. If there is a single, morally best creatable world, God enjoys neither sort of freedom: he is not free not to create and he is not free to select among creatable worlds.[16]
5. If there are a number of morally unsurpassable, creatable worlds, then, although God necessarily creates one or the other of them, he is free (so far as his moral perfection is concerned) to select among the morally unsurpassable worlds the one he will create.[17]

Traditional theists who hold that God is essentially perfect and yet possesses libertarian freedom of will and action have neglected, I believe, some of the implications that appear to follow from God's perfect goodness. For all we know about possible worlds, it may well be that God's perfect goodness is inconsistent with any degree of divine freedom in whether he creates or what world he creates. In any case, it would seem that

---

[15] This point is a plausible extension of our earlier principle: If a being creates a morally inferior world to one it can create, then it is possible that there be a being morally better than it. Extending this principle, it is plausible to hold that if a being can but does not create a world that is morally better than the one it merely inhabits, then it is possible that there be a being morally better than it.

[16] The plausible assumption here is that if there is a single, morally best creatable world, then that world is morally better than any world God inhabits but does not create.

[17] See footnote 16.

his perfection places rather severe limitations on the scope of his freedom in creating a world.

It is now time to see how the problem of divine perfection and freedom can be solved or at least diminished. If our reasoning has been correct, the problem is rooted mainly in the conception of God as essentially both a perfectly good being and a being who has libertarian freedom with respect to many of his creative acts. And the two solutions that immediately suggest themselves are (1) giving up the idea that God has libertarian freedom, and (2) abandoning the idea that God is essentially perfectly good. Let's consider how each of these moves would diminish or solve the problem.

If there is a unique best among creatable worlds, God's being essentially a perfectly good being leaves him no choice, he cannot refrain from creating and he cannot create some world less than the best. This generates a problem only if we ascribe *libertarian freedom* to God with respect to creation. Perhaps, instead, we should ascribe to God what some have thought to be a superior sort of freedom, the power always to choose and act in accordance with one's knowledge of what is best.[18] On this idea of freedom, there need be no power to choose otherwise or to refrain from choosing. So, God necessarily and freely chooses to create the best. Thus, by abandoning the idea that God has libertarian freedom with respect to creating a world, the problem we are discussing can be significantly diminished. However, should there be no morally unsurpassable world, there would still be the difficulty of how God could create and, nevertheless, be essentially a perfectly good being. Denying that God enjoys libertarian freedom with respect to creation would do nothing to diminish this problem.

Our second suggestion was to abandon the idea that God is *essentially* perfectly good. If God's perfect goodness is not essential to him then he may be free to create less than the best he can. Indeed, he may even be free to do evil. Should he do evil, he would cease to be perfectly good; and should he create less than the best he can he would not be a being than which a better is not possible.[19] But neither of these consequences are surprising once we abandon the idea that God's perfect goodness is a part of God's nature.[20]

It must be admitted that the two solutions I've just described constitute significant revisions of a major stream of thought in traditional theism. Clearly, from the perspective of classical theism it would be preferable to uncover some mistake in the reasoning leading to the conclusion that there is a serious problem involving God's essential perfection and freedom. I'll conclude this essay by looking at two objections to the reasoning that has led us to that conclusion.

---

[18] In *The City of God* Augustine ascribes something like this sort of freedom to God.

[19] A less drastic revision of the idea that God is perfectly good would be to allow that God's moral goodness is surpassable, but surpassable only in the sense that God himself might have been morally better than he is. See, for example, the suggestion by William Wainwright (drawn from Charles Hartshorne) that God's perfection might require only that he be unsurpassable by some *other* being (*Philosophy of Religion*, p. 9).

[20] For an argument that God cannot cease to be perfect even if he is contingently perfect, see Thomas Morris, 'Properties, Modalities, and God,' essay 5 in *Anselmian Explorations*.

In an excellent study of the problem of divine creation, Norman Kretzmann reaches two conclusions.[21] His first is that God is not free not to create at all—God must create some world.[22] Moreover, since Kretzmann agrees with Aquinas in holding that for any world God might create there is a better world he could create, Kretzmann's first conclusion, when conjoined with the thesis that there is no best world, implies 'that perfectly good (omniscient, omnipotent) God *must* create a world less good . . . than one he could create.'[23] Kretzmann's second conclusion is that it is a *mistake* to think (as I do) that if God cannot avoid choosing something less good than he could choose, then God cannot be essentially perfectly good. And he proceeds to explain why he thinks it is a mistake.

Like Aquinas, I think that the logical truth that God's actions conform to the principle of noncontradiction entails no limit on his power. And if it would be a violation of the principle of noncontradiction for God to create a world better than any other world he could create, then a fortiori that logical truth which does not diminish his power also leaves his *goodness* undiminished. God's being that than which nothing better can be conceived of cannot entail his producing a world than which none better can be conceived of. No matter which possible world he actualizes, there must be infinitely many possible worlds better than the actual world in some respect or other.[24]

Kretzmann relies on what he takes to be an analogy or parallel between power and goodness. His idea is this. Since we agree that failure to bring about what is logically impossible does not imply any limit on God's power, we should also agree that failure to bring about what is logically impossible does not diminish God's goodness. Given that there is no best world, Kretzmann points out that it is logically impossible for God to create a world better than any other world he could create. So, the fact that God does not do this diminishes neither his power nor his goodness.

Perhaps we can view Kretzmann as appealing to the following principle.

A. If S is a logically impossible state of affairs, then the fact that a being does not bring about S does not entail that the being in question lacks power or perfect goodness.

This principle strikes me as self-evidently true. The fact that God fails to do what logically cannot be done is a bad reason to think that God is morally imperfect. But the fact that there is a bad reason to conclude that God is not perfectly good does not mean that there is no good reason to conclude that God is not perfectly good. And the fact that God fails to do what logically can be done may be a good reason to conclude that God is not perfectly good. The principle that provides this good reason is principle B.

---

[21]   See footnote 7.

[22]   In reaching this conclusion Kretzmann parts company with Aquinas.

[23]   'A Particular Problem of Creation,' p. 238 (emphasis mine).

[24]   Ibid.

B. If a being creates a world when there is a morally better world that it could have created, then it is possible that there exists a being morally better than it.[25]

If B is true, as I think it is, and if it is also true that

C. If a being is essentially perfectly good then it is not possible that there exist a being morally better than it,

then if it is true that for any creatable world there is another creatable world better than it, it is also true that *no* omnipotent, omniscient being who creates a world is essentially perfectly good. Moreover, if we add to this Kretzmann's first conclusion that a perfectly good, omnipotent, omniscient being *must* create, it will follow that there is no omnipotent, omniscient, perfectly good being.

Suppose Aquinas and Kretzmann are right in believing that for any creatable world there is another creatable world that is better than it. Our second objection emerges when we consider what the theistic God is to do in this situation. If some creatable world is better than any world God simply inhabits, then, on my principle B (slightly extended) it appears that God must create some world. On the other hand, as we've just seen, on my principle B it also follows that he cannot create a world if some other creatable world is better. 'So,' the objector now concludes, 'on your principle B it follows that God must create a world and also must not create a world. Surely, then, since your principle leads to a contradiction, however plausible principle B sounds, we must reject it.'

My response to this objection is that on the supposition that for every creatable world there is another world that is better than it, principle B does not lead to a contradiction. What principle B leads to is the conclusion that there is no essentially omnipotent, omniscient, perfectly good being.[26]

---

[25] As we noted earlier, a being may be perfectly morally correct in the sense of never failing in its obligations and still be such that it could be morally better by virtue of the performance of some supererogatory act.

[26] George Mavrodes and I were graduate students together at the University of Michigan. His philosophical talent is extraordinary. In the years since we were students together I have more than once read through his remarkable book *Belief in God: A Study in the Epistemology of Religion*. I am pleased to provide an essay for a book dedicated to him. The essay is a revised version of my paper 'The Problem of Divine Perfection and Freedom' in Eleonore Stump (ed.), *Reasoned Faith* (Cornell University Press, 1993), pp. 223–33.

11

The Many Gods of Hick and Mavrodes

William Hasker with a response by John Hick

Where contemporary philosophy of religion is concerned, polytheism is off the radar screen. It's not just that no one professes to be a polytheist, or mounts a philosophical defense of polytheism. Among the multitude of isms that are discussed in the philosophy of religion, polytheism hardly even gets mentioned. In the history of religions, to be sure, polytheism commands attention, but for philosophy of religion, it virtually doesn't exist. All the more striking, then, when two leading philosophers of religion are found having an animated discussion concerning which of the two is the most important philosophical defender of polytheism. Not that the two men are vying with one another for this title! Rather, with a becoming modesty that is all too rare among eminent scholars, each is eager to award the distinction in question to the other. Clearly, this is a situation that merits further investigation.

The two philosophers in question are John Hick and George Mavrodes. The exchange began with Mavrodes' essay, 'Polytheism,' in which he asserts that Hick is 'probably the most important philosophical defender of polytheism in the history of Western philosophy.'[1] He immediately adds, however, 'But I think he does not much care for that description himself.' In a subsequent article Hick confirms his dislike of the description, which he at first supposed to be 'either an extravagant compliment or a

[1] George I. Mavrodes, 'Polytheism' in Thomas D. Senor (ed.), *The Rationality of Belief and the Plurality of Faith* (Ithaca, Cornell University Press, 1995), pp. 261–86; quotation from p. 262. Mavrodes was of course discussing Hick's views as set forth in John Hick, *An Interpretation of Religion: Human Responses to the Transcendent* (New Haven, Yale University Press, 1989, second edition 2004). Hick subsequently published an article, 'The Epistemological Challenge of Religious Pluralism' (1997), *Faith and Philosophy* 14:3, pp. 277–86, which includes replies to Mavrodes and several other contributors to the Senor volume; this was followed in the same issue by responses from the philosophers in question. In 2001 Hick published *Dialogues in the Philosophy of Religion* (New York, Palgrave, 2001), in which he reprinted his article and the responses by Alston, Plantinga, van Inwagen, and Mavrodes, followed in each case by a rejoinder from Hick, and with further responses from Alston and Mavrodes. Finally, Hick continues the discussion with Mavrodes and a number of others in the Introduction to the second edition of *An Interpretation of Religion*.

splendid insult!'[2] After consideration, however, he decides to take Mavrodes' remark as a 'friendly jest.'[3] He claims, however, that the label 'polytheist' does not properly apply to him. And noting Mavrodes' assertion that he, Mavrodes, is himself a polytheist of sorts, Hick proposes that it may be Mavrodes 'who has become the main defender of polytheism in western philosophy!'[4] In reply, Mavrodes states concerning his description that 'To some extent, I meant it as a compliment (though it was not, in my opinion at least, extravagant). Primarily, however, I intended it as a straightforward characterization of Hick's version of religious pluralism.'[5] What, we wonder, is going on here?

With regard to Mavrodes' own polytheism, the answer is quite simple—and as he would be the first to admit, not especially remarkable. Following Richard Swinburne, he defines a 'god' as 'a very powerful non-embodied rational agent.'[6] And Mavrodes is inclined to accept the traditional Christian view that both angels and devils are just that—very powerful, non-embodied, rational agents. This, then, makes Mavrodes a *descriptive polytheist*—that is, he holds that there does in fact exist a plurality of beings satisfying the definition of a god. Mavrodes, however, is also a *cultic monotheist*, in that he himself worships only one of these many gods, namely the Holy Trinity. Furthermore, it seems likely (though Mavrodes does not specifically say this) that he regards only the Holy Trinity as *worthy of worship*; to worship others among the many gods would be to commit the sin of idolatry. Perhaps it is in order to avoid being misunderstood on these latter points that Mavrodes generally does not, in his other writings, describe himself as a polytheist. At any rate, the combination of views he describes as polytheism is actually quite common among orthodox Christian believers. But if this sort of view is to be considered polytheistic, then Mavrodes does not stand alone in being its advocate. In this case, the roster of distinguish philosophical defenders of polytheism would include such worthies as pseudo-Dionysius and Thomas Aquinas, each of whom offered an elaborate account of the nature of the several orders of angels. To my knowledge, Mavrodes himself has not published anything of that sort.

So much for Mavrodes as a polytheist, but what about Hick? Hick's reaction to Mavrodes' characterization is dismissive; he states,

One who accepts the distinction between, on the one hand, an ultimate and (in Kantian terms) noumenal Real *an sich*, and on the other hand its phenomenal appearances to human consciousness as the experienced god-figures (Yahweh, Allah, Holy Trinity, Shiva, etc.) and experienced non-personal absolutes (Brahman, the Dharmakaya, the Tao, etc.) is at one level a poly-something, though not precisely a poly-theist, and at another level a mono-something, though not precisely a monotheist.[7]

---

[2] 'The Epistemological Challenge of Religious Pluralism,' p. 283.

[3] Ibid.

[4] Ibid.

[5] George I. Mavrodes, 'A Response to John Hick' (1997), *Faith and Philosophy* 14:3, pp. 289–94; quotation from p. 289.

[6] 'Polytheism,' p. 264. The definition is taken from Swinburne's *The Concept of Miracle* (London, Macmillan, 1970), p. 53.

[7] 'The Epistemological Challenge of Religious Pluralism,' p. 283.

This may be so, but we need to examine for ourselves Mavrodes' case for calling Hick a polytheist. That case depends on Mavrodes' overall interpretation of Hick's religious pluralism. As is well known, a central move in Hick's program consists in applying Kant's noumenal–phenomenal distinction to the realm of religious diversity. One important difference is that for Hick the shape of the phenomenon is determined, not merely by universally human factors as for Kant, but also by local variations embodied in language, culture, inherited symbol-systems, and the like. Given this framework, the objects of worship in the various religious traditions are related to the ultimate Real, the final ontological ground of religious life and experience, as phenomena to noumena.

In this connection Mavrodes points out a divergence that exists in Kant-interpretation concerning the relation of phenomena to noumena. On one interpretation, the phenomenon 'is the noumenon as experienced'; a phenomenal cantaloupe, for example, just is a noumenal cantaloupe, experienced under the conditions of human sensibility and cognition. Mavrodes illustrates this interpretation with a story about a prince who wishes to obtain undistorted information about the daily lives of his people. In order to do this, he turns up in various towns from time to time in disguise—sometimes as an itinerant monk, sometimes as a stonemason, and so on. On this model, termed by Mavrodes the *disguise model*, there is a strict identity between the prince and each of the individuals who are, in fact, the prince in disguise—and also, therefore, a strict identity between those individuals. 'The (apparent) monk is identical with the prince, and the (apparent) stonemason is identical with the prince, and therefore the monk is identical with the stonemason.'[8] And this means, of course, that the monk, the prince, and the stonemason all have exactly the same properties, even though they may not *seem*, to the casual observer, to have the same properties. Indeed, those who get to know the prince in his disguises will sometimes be misled about his properties; the prince is not in fact a monk, though he appears to be one. Furthermore, some of the disguises may afford the viewer a truer apprehension of the prince, in some respect or other, than do other disguises. For instance, if the prince is in fact a young man, and the monk appears young whereas the stonemason appears middle-aged, then those who know the monk will form a truer picture of the man in question, at least in this respect, than those who know the stonemason.

The other interpretation of the phenomena–noumena relation is termed by Mavrodes the *construct model*. Here it is not asserted that the phenomenon *is* the noumenon, but rather that the phenomenon 'is a human creation in reaction to some influence, input, or the like from the noumenon.'[9] Mavrodes illustrates this model by a story about a group of non-representational painters, all of whom set out to make paintings of the same landscape. When the paintings are done, we find that there is very little resemblance between the different paintings, nor do any of the paintings contain a

---

[8] 'Polytheism,' p. 274.   [9] Ibid. 272.

feature that closely resembles anything in the actual landscape. Yet each of the artists assures us that her painting is 'of' the landscape, and that if the landscape had been noticeably different in some way, then so would be the painting. So is there is real input from the landscape into the paintings, and a corresponding dependence of the paintings on the landscape. Nevertheless, the paintings are surely not *identical* with the landscape, or with any feature of it. Nor is there any reason to suppose that all, or indeed any, of the properties of the landscape are also properties of the painting, or vice versa. And since the paintings are each distinct from the landscape, we are free to see them also as distinct from each other.

Now, supposing we have some grip on these two incompatible models, which of them corresponds to Hick's understanding of the relation between the ultimate Real and the objects of worship in the various religions? Mavrodes' interesting answer is that Hick is ambiguous on this point. There are passages in his writings that point to the disguise model, and passages that point to the construct model, but neither model by itself can handle all of the things Hick says on this topic. When Hick is thinking along the lines of the disguise model, there is simply a single entity (the Real) presented to humans in many different guises. When he is thinking along the lines of the construct model, on the other hand, the various gods are both real and distinct from one another, and it is this that leads Mavrodes to term Hick 'a distinguished modern defender of polytheism.'[10]

According to Hick, both of Mavrodes' models are 'radically misleading' as applied to his pluralistic hypothesis. This is true of the disguise model because the Real, unlike the prince, 'has no humanly conceivable intrinsic characteristics (other than purely formal, linguistically generated ones), and is accordingly not a person carrying out a revelatory plan.'[11] The analogy used to explain the construct model, on the other hand, assumes that 'the artists directly perceive the landscape, and then through their own creativity represent it in their different ways,' but 'on the pluralistic hypothesis ... there can be no direct experience of the Real *an sich* which could then be imaged in a range of ways analogous to that in which the painters creatively represent the landscape.'[12] Hick admits, however, that 'Mavrodes' two models do nevertheless each single out an aspect of the pluralistic hypothesis. The disguise model points to there being only one Real, whose impact upon us is experienced in different ways. And the construct model points to the positive contribution of the human mind in all awareness.' He then goes on to suggest an analogy of his own, in

the difference between ... the wooden table top that we experience as a solid, hard, brown, partly shiny, enduring three-dimensional object, and the account of it give by the physicists, as (very roughly) mostly empty space in which infinitesimal packages of discharging energy are

---

[10] Ibid. 268.
[11] 'The Epistemological Challenge of Religious Pluralism,' p. 284.
[12] Ibid.

moving about at a great pace, none of these having any of the properties of the table top that we perceive—neither colour nor weight nor extension nor density nor even fixed position.[13]

In assessing this part of the discussion, we need to keep in mind that stories told in order to illustrate the models are bound to be somewhat misleading, since they involve using the relations between elements in the experienced world to depict the relations between that world and something that lies beyond all experience. Such distortions are not necessarily harmful, so long as we keep in mind the limitations of the examples. In any case, Hick's own suggested analogy is subject to similar criticisms; it certainly does not mirror exactly the relation supposed to exist between the Real and the objects of worship. (Hick admits that his analogy is 'still capable of misleading', but 'less so than Mavrodes.')[14] Our ideas about the sub-atomic realm, unlike our ideas about the Real, are derived from experience using detailed experimental evidence and a rigorous chain of scientific reasoning. Furthermore, we have a detailed and well-confirmed account of how the elements of the sub-atomic realm operate in 'creating' the world of ordinary experience. We have nothing at all like this in the case of the Real—a point which Mavrodes emphasizes heavily at a later point in his exchange with Hick.[15] But if we keep these points of difference in mind, we may still be able to gain some insight from the examples.

There is, however, a formal feature of Mavrodes' disguise model that is more seriously problematic. The feature in question is the relation of *identity* emphasized by Mavrodes: 'The (apparent) monk is identical with the prince, and the (apparent) stonemason is identical with the prince, and therefore the monk is identical with the stonemason.' This identity relation cannot possibly apply *either* to the relation between Kantian noumena and phenomena *or* to Hick's account of the relation between the Real and the various divine *personae* and *impersonae*. There is a simple and clear reason why neither a Kantian cantaloupe nor a Hickian divine *persona* can be identical with any noumenal entity: the cantaloupe and the *persona* really do have the properties they seem to us to have, but neither the *Ding-an-sich* nor the Real can have those properties. It would be absurd to suppose that people are mistaken when they say that cantaloupes are rounded in shape, with greenish skin, peach-colored flesh, and a delicious flavor when ripe. And Hick would certainly not countenance the claim that Hindu Shaivite believers (for example) are all completely deceived concerning the properties of Shiva. The relation of identity has to be eliminated if we are to arrive at an even approximately correct understanding of the situation.

What seems to be needed, then, is some relation between noumenon and phenomenon other than strict identity: perhaps we could say that the phenomenal cantaloupe is *the noumenal cantaloupe as manifested under the conditions of human sensibility*, which does indeed have the familiar properties, whereas the *noumenal cantaloupe in itself* does not

---

[13] 'The Epistemological Challenge of Religious Pluralism,' p. 285.

[14] Ibid.

[15] See the response from George Mavrodes in John Hick (ed.), *Dialogues in the Philosophy of Religion*, pp. 72–5.

have these properties. Similarly, the various *personae* and *impersonae* would be *the Real as manifested within a particular cultural matrix*, and would possess the various properties attributed to them in the religious traditions, even though *the Real in itself* does not. (As a replacement for Mavrodes' story of the prince, I suggest the analogy of a translation. A translation of Plato's *Republic* into English is clearly distinct from a translation of the same book into German, yet it is equally clear that each is a manifestation, in the respective language, of the original work composed by Plato in Greek. It can even be said truly of each book that it *is* Plato's *Republic*, provided that the 'is' here is not the 'is' of strict identity.) Understanding the relation between them in this way would still preserve the distinction Mavrodes wants to make between the disguise model and the construct model, but without the misleading suggestion that either the *Ding-an-sich* or the Real can be identical with some experienced item. I suggest, tentatively, that the disguise model thus modified be re-labeled as the 'manifestation model.' We will say (for example) that the Real as manifested within the Muslim tradition really has the properties that Allah is experienced in that tradition as having; and so for the other religious traditions encompassed in Hick's pluralism.

At this point a pair of questions emerges. First, are the construct model and the manifestation model (as we will now call it) really as sharply opposed as seemed to be the case with the construct model and the disguise model? And what bearing, if any, does this shift have on Mavrodes' reasons for calling Hick a polytheist? Beginning with the first question, it seems that the opposition between the two models has been considerably lessened, if not eliminated entirely, by re-construing the disguise model as the manifestation model. As Mavrodes clearly sees, it is one thing to see the various divine *personae* and *impersonae* as each being strictly identical with the Real, as postulated by the disguise model, and quite another thing to see each of them as a human construct, created with some input from the ultimate Real. These two descriptions of the ontological status of the objects of worship really do seem to be incompatible. The first of the two characterizations, furthermore, would have the implication that the worshipers in the various traditions are systematically and radically mistaken about the nature of the objects of their worship—an implication which Hick is quite unwilling to accept.

Things are significantly different, however, when we shift from the disguise model to the manifestation model. On the latter model, the various objects of worship are identical, not with the Real in itself, but with the Real *as manifested in the context of a particular tradition*. And now there does not seem to be such a radical difference between saying of Shiva (for example) that Shiva is the manifestation of the Real within the Shaivite tradition, and saying that Shiva has been constructed by the Shaivites on the basis of a certain input from the Real. Perhaps the first way of putting it has a slightly more 'realist' flavor than the second, but there is a considerable similarity in the fundamental claim that is being made: the Real does indeed have an 'input' into the situation, but the particular characteristics attributed to the deity are strongly conditioned by the human cultural and religious situation of the worshipers. It remains true, to be sure, that there are many constructs but only one Real. But while there is only one ultimate Real, there are many different *manifestations* of the Real; these manifestations are really distinct from one another, and have different, and in some cases incompatible, properties. The two descriptions of this situation, as represented in these two models, now seem to differ more in their respective emphases than in their fundamental assertions.

It is clear, then, that the shift from the disguise model to the manifestation model has had the effect of narrowing the difference between that model and the construct model. But it is on the construct model that Mavrodes hangs his case for Hick as a polytheist, so we need to examine that argument more closely. The argument hinges on two points concerning the construct model: the different constructs are real entities, and they are really distinct from each other. It is very clear on the construct model that the different constructs are distinct from one another. With respect to the reality of the constructs, Mavrodes paraphrases Hick as follows: 'We regard as real the gods and absolutes of our own religion, *and we are to regard the gods and absolutes of the other religions also as real.*'[16] Alluding to Hick's use of Kantian terminology, he states that 'on Hick's view, all the gods are real *in the same sense that cantaloupes are real on the Kantian view*' and goes on to add that 'a cantaloupe is a real entity, a force to be reckoned with, something to be sought for the enrichment of human life.'[17] Mavrodes concludes: 'Thinking of the gods in accordance with this [construct] model yields a straightforward polytheism. The various gods are real—at least as real as the more ordinary furniture of the world, and possibly more real—and they are distinct from one another, again as the more ordinary entities of the world are distinct.'[18] What more is needed for polytheism?

It seems to me, however, that in arguing this way Mavrodes is overlooking certain subtleties in Hick's use of the concept of reality. Immediately after saying that we should regard as real both the object of our own worship and contemplation, *and also* the objects of worship or contemplation within the other religious traditions, Hick goes on to say, 'we are led to postulate the Real *an sich* as the presupposition of the veridical character of this range of religious experience.'[19] Just why are we led to do this? The clear implication is that these objects of worship can be real, and the religious experiences veridical, because *and only because* each such object of worship is a manifestation of the one ultimate Real. In saying this, to be sure, I am bringing together the construct model and the manifestation model, rather than opposing them to each other as Mavrodes wants to do. We must not forget that Hickian gods and absolutes are *phenomenal* gods and absolutes, just as Kantian cantaloupes are phenomenal cantaloupes. The 'reality' that each has is not that of a fundamental, ontologically ultimate being, but rather that of a being whose reality is dependent both

---

[16] 'Polytheism,' p. 269; emphasis in original.
[17] Ibid. 272; emphasis in original.
[18] Ibid. 275.
[19] *An Interpretation of Religion*, p. 249; cited in 'Polytheism,' p. 269.

on its noumenal source and on the minds and conceptual systems of those who experience it.[20]

With this in mind, it seems that Hick may be able to turn back the charge of polytheism. He is not saying that there are many different gods, in the sense that there are many different, ontologically distinct and independent, beings, each of which has the attributes requisite for a god. He is indeed saying that there are many different *manifestations*, and these manifestations really do have divergent properties, so that they cannot be equated with each other. But each of them is a manifestation of the same, ultimate Real, so in the final analysis there is not a plurality with respect to the ultimate object of worship. This is not classical monotheism, to be sure (nor does Hick claim that it is), but neither is it polytheism in the usual sense of that term.

So far, then, Hick seems to emerge from the debate largely unscathed. But there is another chapter to be written—or rather, that has been written by Hick himself, in a section of his book that seems to have been overlooked or ignored by many of the commentators.[21] This is section 16.5, in which he investigates 'The Ontological Status of the Divine *Personae*.' After some preliminary moves, Hick focuses on the Buddhist *trikaya* doctrine, and specifically on the relation between 'the ultimate Dharmakaya, the eternal truth or reality of the Buddha nature,' and 'the Sambhogakaya, the "Body of Bliss," consisting of a plurality of transcendent Buddhas,' including among others Amitabha and Vairocana. Hick points out that

there are two different understandings of the ontological status of the Sambhogakaya...Buddhas, and these suggest two alternative models for the status of the divine *personae*. According to one conception...the transcendent Buddhas are to be understood 'as mental creations, as ideations of the Bodhisattvas: to the Bodhisattva his ideal becomes so vivid and alive that it takes shape as a subjective reality.'... They are thus projections of the religious imagination. They are not, however, random projections, but appropriate expressions of the Dharmakaya.[22]

This is admirably clear, and it fits reasonably well with Hick's Kantian pluralism as we have seen it to this point. The other model, however, is strikingly different:

---

[20] Mavrodes himself later reached the conclusion that he had been mistaken in the sort of reality he attributed to the Hickian gods and absolutes. He wrote, 'I now suspect...that Hick (despite what he sometimes says) does not think that the gods, etc., of the actual religions—Allah, Shiva, Brahman, the Holy Trinity, and so on—are real at all. Or, to put it more cautiously, they have at best a very tenuous and weak reality. They are much less real than, say, cantaloupes' (George Mavrodes, 'A Response to John Hick' (July 1997), *Faith and Philosophy* 14:3, pp. 289–94; quotation from p. 290).

[21] I make no claim to having read all or even most of the vast literature that has grown up around Hick's proposals. But almost all of the considerable amount of commentary that I have read completely ignores this section of the *Interpretation*. Mavrodes does mention it; he points out that one of the two models proposed is 'radically realist', and states (correctly, I think) that 'it is hard to image what more a person would have to assert to be taken to be a polytheist' ('Polytheism,' p. 283). I differ from Mavrodes in thinking that it is *only* to the extent that he endorses this realist model that Hick can be termed a polytheist.

[22] *An Interpretation of Religion*, pp. 272–3; the embedded quotation is from *Buddhism*, by Wolfgang Schumann.

The other kind of model found in the history of the *trikaya* doctrine . . . is that the transcendent Buddhas of the Sambhogakaya are 'objectively existing, supramundane and subtle beings.' . . . On this view Amida, Vairocana, Ratnasambhava and the others are real persons, of immense but not limitless proportions. Applying this conception to Yahweh, Vishnu, Allah, Shiva, the heavenly Father and so on it would follow that they are real personal beings, independent centres of consciousness, with thought and emotion. We have already seen, however, and must not at this point forget, that it is entailed by the plurality of the gods that each of them is finite; for each exists alongside and is limited by the others with their own particular natures and capacities. Although the power of any one of this plurality cannot therefore be infinite it may nevertheless be so great as to be virtually infinite from our human point of view, as the gods exercise their powers in response to prayer and in the providential ordering of nature and history.[23]

Most striking of all, however, is Hick's final gloss in commenting on the two models:

As I have already indicated, the pluralistic hypothesis being propounded here could accommodate either of these models and does not require a decision between them. It therefore seems wise not to insist upon settling a difficult issue which, in logic, the hypothesis itself leaves open.[24]

I must confess that my own appreciation of this passage has gone through several stages. At first I was inclined to see this as a mere lapse on Hick's part—a position insufficiently considered, one that upon reflection he would wish to retract. But that is certainly not the case; in one of his responses to Mavrodes he reaffirms that his pluralism is consistent with either of these two models.[25] So we must take these claims seriously as an important, though neglected, part of his religious thought. When we do this, two conclusions stand out.

First of all, it is either false or (at best) true in a highly qualified sense, that both models are consistent with Hick's pluralistic hypothesis. With regard to the first, or subjective model, there is little if any problem. As already noted, this model seems quite consistent with Hick's pluralism as we have seen it to this point. Things are very different, however, when we turn to the 'objective' model in which 'Yahweh, Vishnu, Allah, Shiva, the heavenly Father and so on . . . are real personal beings, independent centres of consciousness, with thought and emotion.' Here there is a serious problem of consistency. To be sure, if the various heavenly *personae* are real, independently existing personal beings, Hick would nevertheless want to insist that each of them is a manifestation of the Real. And to that extent, the view fits with the pluralistic hypothesis well enough. But if each is an ontologically real, independent center of consciousness, the entire Kantian apparatus becomes superfluous. It will no longer be the case that, because of their particular religious and cultural history, Hindus apprehend the Real as Vishnu whereas Hebrews apprehend it as Yahweh. The truth is, rather, that it *really was* Vishnu who revealed himself to the Hindus, and Yahweh who

---

[23] *Interpretation of Religion*, pp. 274–5; again, the embedded quotation is from Schumann.
[24] Ibid.
[25] See Hick's response to Mavrodes in *Dialogues in the Philosophy of Religion*, p. 69.

revealed himself to the Hebrews. And it will be literally the case that Christians, Muslims, and Hindus are worshiping different gods. No doubt cultural influences would still affect the ways in which the respective deities are perceived—for instance, such influences might explain the regrettable tendency in monotheistic religions to absolutize and 'infinitize' the attributes of one's own deity. But the deities would really and objectively possess whatever attributes are theirs, such as the very great, but not unlimited, power ascribed to them in the quotation from Hick. To the extent that this sort of view is a serious possibility, it is also a serious possibility that Hick's pluralistic hypothesis as he previously expounded it is largely mistaken.

The other conclusion that stands out is that in all likelihood few, if any, of Hick's readers would find this second model attractive or plausible. I suspect Hick is aware of this; he writes, 'Clearly this model will involve extremely awkward issues concerning the relations between the deities and their respective spheres of operation.'[26] I believe he is also aware that the requirement that each of the deities be finite will make the model unacceptable to his monotheistic readers, be they Christians, Jews, or Muslims. But if the model has such limited appeal, and if in addition it conflicts with the Kantian interpretation which is otherwise central to his pluralism, one might wonder why Hick is so insistent on leaving it as an open option.

That way of putting the question assumes that Hick would agree that this model is not, all things considered, a very attractive option. At this point, however, a still more recent writing of his comes into play, namely the Introduction to the second edition of *An Interpretation of Religion*. Once again he cites the two possible accounts of the ontological status of the *personae* and *impersonae*, repeating the claim that both are consistent with his pluralistic hypothesis. He then goes on to say,

I now think that it is possible to venture a step further by combining elements of these two options. In moments of individual prayer and communal worship there is often, or at least sometimes, an experience of being in the presence of God and of being in an I–Thou (or We–Thou) relationship with God. I do not think that this is illusory, but neither do I think that the Thous with whom people of different faiths are in contact have the infinite attributes—as the omnipotent and omniscient etc., creator of everything other than oneself—that the developed monotheistic theologies have come to ascribe to them. For it is not possible to experience that an encountered being has *infinite* dimensions—infinite power, infinite knowledge, etc. The omni-qualities are the result of philosophical thinking congealed into religious dogma. And the possibility that I am proposing is that in each case the experienced Thou is a being analogous to the *devas* (gods with small g) of Indian religion or to the angels and archangels of traditional Jewish, Christian, and Muslim belief, or to the heavenly Buddhas—Amida, Vairocana, etc.—of some understandings of the *trikaya* doctrine of Mahayana Buddhism, each being the object of veneration by their own devotees. These are intermediate beings between ourselves and the transcategorial Real. But in our awareness of these beings we tend, at least within the western

---

[26] *Interpretation of Religion*, p. 275.

traditions, to invest them in our minds with the omni-attributes created by the vast super-structures of theology that have been developed over the centuries.[27]

I have quoted the passage at length, because I find its content so astonishing that I am unwilling either to omit part of it, or to paraphrase and risk being suspected of misinterpreting Hick's assertions. This proposal raises a whole host of issues, of which I will highlight a few of the most pressing. First of all, no explanation has been given of how the 'realistic' model is to be reconciled with the Kantian interpretation which has been central to Hick's exposition of his pluralism. Nor is there any explanation of how it is that this proposal 'combines elements of' both the realist and the phenomenalist models. On the face of it, it seems realist through and through. Perhaps there is a small movement away from all-out realism in the assertion that the omni-attributes of the monotheistic deities are the result of philosophical speculation congealed into dogma. The basis for this assertion apparently lies in the fact that if any of the supernatural persons involved really possessed the omni-attributes this would upset the parity between religions in a way that is uncongenial to the pluralist hypothesis. (Is this a case of the pluralist tail wagging the metaphysical dog?) But such metaphysical over-reaching, if it occurs, can be discussed and disposed of without reference to Kant. And it will still be the case that the different religions really are worshiping different deities—not merely that they conceptualize their gods differently, but that there really are *actual, existing deities* who are the objects of devotion in the rival religions. Or should we rather say, there are actual, existing deities who *rival one another* in drawing adherents to the different religions in which each is featured? If this is the case, the competition among religions will be, quite literally, the rivalry of the gods themselves! And presumably this rivalry will take the form of each god's attempting to provide its worshipers with a sufficient amount of what they most desire from their deities. So the ancient interpretation of battles between nations as the warfare of the gods may not be as far from the truth as we have been accustomed to think!

Perhaps, however, I am being overly flippant; readers will by now be aware that I have difficulty taking this proposal seriously enough to give it sober consideration. Still, the issues are there, and they must be dealt with if Hick's proposal is to gain even a modicum of credibility. All the more, then, one is led to ask: Why does Hick apparently perceive this option in a positive light, to the extent that he seems actually to favor it over the available alternatives? I can think of two possible answers to this question, but they are both very tentative, and I certainly do not rule out the possibility that other and better answers may be available.

A first possibility is that this preference is motivated by Hick's desire to maintain an open, affirming relationship to as many forms of religious belief and practice as possible. It is entirely obvious that this is a strong motivation for his overall pluralistic hypothesis. (I say this without prejudice to the merits or demerits of arguments he may offer for

---

[27] *An Interpretation of Religion,* Introduction to the second edition, pp. xxix–xxx.

that hypothesis.) Consistent with this motivation, he may be disinclined to rule out specific forms of belief as unacceptable when it is possible to avoid doing so. Certainly the experience of being in an I–Thou relationship with a divine Person is of central importance in many religious traditions; not least in the evangelical Protestantism which was Hick's own faith for a number of years following his conversion. The realistic model allows Hick to regard these experiences as essentially reliable, and this is something that is congenial to his overall approach to religious epistemology.

Such motivation on Hick's part is surely generous and admirable. There is, however, a price to be paid for this kind of generosity—namely, one may end up compromising one's own view and encumbering it with the need to defend what may actually be indefensible. Hick's openness does not extend to all religious views whatsoever; consider his sometimes acerbic remarks about orthodox Christians who resist his pluralistic hypothesis! One wonders whether in this case he might not have been better advised to bite the bullet and reject the 'realistic' interpretation of the transcendent Buddhas, and of the divine *personae* generally.

My other suggestion is even more conjectural; it stems from some passages in Hick's very readable and engaging autobiography. In the chapter on 'Religious Exploration and Conversion', Hick describes something of his religious and philosophical frame of mind at age 18, during the period just prior to his evangelical conversion. Though completely unimpressed by conventional religion, he was by no means an atheist. He writes, 'I believed absolutely in some sort of divine reality, though not the God of Christian orthodoxy.'[28] Concerning the 'divine reality,' we have the following excerpt from a notebook of philosophical reflections:

Reality is ethical and consists of God, who cannot be regarded as finite or infinite, or as having any or no form, or by any other analogy from the physical universe, but can only be comprehended 'mystically', by reason of the divine spark in each of us.[29]

This is not yet the Real of Hick's mature thought, but clearly shows signs pointing in that direction. Even more provocative, in the present context, is another aphorism Hick presents immediately after the one just quoted:

To be personal is to be finite. God is not finite and therefore not personal. But the personal being with whom we can get into contact in prayer etc., whilst being finite, may yet be larger than the extent of our consciousness and therefore infinite in relation to us and our needs.[30]

Is this not quite remarkable? 'God'—meaning here the ultimate reality—is not personal, though in view of the preceding quotation perhaps Hick would not have said either that God is impersonal. If that is correct, then this is a striking anticipation of his later thought. But there is also a 'personal being with whom we can get into contact in

---

[28] John Hick, *An Autobiography* (Oxford, One World, 2002), p. 33.
[29] Ibid. 32.   [30] Ibid.

prayer'; this being is not God and not infinite, yet may well be 'infinite in relation to us and our needs'—just what Hick later says about the various gods, on the second or 'realistic' interpretation. There is no indication here that religious diversity had yet become a pressing issue for Hick; if it had, it might very well have seemed plausible to him that there could be more than one of such 'personal beings with whom we can get into contact', corresponding to the personal gods of the various religions. Is it straining a point too far to conjecture that Hick's attraction to such an idea in his youth might go some way towards explaining his retention of it as a live option in his mature religious pluralism? It is after all Hick himself who has written, 'Reading all this now [viz. his early philosophical reflections] I see how my intellectual development has been surprisingly consistent apart from the interruption of the evangelical years.'[31]

Finally, who takes the prize? That is to say, which of our protagonists has a better claim to being the most distinguished defender of polytheism? If Mavrodes' view is to be considered polytheistic, then it is quite clear that, since he does defend his own view, he must be considered a defender of polytheism. Perhaps not its most important defender, however; as already noted, some earlier thinkers have gone much farther than Mavrodes himself in setting out the natures and activities of angels and devils. But I suspect I may not be alone in thinking that his view is not, after all, a species of polytheism. It seems to me that in order to qualify as a (descriptive) polytheist a thinker must not only recognize a plurality of 'very powerful non-embodied rational agents,' as per Swinburne's definition, but must consider that more than one of these agents is *worthy of worship*—whether or not the thinker himself worships more than one of them. Since Mavrodes, as I understand him, thinks that only the Holy Trinity is worthy of worship, his name must be deleted from the roster of polytheists.

With regard to Hick, the situation is more complicated. I have argued at some length that Mavrodes' attempt to classify Hick's Kantian pluralism as polytheistic does not succeed. It is true that the various *personae* and *impersonae* are distinct from one another, and it is also true that each of them is 'real' in an important sense. But the reality ascribed to them in the Kantian model is not the full-blooded sort of reality that would be needed to qualify the view as polytheistic. (As we've seen, Mavrodes came to think he had been mistaken in the sort of reality he ascribed to these entities.) Theirs is a phenomenal reality, a reality in the minds and experience of their worshipers, but this is entirely consistent with holding that their ontological status is that of manifestations or appearances of the one ultimate Real. It seems, then, that polytheism remains bereft of defenders.

Things change, however, when we consider the second, 'realistic' interpretation of the *personae*, as derived from the Buddhist *trikaya* doctrine. If indeed the *personae* are held to be 'objectively existing, supramundane and subtle beings' there is no remaining barrier to classifying such a position as straightforwardly polytheistic. It may be that

---

[31] *Autobiography*, p. 33.

Hick himself does not fully endorse the position, though the selection from the Introduction to the *Interpretation* certainly portrays him as leaning in that direction. In any case he insists that this view is consistent with his pluralistic interpretation of religion, and his official stance is that he need not choose between the 'phenomenalist' and the 'realist' views concerning the ontological status of the *personae*. Since this is the case it follows that, in defending his pluralist view, he is defending polytheism, whether or not he embraces polytheism as his personal belief. It seems, then, that Mavrodes was right after all: Hick is indeed a defender of polytheism, and without doubt one of its most important defenders![32]

Response to Hasker

John Hick

This is a brief response to William Hasker's admirable essay.

As a preliminary point, Mavrodes and Hasker both seem to agree in an interpretation of Kant from which I (and many others) differ. For Mavrodes and Hasker there is a noumenal cantaloupe as well as a phenomenal cantaloupe—and presumably noumenal and phenomenal individual leafs and blades of grass and pens and pencils and horses and humans and sun and moon and everything else. This is not how I read Kant. The *Critique of Pure Reason* is certainly open to differing interpretations, and indeed to the probability that Kant is not entirely consistent. But as I understand him, the sensory manifold is ordered in terms of the mind's innate forms and categories in order to appear in the unitary consciousness of the perceiver (the transcendental unity of apperception). On this view the world in itself does not consist of discrete objects (cantaloupes, etc.) arranged in space and time and causally connected with one another, although it can only be experienced by us in this way. And so Mavrodes' question, Are the gods as real as, or more real or less real than, cantaloupes does not arise. Another analogy that captures the situation better than any of either Mavrodes' and Hasker's or my own taken from physics, but still very imperfectly, would be the way in which the light of the sun is refracted by the earth's atmosphere into the different colors of a rainbow. In order to affect us the light has to pass through the earth's atmosphere, which divides it into the different perceived colors. Religiously, the 'light' of the universal presence of the Real is refracted by the human religious cultures into the different Gods and Absolutes.

However, independently of this, Hasker reminds us of my suggestion that the heavenly Buddhas, according to one interpretation of the *trikaya* doctrine, may, consistently with the pluralistic hypothesis, be independent centres of consciousness. The way that I presented this, I now see, was confused and confusing. Let me now

---

[32] But perhaps not its *most* important defender? Plato, after all, was a polytheist, and it is no slight to Hick to suggest that he may not outrank Plato in this regard!

straighten it out. I want to distinguish between the God figures (Yahweh etc.) of the different monotheistic traditions, with their omni-properties, and the personal presence of which we are aware in religious experience. My suggestion is three-fold: (1) The monotheistic God figures are human projections, existing only in the religious imaginations of a particular faith community—the Jews, the Christians, the Muslims. This by no means a new idea. The fifteenth century Indian Kabir wrote, 'Every votary offers his worship to the god of his own creation.'[33] (2) These projections are human responses within a particular cultural situation to the continuous impact upon humanity of the universal presence of the Real. (1 and 2 must be taken together. To quote one alone would be misleading.) And (3) The thou experienced in prayer and revelation is quite likely an intermediate figure between us and the Real. The Gods, then, are phenomenal appearances of the Real existing, with their omni- and other properties, in the thought of the worshipping community. But in praying to them we may in fact (unknown to us) be in contact with a real personal presence which is an 'angel,' in the sense of an intermediate being between ourselves and the Real, corresponding to the angels, archangels of the western monotheisms, or devas (gods with a small g) of Indian religion, or the heavenly Buddhas of one interpretation of one strand of Mahayana Buddhism. These are independent centres of consciousness, finite in their qualities. This suggestion is an attempt to make sense of what I take to be the actual situation— on the one hand, the transcendent transcategorial Real and, on the other, personal presences known in some forms of religious experience. It is worth noting that in the Qur'an it is stated that the presence that gave Muhammad the words that became the Qur'an was the archangel Gabriel (2: 97).

This will of course be quite unacceptable to traditional monotheists. Indeed the very idea of angelic beings is today unmentionable in the western world, dominated as it is by the pervasive naturalistic assumption. But this is only an assumption, and it is one that I reject. I see no reason why there should not be angels—not, of course, physical beings with wings and white garments, but spiritual beings, perhaps with the *soma pneumatikon* to which St Paul refers (I Cor. 15: 44). And if there are, it seems to me entirely possible that a Christian in prayer is addressing an angel, or indeed different Christians addressing different angels, and not an infinite, omnipotent, omnipresent, omniscient etc. Being.

In using the Kantian noumenal/phenomenal distinction there is however an important difference when we apply it (as Kant did not) to the relation between, on the one hand, the unknowable, transcategorial ultimate reality that I refer to as the Real and, on the other hand, the Gods and Absolutes of the human religions. The phenomenal world for Kant was the perceived physical world. Here the categories of the mind are schematized, or made concrete, by what Kant calls 'imagination' in terms of abstract time as causally interacting spatial substances. But the phenomenal Gods and Absolutes

---

[33] *Songs of Kabir*, trans. Rabindranath Tagore (New York, Weiser, 1977), p. 56.

are not physical things. Here the religious categories of transcendent personality and non-personal absoluteness are schematized, again by the human imagination, in terms of the filled time of history and culture to form the different God-figures and non-personal Brahman, Tao, Dharmakaya etc. The God-figures are not independent centres of consciousness, like the angels, and I was wrong when I proposed that the second interpretation of the *trikaya* doctrine was equally compatible as the first with the pluralistic hypothesis. I said that, 'Applying [the idea of the heavenly Buddhas, and angels etc.] to Yahweh, Vishnu, Allah, Shiva, the heavenly Father and so on it would follow that they are real personal beings, independent centres of consciousness, will, thought and emotion.'[34] This would indeed follow, and would indeed make me a polytheist, as Hasker argues, and the mistake was in accepting this as compatible with the pluralistic hypothesis. Hasker has enabled me to see this, and I am grateful to him. We ought never to operate on a 'sub-prime' level, but I am afraid that some of us sometimes do.

---

[34] *An Interpretation of Religion*, p. 274.

Bibliography

Adams, Marilyn McCord. 1995. 'Praying the *Proslogion*: Anselm's Theological Method.' In Senor (ed.) 1995, pp. 13–39.

Adams, Robert. 1972. 'Must God Create The Best?' *Philosophical Review* 81, pp. 317–32.

—— 1999. *Finite and Infinite Goods*. Oxford, Oxford University Press.

Alston, William. 1986. 'Epistemic Circularity.' *Philosophy and Phenomenological Research* 47, pp. 1–30.

—— 2005. *Beyond Justification: Dimensions of Epistemic Evaluation*. Ithaca, NY, Cornell University Press.

Audi, Robert and Wainwright, William. 1986. *Rationality, Religious Belief and Moral Commitment*. Ithaca, NY, Cornell University Press.

Axelrod, Robert. 1984. *The Evolution of Cooperation*. New York, Basic Books.

Baier, Kurt. 1958. *The Moral Point of View: A Rational Basis of Ethics*. Ithaca, NY, Cornell University Press.

Beilby, James (ed.). 2002. *Naturalism Defeated? Essays on Plantinga's Evolutionary Argument Against Naturalism*. Ithaca, NY, Cornell University Press.

Bergmann, Michael. 2004. 'Epistemic Circularity: Malignant and Benign.' *Philosophy and Phenomenological Research* 69, pp. 709–27.

—— 2006. *Justification without Awareness: A Defense of Epistemic Externalism*. Oxford, Oxford University Press.

—— Forthcoming. 'Evidentialism and the Great Pumpkin Objection.' In Dougherty (ed.). Forthcoming.

Binmore, Ken. 1992. *Game Theory and the Social Contract*, Vol 1. Cambridge, MIT Press.

Bonjour, Laurence. 1978. 'Can Empirical Knowledge Have a Foundation?' *American Philosophical Quarterly* 15, pp. 1–14.

Broome, John. 1992. 'Deontology and Economics.' *Economics and Philosophy* 8, pp. 269–82.

Carnap, Rudolph. 1950. *Logical Foundations of Probability*. Chicago, University of Chicago Press.

Chadwick, Owen. 1990. *The Secularization of the European Mind in the Nineteenth Century*. Cambridge, UK, Cambridge University Press.

Christensen, David. 2007. 'Epistemology of Disagreement: the Good News.' *Philosophical Review* 116 (2), pp. 187–217.

Clayton, John. 1987. 'Religions, Reasons, and Gods.' *Religious Studies* 23, pp. 12–13.

—— 1990. 'Piety and the Proofs.' *Religious Studies* 26, pp. 19–42.

Cohen, Stewart. 1984. 'Justification and Truth.' *Philosophical Studies* 46, pp. 279–95.

Collingwood, R. G. 1956. *The Idea of History*. Oxford, Oxford University Press.

Comesaña, Juan. Forthcoming. 'Evidentialist Reliabilism.' *Nous*.

Conee, Earl, and Feldman, Richard. 2004. *Evidentialism*. New York, Oxford University Press.

—— —— 2008. 'Evidence.' In Smith (ed.) 2008, pp. 83–104.

Craig, William L. and Smith, Quentin. 1993. *Theism, Atheism and Big Bang Cosmology*. New York, Oxford University Press.

Danielson, Peter. 1991. 'Closing the compliance dilemma: How it's rational to be moral in a Lamarckian world.' In Vallentyne (ed.) 1991, pp. 291–322.

Dawkins, Richard. 1986. *The Blind Watchmaker*. New York, W. W. Norton.

—— 2008. *The God Delusion*. New York, Houghton Mifflin Publishers.

Delaney, C. F. (ed.). 1979. *Rationality and Religious Belief*. Notre Dame, IN, University of Notre Dame Press.

DePaul, Michael (ed.). 2001. *Resurrecting Old-Fashioned Foundationalism*. Lanham, MD, Rowman and Littlefield.

Dougherty, Trent (ed.). Forthcoming. *Evidentialism and its Discontents*. New York, Oxford University Press.

Draper, Paul. 1989. 'Pain and Pleasure: An Evidential Problem for Theists.' *Nous*, 23, pp. 331–50.

Earman, John. 1992. *Bayes or Bust*. Cambridge, MA, MIT Press.

Edwards, Paul. 1967. 'Common Consent Arguments for the Existence of God.' In Paul Edwards (ed.) *The Encyclopedia of Philosophy*, vol. 2 (New York, Macmillan Publishing), pp. 147–55.

Egan, Andy and Elga, Adam. 2005. 'I Can't Believe I'm Stupid.' In Hawthorne (ed.) 2005, pp. 77–93.

Evans, C. Stephen. 2004. *Kierkegaard's Ethic of Love: Divine Commands and Moral Obligations*. Oxford, Oxford University Press.

—— 2010. *Natural Signs and Knowledge of God: A New Look at Theistic Arguments*. Oxford, Oxford University Press.

Fales, Evan. 2002. 'Darwin's Doubt, Calvin's Calvary.' In Beilby (ed.) 2002, pp. 43–60.

Feldman, Richard and Conee, Earl. 1985. 'Evidentialism.' *Philosophical Studies* 48, pp. 15–34.

—— and Warfield, Ted (eds.). 2010. *Disagreement*. Oxford, Oxford University Press.

Fitelson, Brandon and Sober, Elliot. 1998. 'Plantinga's Probability Arguments Against Evolutionary Naturalism.' *Pacific Philosophical Quarterly* 79, pp. 115–29.

Flint, Robert. 1877. *Theism*. London.

Fodor, Jerry. 2002. 'Is Science Biologically Possible?.' In Beilby (ed.) 2002, pp. 30–42.

Foley, Richard. 2001. *Intellectual Trust in Oneself and Others*. Cambridge, Cambridge University Press.

Franssen, Maarten. 1994. 'Constrained Maximization Reconsidered.' *Synthese* 101, pp. 249–72.

Fricker, Elizabeth. 2006. 'Testimony and Epistemic Autonomy.' In Lackey and Sosa (eds.) 2006, pp. 225–50.

Fumerton, Richard. 2001. 'Classical Foundationalism.' In DePaul (ed.) 2001, pp. 3–20.

Gauthier, David. 1986. *Morals by Agreement*. New York, Oxford University Press.

Gendler, Tamar Szabo and Hawthorne, John (eds.). 2005. *Oxford Studies in Epistemology*, vol. 1. Oxford, Oxford University Press.

Goldman, Alvin. 2001. 'Experts: Which Ones Should You Trust?' *Philosophy and Phenomenological Research* 63, pp. 85–110.

—— 2008. 'Immediate Justification and Process Reliabilism.' In Smith (ed.) 2008, pp. 63–82.

Greco, John. 2000. *Putting Skeptics in their Place*. New York, Cambridge University Press.

Hare, John. 1996. *The Moral Gap*. Oxford, Oxford University Press.

Harman, Gilbert. 1965. 'The Inference to the Best Explanation.' *The Philosophical Review* 74, pp. 88–95.

Hawthorne, John (ed.). 2005. *Philosophical Perspectives*, vol. 19, *Epistemology*. Oxford, Blackwell Publishers.

Hazlett, Allan. 2006. 'Epistemic Conceptions of Begging the Question.' *Erkenntnis* 65, pp. 343–63.

Henderson, David and Horgan, Terry. 2006. 'Transglobal Reliabilism.' *Croatian Journal of Philosophy*, pp. 171–95.

Hick, John. 1997. 'The Epistemological Challenge of Religious Pluralism.' *Faith and Philosophy* 14, pp. 277–86.

—— 2001. *Dialogues in the Philosophy of Religion*. New York, Palgrave.

—— 2002. *An Autobiography*. Oxford, One World.

—— 2004. *An Interpretation of Religion: Human Responses to the Transcendent*, 2nd edn. New Haven, Yale University Press.

Hoffman, Joshua. 1979. 'Can God Do Evil?' *Southern Journal of Philosophy* 17, pp. 213–20.

Howard-Snyder, Daniel (ed.). 1996. *The Evidential Problem of Evil*. Bloomington, Indiana University Press.

—— and Moser, Paul (eds.). 2001. *Divine Hiddenness: New Essays*. New York, Cambridge University Press.

Huemer, Michael. 2001. *Skepticism and the Veil of Perception*. Lanham, Rowman & Littlefield Publishers.

—— 2006. 'Phenomenal Conservatism and the Internalist Intuition.' *American Philosophical Quarterly* 43, pp. 147–58.

—— 2007. 'Compassionate Phenomenal Conservativism.' *Philosophy and Phenomenological Research* 74, pp. 30–55.

Hume, David. 2000 (1748). *An Inquiry Concerning Human Understanding*. Tom L. Beauchamp (ed.). Oxford, Oxford University Press.

—— 1980 (1779). *Dialogues Concerning Natural Religion*. Richard Popkin (ed.). Indianapolis, Hackett Publishing.

James, William. 1956 (1897). *The Will to Believe and other Essays in Popular Philosophy*. New York, Dover.

—— 1981 (1890). *Principles of Psychology*, vol. 2. Cambridge, Harvard University Press.

Johnston, Mark. 2009. *Saving God: Religion after Idolatry*. Princeton, NJ, Princeton University Press.

Joyce, George Hayward, SJ 1923. *Principles of Natural Theology*. New York, Longmans, Green and Co.

Kant, Immanuel. 1956 (1788). *Critique of Practical Reason*. L.W. Beck (trans.). New York, Liberal Arts Press.

—— 1960 (1793). *Religion Within the Bounds of Reason Alone*. Theodore M. Greene and Hoyt H. Hudson (trans.). New York, Harper and Brothers.

—— 1965 (1781). *Critique of Pure Reason*. Norman Kemp Smith (trans.). New York, St Martin's Press.

Kelly, Thomas. 2005. 'The Epistemic Significance of Disagreement.' In Gendler and Hawthorne (eds.) 2005, pp. 167–96.

—— 2006. 'Evidence.' In Edward Zalta (ed.), *The Stanford Encyclopedia of Philosophy*.URL <http://plato.stanford.edu/entries/evidence/>.

—— 2010. 'Peer Disagreement and Higher Order Evidence.' In Feldman and Warfield (eds.) 2010.

Keynes, John Maynard. 1921. *A Treatise on Probability*. London, Macmillan and Co.

Kreeft, Peter, and Tacelli, Ronald. 1994. *Handbook of Christian Apologetics*. Downers Grove, IL, Intervarsity Press.

Kretzmann, Norman. 1990. 'A General Problem of Creation.' In MacDonald 1990, pp. 208–28.

―― 1990. 'A Particular Problem of Creation.' In MacDonald 1990, pp. 229–49.

Kripke, Saul. 1980. *Naming and Necessity*. Cambridge, MA, Harvard University Press.

Kuhn, Thomas. 1962. *The Structure of Scientific Revolutions*. Chicago, University of Chicago Press.

Lackey, Jennifer and Sosa, Ernest. (eds.). 2006. *The Epistemology of Testimony*. Oxford, Oxford University Press.

La Follete, Hugh (ed.). 2000. *The Blackwell Guide to Ethical Theory*. Oxford, Blackwell.

Lipton, Peter. 1991. *Inference to the Best Explanation*. London, UK, Routledge.

Locke, John. 1979 (1689). *An Essay Concerning Human Understanding*. P. H. Nidditch (ed.). Oxford, Clarendon Press.

Long, Eugene Thomas (ed.). 1992. *Prospects for Natural Theology*. Washington, DC, The Catholic University of America Press.

MacDonald, Scott (ed.). 1990. *Being and Goodness*. Ithaca, NY, Cornell University Press.

Mackie, J. L. 1982. *The Miracle of Theism*. Oxford, Oxford University Press.

Mann, William E. (ed.). 2004. *The Blackwell Guide to the Philosophy of Religion*. Oxford, Blackwell Publishing.

Markie, Peter. 2004. 'Nondoxastic Perceptual Evidence.' *Philosophy and Phenomenological Research* 68, pp. 530–53.

―― 2005. 'Easy Knowledge.' *Philosophy and Phenomenological Research* 70, pp. 406–16.

―― 2005. 'The Mystery of Perceptual Justification.' *Philosophical Studies* 126, pp. 347–73.

―― 2006. 'Epistemically Appropriate Perceptual Belief.' *Nous* 40, pp. 118–42.

Martin, Michael (ed.). 2006. *The Cambridge Companion to Atheism*. Cambridge, Cambridge University Press.

Mavrodes, George I. 1970. *Belief in God: A Study in the Epistemology of Religion*. New York, Random House.

―― 1979. 'Rationality and Religious Belief—A Perverse Question.' In Delaney (ed.) 1979.

―― 1983. 'Jerusalem and Athens Revisited.' In Plantinga and Wolterstorff (eds.) 1983, pp. 192–218.

―― 1986. 'Religion and the Queerness of Morality.' In Audi and Wainwright (eds.) 1986, pp. 213–26.

―― 1992. 'On the Very Strongest Arguments.' In Long (ed.) 1992, pp. 81–91.

―― 1995. 'Polytheism.' In Senor (ed.) 1995, pp. 261–86.

―― 1997. 'A Response to John Hick.' *Faith and Philosophy* 14, pp. 289–94.

McCarthy, Gerald D. (ed.). 1985. *The Ethics of Belief Debate*. Atlanta, Georgia, Scholars Press.

Mercier, Cardinal Joseph. 1926. *A Manual of Modern Scholastic Philosophy*. T. L. and S. A. Parker (trans.). London.

Merricks, Trenton. 2002. 'Conditional Probability and Defeat.' In Beilby (ed.) 2002, pp. 165–75.

Mill, John Stuart. 1885. 'Theism.' Reprinted in *Three Essays on Religion*. Amherst, NY, Prometheus Books, 1998.

Morris, Thomas. 1987. *Anselmian Explorations*. Notre Dame, University of Notre Dame Press.

Morriston, Wes. 1985. 'Is God "Significantly Free"?' *Faith and Philosophy* 2, pp. 257–64.

Moser, Paul. 2001. 'Cognitive Idolatry and Divine Hiding.' In Howard-Snyder and Moser (eds.) 2001, pp. 129–48.

—— 2003. 'Divine Hiddenness Does Not Justify Atheism.' In Peterson and VanArragon (eds.) 2003, pp. 42–53.

—— 2008. *The Elusive God: Reorienting Religious Epistemology.* New York, Cambridge University Press.

Newman, John Henry. 1979 (1870). *An Essay in Aid of a Grammar of Assent.* Notre Dame, IN, University of Notre Dame Press.

—— 1966 (1943). 'Love the Safeguard of Faith against Superstition.' In *Fifteen Sermons Preached before the University of Oxford.* Westminster, MD, Christian Classics.

O'Briant, Walter H. 1985. 'Is There an Argument *Consensus Gentium?*' *International Journal for Philosophy of Religion* 18, pp. 73–9.

Otte, Richard. 1987. 'A Theistic Conception of Probability.' *Faith and Philosophy* 4, pp. 427–47.

—— Unpublished. 'Science, Naturalism, and Self-Defeat.'

Peterson, Michael and VanArragon, Raymond (eds.). 2003. *Contemporary Debates in Philosophy of Religion.* London, Blackwell Publishing.

Plantinga, Alvin. 1983. 'Reason and Belief in God.' In Plantinga and Wolterstorff (eds.) 1983, pp. 16–93.

—— 1993. *Warrant and Proper Function.* New York, Oxford University Press.

—— 1995. 'Pluralism: A Defense of Religious Exclusivism.' Reprinted in Quinn and Meeker (eds.) 2000, pp. 172–92.

—— 1996. 'Epistemic Probability and Evil.' In Howard-Snyder (ed.) 1996, pp. 244–61.

—— 2000. *Warranted Christian Belief.* New York, Oxford University Press.

—— 2002. 'Introduction.' In Beilby (ed.) 2002, pp. 1–14.

—— and Wolterstorff, Nicholas (eds.). 1983. *Faith and Rationality.* Notre Dame, IN, University of Notre Dame Press.

Pojman, Louis P. 1986. *Religious Belief and the Will.* New York, Routledge & Kegan Paul.

Pryor, James. 2004. 'What's Wrong with Moore's Argument?' *Philosophical Issues* 14, pp. 349–78.

Putnam, Hilary. 1975. *Mathematics, Matter, and Method: Collected Papers* vol. 1. Cambridge, Cambridge University Press.

Quinn, Philip L. 1982. 'God, Moral Perfection, and Possible Worlds.' In Sontag and Bryant (eds.), pp. 197–213.

—— 1985. 'In Search of the Foundations of Theism.' *Faith and Philosophy* 2, pp. 468–86.

—— 1993. 'The Foundations of Theism Again: A Rejoinder to Plantinga.' In Zagzebski (ed.) 1993, pp. 14–47.

—— 2000. 'Divine Command Theory.' In La Follette (ed.) 2000, pp. 53–73.

—— and Meeker, Kevin. 2000. *The Philosophical Challenge of Religious Diversity.* New York, Oxford University Press.

—— and Taliaferro, Charles (eds.). 1997. *A Companion to Philosophy of Religion.* Malden, MA, Blackwell.

Ramsey, William. 2002. 'Naturalism Defended.' In Beilby (ed.) 2002, pp. 15–29.

Rea, Michael C. 2002. *World Without Design: The Ontological Consequences of Naturalism.* Oxford, Oxford University Press.

Reid, Thomas. 1969 (1785). *Essays on the Intellectual Powers.* Cambridge, MIT Press.

Reppert, Victor. 2003. *C. S. Lewis's Dangerous Idea: In Defense of the Argument from Reason.* Downers Grove, IL, InterVarsity Press.

Roeber, Blake. 2009. 'Does the Theist Have an Epistemic Advantage over the Atheist? Plantinga and Descartes on Theism, Atheism and Skepticism.' *The Journal of Philosophical Research* 34, pp. 305–28.

Ross, James. 1985. 'Believing for Profit.' In McCarthy (ed.) 1985, pp. 221–35.

—— 1995. 'Rational Reliance.' *Journal of the American Academy of Religion* LXII, pp. 769–98.

Rowe, William L. 1979. 'The Problem of Evil and Some Varieties of Atheism.' *American Philosophical Quarterly* 16, pp. 335–41.

—— and Wainwright, William (eds.). 1998. *Philosophy of Religion: Selected Readings.* 3rd edn. New York, Oxford University Press.

Schellenberg, John L. 2004. ' "Breaking Down the Walls that Divide:" Virtue and Warrant, Belief and Nonbelief.' *Faith and Philosophy* 21, pp. 195–213.

Searle, John R. 1983. *Intentionality.* Cambridge, Cambridge University Press.

—— 1995. *The Construction of Social Reality.* New York, Simon and Schuster.

Senor, Thomas D. (ed.). 1995. *The Rationality of Belief and the Plurality of Faith.* Ithaca, NY, Cornell University Press.

Sinnott-Armstrong, Walter. 2006. *Moral Skepticisms.* Oxford, Oxford University Press.

—— (ed.). 2008. *Moral Psychology,* Volume 2: *The Cognitive Science of Morality: Intuition and Diversity.* Cambridge, MA, MIT Press.

Smith, Quentin (ed.). 2008. *Epistemology: New Essays.* Oxford, Oxford University Press.

Sobel, J. Howard. 1993. 'Straight Versus Constrained Maximizers.' *Canadian Journal of Philosophy* 23, pp. 25–54.

—— 2003. *Logic and Theism.* Cambridge, Cambridge University Press.

Sontag, Frederick and Bryant, M. Darrol (eds.). 1982. *God: The Contemporary Discussion.* New York, The Rose of Sharon Press.

Sorabji, Richard. 1993. *Animal Minds and Human Morals: The Origins of the Western Debate.* Ithaca, NY, Cornell University Press.

Sorensen, Roy. 1988. *Blindspots.* Oxford, Oxford University Press.

Surowiecki, James. 2004. *The Wisdom of Crowds.* New York, Doubleday.

Swinburne, Richard. 1979. *The Existence of God.* Oxford, Oxford University Press.

—— 1996. *Is There a God?* Oxford, Oxford University Press.

—— 2001. *Epistemic Justification.* Oxford, Oxford University Press.

Tolhurst, William. 1998. 'Seemings.' *American Philosophical Quarterly* 35, pp. 293–302.

Tucker, Chris. Forthcoming. 'Why Open-Minded People should Endorse Dogmatism.' *Philosophical Perspectives.*

Turri, John. 2009. 'The Ontology of Epistemic Reasons.' *Nous* 2009, pp. 490–512.

Vallentyne, Peter (ed.). 1991. *Contractarianism and Rational Choice.* New York, Cambridge University Press.

Wainwright, William J. 1995. *Reason and the Heart: A Prolegomenon to a Critique of Passional Reason.* Ithaca, NY, Cornell University Press.

—— 2004. 'Competing Religious Claims.' In Mann (ed.) 2004, pp. 220–43.

—— 2005. *The Oxford Handbook of Philosophy of Religion.* Oxford, Oxford University Press.

—— 2005. 'Religious Experience, Theological Argument, and the Relevance of Rhetoric.' *Faith and Philosophy* 22, pp. 391–412.

Warfield, Ted. 2008. 'Metaphysical Compatibilism's Appropriation of Frankfurt.' *Oxford Studies in Metaphysics* 3, pp. 283–95.

White, Roger. 2005. 'Explanation as a Guide to Induction.' *Philosophers' Imprint* 5 (2), pp. 1–29.

—— 2006. 'Problems for Dogmatism.' *Philosophical Studies* 131, pp. 525–57.

Wielenberg, Erik J. 2002. 'How to be an Alethically Rational Naturalist.' *Synthese* 131, pp. 81–98.

Wilson, Margaret Dauler. 1995. 'Animal Ideas.' *Proceedings and Addresses of the American Philosophical Association* 69, pp. 7–25.

Wright, Crispin. 2008. 'The Perils of Dogmatism.' *In Themes from G. E. Moore: New Essays in Epistemology and Ethics*. Oxford, Oxford University Press.

Wykstra, Stephen. 1989. 'Toward a Sensible Evidentialism: On the Notion of "Needing Evidence".' In Rowe and Wainwright (eds.) 1998.

Zagzebski, Linda (ed.). 1993. *Rational Faith: Catholic Responses to Reformed Epistemology*. Notre Dame, Indiana, University of Notre Dame Press.

Zuckerman, Phil. 2006. 'Atheism: Contemporary Rates and Patterns.' In Martin (ed.) 2006, pp. 47–68.

Index